Joan Woodcock was born and brought up in Blackburn, Lancashire. Hospitalisation at the young age of four inspired her to enter the world of medicine. At sixteen she started as a cadet nurse, before beginning formal nurse training two years later under the traditional matron system.

MATRON KNOWS BEST

Joan Woodcock became a nurse in 1966, when she began as a naïve sixteen-year-old cadet. Joan's story spans over forty years in NHS nursing. Working on hospital wards, casualty units and out in the community — as well as stints in a prison and a police unit dealing with sexual assault — Joan has seen it all. Her story is one of a challenging, unpredictable and ultimately rewarding life in nursing. From an early encounter with a horrific axe injury, to the patient who swallowed their suppositories, to daily dealings with difficult patients and bodily fluids, Joan shares memories of laughter, warmth and tragedy. She also describes the methods used by the now defunct matron system that instilled nurses with such high standards of professionalism and patient care.

JOAN WOODCOCK

MATRON KNOWS BEST

The true story of a 1960s NHS nurse

Complete and Unabridged

CHARNWOOD
Leicester

First published in Great Britain in 2011 by
Headline Review
An imprint of
Headline Publishing Group
London

First Charnwood Edition
published 2012
by arrangement with
Headline Publishing Group
An Hachette UK Company
London

British Library CIP Data

Woodcock, Joan.
    Matron knows best.
    1. Woodcock, Joan. 2. Nurses- -Great Britain- -
    Biography. 3. Large type books.
    I. Title
    610.7'3'092–dc23

    ISBN 978–1–4448–1019–6

Printed and bound in Great Britain by
T. J. International Ltd., Padstow, Cornwall

This book is printed on acid-free paper

This book is dedicated to my dear son, Mark.

Acknowledgements

My thanks to Bill Cribb, one of nature's true gentlemen, for his invaluable help in getting this book off the ground. Thanks also to John, Michael and Toni for their advice and expertise along the way, and my appreciation to Glyn, Jeanne and Christine, who have graciously allowed me to relate some of my memories of them in print. Finally, not forgetting my husband, Bill, without whose constant help and support my book probably wouldn't have been completed.

Introduction

This book is a true recollection of events since my first day as a naïve sixteen-year-old standing nervously outside Matron's office at Blackburn Royal Infirmary in September 1966. It recalls the struggles and fears of coping not only with the fierce expectations of Matron and the senior nursing staff, but also the battle to deal with the unfamiliar sights and sounds of hospital life in the raw. The memories span forty-one vastly interesting and enjoyable years spent working in numerous busy wards and casualty departments, as well as working in the community as a practice nurse and a Marie Curie nurse. They include two years looking after the inmates of an all-male prison and ending my career working for Lancashire Police in an acute unit dealing with cases of sexual assault. Some sad memories are interspersed with many amusing ones, but my main reason for writing this book was to highlight the very high standards of patient care demanded under the now-defunct, old-fashioned matron system. During my working life there have been undreamed of advances in medical science, but I remain intensely proud of the training I received all those years ago and the obligation which was instilled in me to maintain the highest levels of professionalism when caring for my patients.

My stories are as accurate as memory will

allow. All patient names have been changed to protect confidentiality, although a number of staff names have been included as a mark of my respect for their outstanding ability and professional qualities.

1

It was September 1966 when I found myself standing outside Matron's office at Blackburn Royal Infirmary (BRI) with about twenty other girls, all sixteen or seventeen years of age, anxious and giggling nervously, waiting to start our first day as cadet nurses. This had been my sole ambition since having my tonsils removed at the age of four. The nurses who had looked after me had been so kind and caring that they had held a complete fascination for me from then on. By the time I was sixteen I couldn't wait to start work at the hospital. I had been interviewed by Matron some eight weeks earlier and she had asked why I wanted to become a nurse. She carefully noted my answer, and occasionally nodded and smiled encouragingly as the short interview proceeded. I was then directed to a room down the corridor to take both a maths and an English test. On their completion, I was informed that I would receive a letter in due course advising me whether I had been accepted. Two weeks later I received the confirmation that I had indeed been successful and should attend my induction at the end of summer. A list of essential items which I was expected to provide and bring with me on my first day was included with the letter and consisted of: a navy blue cardigan, flat black shoes, a fob watch, a pen, a small torch and a pair of round-ended scissors. I was elated; terrified but elated. Flippin' 'eck, I was going to be a real nurse!

How hard could it be, though? I could see little problem in holding the hands of a few sickly people and mopping an occasional brow. Yes — I was definitely going to be a great nurse, second only to Miss Nightingale herself! Matron had seemed reasonably friendly during my interview, quite human really. Mind you, I wasn't enamoured with the navy blue Crimplene uniform she wore, though I quite fancied the crispy, little, white ensemble propped on top of her head. Mmm, when I become matron the Crimplene would have to go, but the hat would definitely stay!

I remember the butterflies in my stomach as I stood with the other girls outside the office. My heart was pounding and my mouth was so dry that my lips stuck to my teeth. Looking around it was comforting to see that I wasn't the only nervous person there. Indeed, one girl who had short, bright red hair was looking decidedly iffy.

It was 9.15am and everyone was getting restless as we waited for something to happen. The hospital was already a hive of activity, though, with people rushing around like headless chickens: porters pushing trolleys and wheel-chairs with nurses accompanying them; office staff dashing to and fro with files and case notes; doctors striding along purposefully with stetho-scopes dangling around their necks; and members of the public milling around, obviously lost, carefully scrutinising the numerous over-head signs. Suddenly I saw, bearing down on us

2

at high speed, a very thin, sour-faced woman in a dark green uniform and white frilly cap carrying an armful of files, looking particularly fierce and extremely agitated. She scowled at us and barked an order to wait in silence as she knocked on Matron's door and hurried inside. Seconds later she came back out and demanded instant attention.

'Listen carefully and answer your names when called.'

She read out all the names on her list and appeared satisfied that we were all present and correct. I couldn't help thinking how pinched and miserable she looked, not at all welcoming. It beggared belief that this woman could be a member of the caring profession. I swear she could have turned milk sour with a single glance. We were ordered to line up in twos and follow her. It took a minute or so for everyone to organise themselves and then we were off down the corridor, marching like soldiers behind a Regimental Sergeant Major.

One or two brave souls mimicked the nurse and only just avoided getting caught when she unexpectedly turned around to demand complete silence. There was some muffled tittering in the ranks but another smouldering look quickly quelled the indiscipline. When we reached the end of the corridor we were led down a wide, tiled stairwell that led to the nurses' quarters (lovingly referred to by the doctors as 'The Virgins' Retreat'). The whole area was tiled in drab green, brown and white and looked not unlike a public convenience. Eventually we were ushered into a cold, dark basement, which was to be our changing room for the next two years. The only objects in the room were dozens of lockers and several very large cardboard boxes. Some of the lockers were already occupied and displayed stickers with names on, while others had keys hanging from their locks awaiting new owners. The nurse in green (who was soon identified as Miss Hanlon, one of Matron's assistants) proceeded to open the cardboard boxes, which were full of freshly laundered but obviously pre-owned mauve uniforms. Gathering us around, she made it very clear that it was strictly forbidden (apparently on pain of death) for any cadet to go out of the hospital grounds wearing their uniform. She then called out our names once again and, on being summoned, we stepped forward. Eyeing us up and down, she rummaged in the boxes and threw four uniforms at each new recruit. Never once did I hear her ask anyone their size; and I don't think she really cared. When it came to my turn she threw me two size 14s and two size 18s; the fact that I was a size 12 seemed to be quite irrelevant to her. She then left the room, giving us ten minutes to find ourselves a locker, change into uniform, put on our cardigans and work shoes and be ready for her inspection.

There was an immediate scrum to find a vacant locker. Civvies were discarded and everyone hurriedly changed into uniform. One or two cadets exchanged their ill-fitting dresses with each other. There was a lot of laughter, although I was more than a little put out because most of the girls were shorter than my five feet ten and no one was willing to swap with me — I looked like an advert for Oxfam or an escapee from an institution. In point of fact, we must have been a sorry sight but there was nothing we could do about it. Miss Hanlon came back precisely ten minutes later and we lined up for inspection. Anyone who had the audacity to complain was sent to the sewing room with a note saying that their uniform had to be lengthened; no matter that it was already touching the floor. This was the punishment for making waves. I made a mental note to avoid this woman at all costs.

The inspection didn't go well. Two girls had forgotten to bring black shoes and two others had shoes that weren't flat. They were warned, in no uncertain terms, to bring the correct footwear the next day or be sent home. Our cardigans also created problems; one cadet had brought a black one, and another girl paraded a beige, hand-knitted creation. Miss Hanlon tut-tutted and sighed in irritation; it was navy blue or nothing. Hair had to be off the collar, no wispy bits were allowed, no shiny slides and only navy blue hair ribbons were permitted. Make-up was definitely out of the question and anyone found wearing eye shadow, eyeliner, lipstick or nail varnish had to remove it immediately. A plain wedding ring would be the only jewellery allowed and a fob watch the only timepiece permitted. Anyone not obeying these basic rules would be reprimanded and sent to Matron. I was beginning to wonder if I had strayed into an army barracks instead of a hospital but, as we all were in those days, I had been brought up to respect my elders and accept instructions without argument, whether I agreed or not, so I held my tongue. With uniform inspection over, Miss Hanlon ordered us to line up in twos once again. We were to have a medical.

Our letters of confirmation hadn't mentioned this at all, but we lined up as instructed and were again ordered to follow our new RSM in silence as she led us further down another long, lonely corridor into the bowels of the nurses' quarters. We were shown into a cold, musty room that, apart from six large upright wooden chairs along one wall, was completely empty. A door at the far end led to a block of toilets and opposite these was the room where we were to have our medical. We were abruptly instructed to strip down to our bra and knickers and provide a urine specimen in the containers which were handed out. I was mortified. Did this woman not realise that, apart from my family doctor, no one had ever seen me undressed before? If I had known in advance I would have asked Mum to buy me some new underwear, instead of having to stand there feeling very embarrassed in tatty school knickers and a greying M&S bra. Holding a container of wee and trying to cover up at the same time was no easy task. We weren't even allowed the luxury of a gown to hide our blushes. But at least I could see I wasn't the only one wearing school drawers.

When it was my turn, Miss Hanlon shouted my name and I made my way into the medical

6

room. She took my specimen, handling it as though it was an explosive device, and dipped a multicoloured strip from a bottle into the urine, checked it against a chart and wrote something in a file. Not a word was spoken. I had to be weighed and measured before I clambered on to the examination couch — a huge, dark brown leather bed, which necessitated standing on a footstool in order to reach it. How all the shorter girls managed the climb I could only imagine. The head end of the couch tilted forward like a deck-chair, the bedcover was a rough paper sheet and there was no blanket or pillow. I felt exposed and vulnerable. An elderly, white-haired doctor was sitting at a desk near my feet still scribbling notes on the previous victim. He didn't look up or speak until he had finished writing, but eventually came over to me with a friendly smile on his face. He seemed perfectly amiable and down to earth; until he asked if I had ever been pregnant! I felt myself blushing to the roots of my hair and couldn't speak. I simply shook my head. (Periods, pregnancy and boys were never discussed in our house. I even remember Dad switching off wildlife programmes on the telly, especially if there was a risk of seeing naked people or copulating animals.) He then asked me when my last period was. The man was obsessed; it was all he seemed to be concerned about. And I felt myself getting hotter by the minute. Having acknowledged my answers he listened to my heart, checked my blood pressure, prodded my stomach, looked into my eyes and my ears and then bawled, 'Right, off you go.' I couldn't get out of there fast enough. Damn cheek of the man! Several remaining cadets had yet to be seen but those who had already been examined were allowed to go for coffee in an adjacent room, where some of the girls were muttering and complaining. One or two had been told off for being overweight and those cadets who smoked were positively glowered at and had 'SMOKER' emblazoned in large red letters across the top of their notes. (Quite funny really, as I was sure that I saw a pipe and an ashtray on the doctor's desk and he wasn't exactly sylph-like either!)

After everyone had been tapped, poked, pummelled and insulted, Miss Hanlon offered us a tour of the hospital. This was to be followed by lunch and then we were to find out our work placements.

Our first port of call was the pathology laboratory. This department was situated on the ground floor just around the corner from Matron's office. Now dressed in our tasteful mauve uniforms and feeling very excited and proud of ourselves, we followed Miss Hanlon into the laboratory. Passing through the double swing doors we came across a solitary domestic, heavily laden with mops, buckets and all manner of cleaning materials. She was totally engaged in the scrubbing and polishing of an already spotlessly clean corridor and was less than pleased when she realised we were all about to venture on to her newly mopped floor. She had dutifully put out a sign warning people about the wet surface but, when she saw all of us bearing down on her, she grudgingly pointed at her sign

8

and barked at us to be careful where we walked. Miss Hanlon sniffed haughtily and completely ignored her, before proceeding through a narrow door marked 'Reception Office'. All patients attending the laboratory for an appointment (whether it was to have a blood sample taken or to go to a specialised clinic) had to book in at the reception window before being shown through to where they had to wait. Similarly, permission had to be sought before we could enter the department. After a quick telephone call made by the office receptionist, a tall, thin, middle-aged lady dressed in a white coat appeared from down the corridor and introduced herself as the supervisor who had been designated to show us around.

Starting at the end of the corridor, the first room we entered was Bacteriology. We all shuffled en masse into this untidy-looking section of the laboratory and were instantly transfixed at the scene that greeted us: men and women in surgical masks, white coats and surgical gloves were surrounded by dozens of samples of sputum, urine, stools, blood and heaven knows what else. Individual plastic containers were being examined, dipped into and their contents spread on to small glass culture dishes, which were then placed in incubators to see if they grew any of the myriad types of germs that could be causing a particular patient's ill health. The process could sometimes take several days to complete; during which each specimen was meticulously and regularly checked by laboratory staff to see if any organisms had begun to grow. If so, a sample was taken and placed under a microscope which would then hopefully identify the culprit, after which an appropriate antibiotic could be recommended to the doctor who was responsible for that patient.

We were allowed to look down a number of microscopes while a laboratory technician explained in detail what each specimen showed and what symptoms a patient would be likely to present with, if they were unlucky enough to catch one of them. I have to say that they all looked very similar to me, but the technician assured us that some were bacteria or fungi, which needed treating with antibiotics or antifungal medication, others were viruses, for which no amount of antibiotics would be of any value because they went through pre-defined stages and caused unpleasant symptoms but once they had run their natural course would disappear and the patient would recover naturally. It was simply fascinating, but the one thing that was stomach churning was the smell: a mixture of disinfectant, cleaning materials, open specimen containers and the general heat within the department all seemed to mingle together to result in a nauseating stink. It was no wonder they had to wear masks. As well as protecting the wearer from germs, perfume sprayed inside the mask made the job a little more bearable. Air fresheners were in evidence on a number of window ledges but were virtually ineffective and, before too long, a number of cadets were pinching their noses and groaning in discomfort. How anyone in their right mind could work in there was beyond my comprehension.

In the next part of the laboratory designated Histology, there were seemingly endless shelves laden with different-sized jars filled with formaldehyde (a preservative of formic acid), each containing a different organ of the body. We were shown an appendix (which we were assured had been removed from a patient that very morning), together with a cancerous lung, which could only be described as gruesome and came with a stern lecture from Miss Hanlon to all the smokers present. There were stomachs and diseased wombs and a wide variety of other organs, some of which had been there for many years and were now used solely for teaching purposes.

One specimen that caught my eye was a jar containing an aborted foetus. I was fascinated to see the tiny arms, legs and face, all in the early stages of development. It made me feel quite humble knowing that I could have been in that jar. My sister had been born two years earlier than me and Mum had endured a very difficult pregnancy due to an underlying heart condition and had spent many weeks on hospital bed rest prior to the birth. She had been warned by her doctors at the time never to have any more children as there was a high risk of mortality for both her and any subsequent baby. However, two years later Mum had an unplanned pregnancy and she was strongly advised to terminate as soon as possible. She refused and thankfully the pregnancy went well before I emerged fit and healthy.

One of the other cadets called Kathleen had to

choke back tears when she saw the foetus because she found the reality of abortion so difficult to come to terms with. There was a reflective silence within the group, but we realised that inevitably we were going to come across such sights time and time again. We all needed to deal with it as best we could and not make judgements, although it certainly affected Anne as well (the redhead who had looked uncomfortable outside Matron's office), who had turned white as a sheet and almost fainted. A chair appeared as if by magic and her head was unceremoniously pushed between her knees. There were nervous giggles from one or two of the other girls but Anne looked pretty ghastly. Without further ado we were told to continue with the tour and leave our fellow cadet to recover. Much later Anne was to confide in me that she had absolutely no wish or vocation to train as a nurse, but it was a tradition in her family dating back several generations that all first-born daughters become nurses and, like them, she was expected to continue this unreasonable expectation regardless of her own wishes. I wondered how on earth she would ever cope.

The last area we were allowed to see within the laboratory before moving on was Haematology. This was a department in itself and, apparently, was always chaotically busy. Every out-patient and in-patient's blood was dealt with here, whether it was for routine checks or for emergency transfusions. Specialised clinics were also held within Haematology to monitor people who had cardiac problems and were being treated with anticoagulants (anti-blood-clotting tablets), or for people suffering with a variety of blood-borne cancers such as leukaemia, who were on chemotherapy and needed to be monitored regularly. The consultant haematologist would see literally dozens of people at every clinic at any one time, his work was frantically busy and, as we walked around the area, patients were already gathering at the receptionist's window waving their appointment cards in the air anxious to be seen promptly (it was a first-come, first-served basis). Considering how busy the department was, the haematology staff were very patient with us, trying their best to answer our questions without hurrying us, but it was soon very evident from the volume of grumbles coming from the growing number of waiting patients that the natives were getting restless. Miss Hanlon felt it better that we moved on.

After leaving the laboratory, she advised us that she was going to show us two very different wards. The first was situated in the old part of the hospital, which had wards laid out in the traditional Nightingale fashion, and the second was in the newly built modern wing. To get to the old wing we came out of the laboratory on to the main corridor, heading back in the direction of the nurses' quarters, and turned to climb a wide, poorly lit flight of stairs on the left which brought us out on to the top corridor. Some cadets, already out of breath at the effort of climbing the stairs, stood mesmerised looking both right and left, awestruck at the sheer length of the corridor, which seemed to stretch for miles. Even though the whole area was obviously old and was decorated in the most miserable, drab colours, it was sparklingly clean, thanks to a team of domestics in their blue check overalls who were still in the process of mopping floors and washing down the old flaky paintwork, clearly proud of their efforts. In 1966 these workers were employed directly by the hospital to clean their own specific areas on a daily basis and, for many of them, it was a matter of pride that high standards were maintained. But they also knew that if anything was not up-to-scratch, Matron would be on to them like a ton of bricks.

Miss Hanlon urged us along and, as we neared the ward, a large cage-like lift to our right rattled and squeaked to a halt. Two porters in long grey coats emerged; both were pushing heavy trolleys bearing large, black-and-white metal cylinders that Miss Hanlon informed us contained oxygen. The sisters on the old wards had to request these cumbersome monstrosities as and when they were needed, and they were then brought up from the basement and transported directly to the patient's bedside.

As we reached the end of the corridor it opened out into an atrium with a large central well in the floor, surrounded by an ornate metal and highly polished wooden railing, which fell some thirty feet to ground level where the surface was a beautiful and intricate mosaic tiled pattern. The whole area was wonderfully light due to large, stained-glass windows and a glass roof. The effect was stunning and the workmanship breathtaking. Two wards led off this atrium and we were shown into what we were told was a female medical ward.

The ward itself was spacious, light and airy, and metal-framed beds lined three sides of the ward with a large wooden writing desk in the centre. We were advised that this desk was for the nurses to write their patients' reports on, and was especially useful at night as the night nurses could see at a glance if any patient needed their help.

The ward sister, a tall slim redhead, quickly came over to greet us. She acknowledged Miss Hanlon with a smile and within seconds was taking us around the ward, introducing us to her patients and the nurses who were caring for them, giving us a short talk about the type of patients who were on her ward. They tended to be coronaries, asthmatics and chest patients, together with a diverse range of other medical conditions such as diabetes and anaemia. She spoke to us in simple terms so we could all understand but without being the least bit patronising, and it was evident that she was very proud of her ward and her staff.

The whole ward was immaculate and there was a military precision to the way the beds were in complete alignment but, most importantly of all, the patients were smiling, comfortable and appeared content. The porters we had seen a few minutes earlier were now busy exchanging the empty oxygen cylinders for full ones and were making quite a din as they successfully attempted to unscrew a sticking valve that needed loosening in order to release the oxygen. A nurse immediately went to the patient's bedside and transferred the mask and tubing from the empty to the full cylinder and the flow was switched on with a distinctive whoosh. Once it was established that the exchange was satisfactory, the two porters apologised for the noise and trundled away with the now-empty cylinders, puffing and panting from the struggle.

Some patients had curtains around their beds and were being washed, changed and made comfortable; others were being helped to the dayroom (a small, comfortable room situated within the ward itself on the left-hand side as you entered). There was a large television for them to watch or an assortment of newspapers and out-of-date magazines to read. It was chaotically busy but seemed to run like clockwork. The thing that struck me most was the way the nurses were scurrying around doing umpteen jobs at the same time, while still managing to remain quiet, friendly and efficient. One nurse was responsible for taking temperatures, blood pressures and pulses, which she recorded on charts hanging from the foot of each bed, while two others were giving out medicines from a large trolley, making sure that each patient had actually swallowed them before moving on to the next. The ward cadet, who we recognised by her mauve uniform, was pushing a trolley around collecting water jugs and glasses, in order to wash and replace them, as well as taking the flower vases that needed water changing. An auxiliary (nursing assistant) was helping one of the nurses behind a curtain and kept popping in and out for one thing or another. All in all I was very impressed and couldn't wait to start doing it all myself.

The thing that did confuse some of us was the number of different uniforms that the staff wore. One cadet plucked up the courage to ask the ward sister if she could explain why there were so many different types. Sister smiled and agreed that it did take some getting used to at first, but she was happy to describe the hierarchy of the nursing structure within the hospital for us. Matron was the senior nurse in every hospital, responsible for all nursing and domestic staff, patient care, general standards and the efficient running of all wards and departments. Usually career nurses, their entire lives were devoted to the care and interests of their staff and patients. Matron's uniform varied from hospital to hospital according to preference, but our own matron wore a long-sleeved, below-the-knee navy blue dress that sported a particularly frilly white broderie anglaise starched collar and matching cap. She had a deputy matron who wore dark green and who deputised for her when she was absent.

On every ward and in many of the departments, there were two sisters, one senior and one junior; both wore identical navy blue dresses with starched aprons, caps and cuffs. Staff nurses came next in the pecking order, the number depending on the size of the ward or the type of department but usually there were two of them and they wore royal blue. The staff nurses were expected to deputise for sister if she was absent on holiday or off the ward for whatever reason, and they were also responsible for helping to train and support students and pupil nurses who were working on their ward.

In the 1960s, hospitals used an apprenticeship system for training nurses. The trainees attended lectures part-time and worked on the wards the remainder of the time. There were two types of training available; one was a reduced training that lasted only two years and enabled the nurse to attain the State Enrolled Nurse (SEN) qualification. During training these nurses were regarded as pupils rather than students and wore green-and-white striped uniforms with a plain white cap in their first year and a white cap with a green stripe across the front in their second year. This was for identity purposes only, so that other medical or nursing staff could tell at a glance what level of education they had reached. Once they had qualified they wore dark green and were addressed simply as nurse.

Student nurses, on the other hand, completed a three-year course and were expected to pass both theoretical and a series of hands-on practical assessments, as well as a practical examination set by the General Nursing Council, before qualifying as a State Registered Nurse (SRN) and being appointed to a staff nurse post. Promotion beyond the post of staff nurse was not generally open to anyone without the SRN qualification. All students, regardless of their year, wore sky

18

blue and (like the pupils) their caps denoted their level of training. A first-year student wore a plain white cap, a second-year student had a tiny blue squiggle across their cap and the third years had a broad blue band across theirs.

And then there were the auxiliaries. Their job was to help the nurses wherever they were needed, whether it was making beds or helping to give bed baths to patients. They also carried out many domestic duties such as cleaning lockers, washing and changing beds, and even mopping the floors after spillages. These untrained ladies (there were some male orderlies, but they were few and far between) were the backbone of the wards and some had worked on the same ward for many years. They wore green-and-white check dresses with a green apron.

Last but not least were the cadets. They could start work in the hospital at the age of sixteen but had to be at least eighteen before being considered for formal training. In my case, during the two years I would be a cadet, I could expect to be sent on day release to the local polytechnic college to study basic biology, chemistry and physics (as they had not necessarily been studied at school), along with anatomy and physiology, and we would also be taught the basics of invalid cookery (dealing with the various different dietary requirements for specific illnesses). This would culminate in my taking the NHS State Preliminary Examinations. Every hospital operated differently as far as cadets were concerned, but at Blackburn Royal the first-year cadets were never allowed to work on the wards. Instead they were allocated posts in the numerous departments, where they learned how these hives of activity played a vital role in the day-to-day running of the hospital. It was only when we had turned seventeen that we were allowed to go on the wards. Other hospitals sometimes worked differently, it was down to the individual matron and the number of candidates they had decided to take on. Cadets' uniforms were mauve and there was no distinction made between first and second year. Every single item of uniform was expected to be pristine at all times, regardless of position or title. The hospital laundry provided this essential service for every member of staff.

After this run-through, Miss Hanlon was desperately looking at her watch as we still had a lot to see and not much time left before lunch. We quickly left the ward itself and moved on to the sluice, which was the room where all the bedpans were washed, cleaned and sterilised, and the treatment room, which was where the sterile dressings, syringes, instruments and refrigerators containing the numerous injections were stored. We didn't have much time to see either of these in great detail and had to content ourselves with a brief glance before giving our genuine thanks to Sister for her time before heading back down the two flights of stairs into the basement.

The basement was very old and dilapidated with massive heating pipes running the full length of the ceiling, which made the corridors hot and humid. Unbelievably, even down here the domestics were slaving away! I felt quite sorry for these ladies as their work was not only hot but, regardless of the state of the floors, they still had to be mopped and the surfaces cleaned and who was even going to notice? The paint-work on the walls and window frames was in desperate need of decoration, yet the floor was spotlessly clean despite being almost worn away. It was certainly a labour of love for these people working in these difficult conditions.

As we walked down the corridor, Miss Hanlon pointed out a department on the right-hand side where all the medical and surgical instruments, syringes, dressings and theatre garments were cleaned, sterilised and stored. Known as CSSD (Central Sterile Supply Department), the temperature was absolutely stifling and at first glance it looked very much like a mini factory. This busy department provided an outstanding service to every ward and department throughout the hospital. Not having the benefit of pre-packed sterile disposable instruments or dressings in those days, everything had to be re-used, so this department scrubbed, sterilised and re-distributed all these essentials on a daily basis. Without this service, the hospital would no doubt have quickly ground to a halt.

Next we visited the hospital kitchens. For hygiene purposes you were not allowed into the kitchens without first changing into appropriate clothing but, because of our numbers, this clearly wasn't going to happen so we had to content ourselves with peering over each other's shoulders. We could see both men and women dressed from head to toe in white overalls, hats and hard, flat shoes doing a whole variety of jobs, from peeling vegetables to chopping up meat. The smell was not exactly appetising and the mixture of soggy cabbage and rice pudding reminded me of school dinners. But one of the cooks was stirring what looked like a massive vat of custard while another lady was preparing huge trays of jam roly-poly and several stomachs began grumbling in unison. Obviously beginning to feel hungry herself, Miss Hanlon decided to take us swiftly to our final destination — Ward 2. This was the basement ward in the new tower block and was situated next to the staff canteen. The New Wing, as it was called, was a great source of pride within the hospital and had been opened only a few months earlier by Princess Anne, and Miss Hanlon couldn't wait for us to see it.

She took us to the sister's office and asked the senior sister on duty if it was convenient to give us a tour. Unfortunately she was very short-staffed and was inundated with queries that only she could deal with so, much to the annoyance of Miss Hanlon, she declined to offer her own services but said she was more than happy for Miss Hanlon to show us around without a chaperone.

Miss Hanlon did not look very pleased but said nothing; instead she turned to us and explained that there were six wards in the New Wing numbered from 2 to 7 (no one knew what happened to Ward 1) and each housed thirty-two patients. Every ward was a mirror image of the others, in that they were divided into sixteen male patients on the left-hand side and sixteen female patients on the right. A large double dayroom, which was full of comfortable easy chairs and a television, was divided by a folding partition down the middle, to separate the men from the women. The rooms were light and positively luxurious compared to the older ward. Thick carpets covered the floors and colourful floral curtains hung at the enormous, double-glazed windows; there were even paintings and ornaments on display, which made an even starker contrast to the old wing.

Miss Hanlon decided to take us on to the female side where it was a little bit quieter at the time. There were three four-bed cubicles and four single side-wards on both sides, along with an oval-shaped nurses' station, a toilet block, a bathroom and a sluice. As each cubicle was the same as the other, it was only necessary to show us the first one, where we found four lovely ladies sitting happily by their beds chatting to each other and comparing notes on their progress. The cubicle looked virtually brand new; a fresh smell of paint still lingered all those months later. There was not so much as a finger mark or a speck of dust anywhere, yet two female domestics were busily cleaning down the windowsills, chairs and curtain rails; in fact, any and every surface that was likely to hold dust or dirt. They were both middle-aged and looked as though they were really enjoying their job, considering the amount of elbow grease they were using. One of the domestics, a chubby little lady with a beaming smile, was chatting away non-stop to the patients as she cleaned and, from the expression on the patients' faces, this lady was not only a cleaner to them but a friend as well. When the domestics saw us approaching, they made themselves scarce and disappeared into the next cubicle to carry on with their work.

The cubicle had two very large windows that were divided in the centre by a small washbasin where the staff washed their hands. A soap dispenser and paper-towel holder were fixed to the wall above the sink and everything was so neat it looked untouched by human hand. The two beds on the right faced the pair on the left and over each bed was a wheeled table from which the patients ate their meals, all in perfect alignment. The counterpanes were new and perfectly placed; in fact, they were almost standing to attention they were so straight. There wasn't a crease or a mark anywhere; it really had to be seen to be appreciated. Oh, and not to forget the hospital corners; they had a perfect forty-five degree angle to them, and I smiled to myself at the prospect of trying to achieve such precision. Next to each bed was a modern locker for the patients to store their belongings and each one was festooned with Get Well cards and overflowing flower vases.

The most important pieces of equipment were the piped oxygen and suction fixtures behind every bed. No lugging heavy oxygen cylinders here — everything was on tap. Suction was usually only needed if a patient was unconscious and therefore unable to swallow their own saliva. A very fine rubber or plastic tube was placed on to the end of the suction outlet coming out of the wall and inserted into the patient's mouth in order to clear the airway fast, acting rather like a vacuum cleaner by sucking away any loose debris, saliva or vomit, enabling the patient to breathe clearly. I can only imagine what a difference this concept must have made to both the nurses and patients. It must have been heaven to be able simply to reach behind a bed rather than to have to run down the ward and drag heavy equipment back to the bedside.

The one other innovation available behind every locker was a handheld buzzer, which allowed every patient to request assistance when needed. Once the buzzer had been pressed, a light would come on outside the corresponding cubicle, as well as on the ceiling between the wards, which told the nurse at a glance whether they were needed on the male or female side and which cubicle needed assistance. It must have been far better to be able to summon a nurse quickly and discreetly, than have to wait and simply hope that someone would arrive in time, especially if it was a bedpan that was needed.

I could see now why Miss Hanlon was so proud of the New Wing; it must have been a godsend to staff and patients alike. There were other areas to see but we had run out of time, so finally we were deposited in the staff dining room and allowed thirty minutes for lunch before being escorted to our initial placements. After our meal, Miss Hanlon produced her list of names, gathered us all together like a mother hen and escorted us around the hospital once more, dropping off new cadets in dribs and drabs at the departments in which they were to work.

2

My initial disappointment, when I realised we were too young to be allowed to work on a ward, had turned to excitement when I learned that I was assigned to the X-ray Department along with two other new cadets. When Miss Hanlon had initially shown us around the hospital she had avoided X-ray because the staff were dealing with a serious road traffic accident, but now she thrust us forward into what was the office-cum-reception to introduce us to the department manager. Audrey was a small, slim, middle-aged lady, who welcomed us warmly and showed us around her department with considerable pride, introducing us to each member of staff in turn. The waiting room, which was more like a corridor than a room, was packed to capacity. People were parked in wheelchairs, on stretchers or balancing on crutches, some pacing up and down impatiently and others sporting a variety of splints and bandages. We picked our way through the chaos, taking great care not to trip over or collide with any outstretched limbs, which were probably painful enough already, as Audrey proceeded to give us the full tour, explaining departmental rules and procedures as we went along.

Naturally, our first and most important introduction was to the boss, the Chief Radiologist, Mr Wilson, who seemed particularly stressed and grumpy that afternoon. He must have been at least sixty years old, which to my sixteen-year-old eyes was very definitely ancient, if not hovering on the point of death. We found him in his office, which was a long, narrow, darkened room, propped up in front of a pile of x-rays and an illuminated screen studying the processed film plates closely and reporting on them. As Chief Radiologist this was his expertise and his lone responsibility. A very attractive young lady called Tracy who looked to be in her twenties, was his secretary, and she was busy scribbling his findings in shorthand as he dictated. As Audrey ushered us into the room, he immediately stood up and I observed that he was wearing a short white jacket, had a pen behind one ear and a cigarette stuck behind the other. He was extremely round-shouldered and scrawny, with grey hair cropped very short in a crew cut and didn't look the least bit friendly. When we were introduced to him, he never said a word, merely peered at us over his glasses as if we were from another planet and grunted. Having actually got up off his backside to leave the room (not simply out of politeness, as I first thought), he scowled and left us standing there feeling distinctly apprehensive. Audrey looked exasperated but assured us this wasn't to be taken personally as he was always the same: a man of few words. She told us we would soon get used to him, but I wasn't altogether convinced.

Next to his office was a large rest room where most of the all-female staff were having a morning cuppa before starting their day's work. There were six radiographers (which was their official title) ranging in age from about thirty to late middle-age, and they all eyed us up and down with friendly interest before welcoming us into the fold. We were told that we would be working alongside each of them at some stage over the next few weeks and not to be afraid of asking questions at any time. Our duties would vary from filing x-rays and forms to chaperoning patients and helping the radiographers wherever necessary. My butterflies hadn't gone away but I felt a little easier knowing that they all appeared to be quite friendly and, in point of fact, they went out of their way to make us really welcome over the next few weeks.

There were four x-ray rooms: two were for patients coming directly from Casualty, one was for diagnostic deep x-rays, and the last room was integrated within a separate clinic upstairs specialising in chest problems. The radiographers there simply took chest x-rays as and when the consultant running the clinic requested them. Patients with tuberculosis or suffering from lung cancer were among some of the most typical categories of patients attending.

The most important rule of the department concerned protecting staff from exposure to radiation. Audrey explained that above the entrance to each x-ray room was an oval red light; if the light was switched on, staff were not allowed to enter as this indicated that x-rays were being taken and radiation was present. For health and safety reasons it was compulsory for all permanent x-ray staff to wear monitoring badges on their uniforms during each shift and these were inspected regularly to check whether the wearer had been exposed to excess radiation. If high levels were found, that particular member of staff could possibly be reprimanded for taking unnecessary health risks. In each room large, lead-lined screens protected staff from radiation exposure and heavy-leaded jackets, worn like tabards, were also provided. These were essential if a patient needed to be held or supported during an x-ray.

After the brief introductions we were given our first tasks. (Audrey reiterated the importance of protecting ourselves and made a point of reminding us that department health and safety rules were to be strictly observed, at the same time as reassuring us that there would always be a member of staff on hand to explain anything of which we were unsure.) Before she left us to our tasks, she showed us into a tiny room where the bedpans and urine bottles were stored. Patients sometimes needed to use them, particularly if they were elderly and on stretchers, so she went through the procedure of how the steriliser worked before disappearing into her office. Sheila, a tall, bespectacled girl, was sent to the office to file x-ray reports, while Anne, the redhead who had nearly fainted in the laboratory, and I were sent to file x-ray films in numerous large boxes that lined the main corridor, which led from Casualty into X-ray. The boxes were in alphabetical order and were the overflow from two storage rooms already bursting at the seams. Although it was repetitive work, the job suited me because I could see everything that was going on in nearby Casualty and there was a constant stream of injured patients meandering back- wards and forwards all afternoon. Poor Anne looked quite sick and very noticeably tried to avert her eyes at every opportunity, but I was in my element.

My first day came to an end and I got changed and hung up my new uniform in the locker room (I made a mental note to try at all costs to exchange them for ones that actually fitted me, at least in one or two places) before heading out to join the bus queue going back to the town centre. Looking back now, the contrast between the solid, traditional stone buildings behind me, erected a century earlier, and the shining concrete and glass new wing, opened only months before, probably never even entered my head, yet in many ways they symbolised the town itself. Built upon the once vastly prosperous but now fading cotton industry, and yet determined to join in the postwar development boom, redundant mill chimneys and new industrial estates and inadequate back-to-back terraced houses mixed with one or two affluent areas with large houses and large numbers of newly constructed square boxes aspiring to be family homes. The Beatles, the Rolling Stones, the swinging sixties, sex, drugs and rock'n'roll . . . it was all happening. But not to anyone I knew!

Blackburn and the whole of that part of east Lancashire had developed throughout the previous century on the back of the cotton industry and a quirk of nature: the weather. The unique microclimate created by damp air rolling

31

off the surrounding moors and down the streams into the valleys, where the mills were built to use the water in their production processes, created particularly humid conditions that vastly reduced breakage of the fine cotton thread when it was being woven into cloth on the old, steam-driven looms. By the end of the nineteenth century, Lancashire was producing most of the cotton cloth exported to the far corners of the British Empire via the sweatshops of Manchester and the ships out of Liverpool, but by the 1960s the industry was in serious decline, overtaken by American technology and cheap labour costs on the Indian sub-continent.

Taking my favourite upstairs front seat on the double-decker Blackburn Corporation bus, I could see the Leeds-Liverpool canal running alongside the road on the left, while on the right were empty mill premises and large areas of rubble, where whole streets of terraced houses had been demolished. Further down on the left were the railway sidings and goods warehouses, no doubt once a hive of activity but now partially abandoned, before coming to Darwen Street bridge, a massive Victorian steel and cast-iron railway bridge across the main road where two branch lines joined before coming in to Blackburn Station.

The bus terminal was directly in the centre of town. Known as the Boulevard, it was a sprawling area of individual bus shelters, bordered on one side by the smoke-blackened stonework of the railway station and on the other by ornate metal railings surrounding the grounds of Blackburn Cathedral, which everyone used as a short cut between the shops and the bus station. After changing buses, my route home took me past the newly rebuilt market hall, all concrete and glass, across the road from the large, red brick buildings of the local Thwaites Brewery, who still used carts pulled by huge dray horses to deliver their barrels of beer to town centre public houses. Further along the road we passed an even more extensive area of demolished properties, all now landscaped and proudly sporting two new, high-rise blocks of local authority flats, together with the Larkhill Health Centre. Soon my journey came to its conclusion at the two-up, two-down terraced house in Florence Street where I was born and lived with my parents and my sister Pat.

Bringing up two young daughters in early post-war Britain couldn't have been easy. Dad had served in the Navy and, after being demobbed, had found work in a factory. Mum was a bookbinder. Money was always tight and it must have been a daily struggle for them trying to make ends meet, yet when I look at the faded photographs of my childhood and see the rainbow-coloured, knitted cardigans, the ill-fitting, hand-me-down dresses and oversized shoes, I can't help but smile and shed the occasional tear. Nothing was ever wasted. Even the hearthrugs, proudly displayed in front of the fire, were homemade using old coats and faded curtains, anything that would keep the cold from our feet.

Like many hundreds of others in Blackburn, luxury came in the form of a tin bath in front of the open fire in the kitchen on Friday nights. We didn't have a bathroom or running hot water; every drop of water had to be heated up on the tiny gas stove until there was enough for both my sister and me to bathe in. The solitary small coal fire had to heat the whole house, so perhaps it wasn't surprising that the subsequent cold and damp took its toll on my health. At the age of four I suffered a serious bout of rheumatic fever followed soon afterwards by tonsillitis. It became necessary to admit me to hospital to have my tonsils out and the nurses on the ward looked after me wonderfully. When I returned home all I could think about was becoming a nurse.

Unfortunately school intervened first and I hated every minute of it, not least because the headmistress (a nun) could have given Attila the Hun a run for his money. Even worse, I was advised by the careers teacher that in order to be accepted as a cadet nurse I needed to demonstrate that I had an aptitude to study, which meant staying on at school for a further year to take my GCEs. With gritted teeth I got my head down, eventually managing to achieve a handful of passes. When I left school, nursing was seen as a vocation rather than a job or a career. The pay was poor and the discipline strict. You didn't have to be exceptionally clever, but what you did need was an abundance of common sense, a willingness to work hard and a genuine desire to care for others.

★　★　★

My first week as a cadet was spent filing hundreds of x-rays and reports, but after a week of filing I was finally asked to look after an actual patient. An elderly lady called Agnes, who had been brought through from Casualty, needed someone to stay with her while she waited on her trolley for her x-ray. The attendant nurse had to return immediately to Casualty as they were overwhelmed with patients and I was thrilled to be entrusted with the task.

Agnes was in her eighties but single-handedly ran her own small tobacconist shop in Blackburn town centre. That day she had turned around to get a box of matches for a scruffy, middle-aged customer when the man vaulted over the counter, without warning, and demanded money from the till. When she screamed, he pulled out an axe and hit her viciously about the head and face several times before callously stepping over her and stealing the takings. Seeing someone about to enter the shop he fled through the back door. The customer who came in heard moaning and found Agnes on the floor behind the counter bleeding profusely, he immediately called for an ambulance and the police, and stayed to comfort her until they arrived. The ambulance men were on the scene within minutes and, after first checking her blood pressure and pulse, covered her wounds with bandages. She was seen immediately on her arrival into Casualty, not least because she looked as though she had been in a massacre, blood was pouring through her bandages and her clothing was soaked with it. She was obviously going to require extensive stitching but first it was necessary to x-ray her in case she had fractures and needed surgery (in which case, any suturing would have been a waste of time as the stitches would have had to be removed for the doctors to have a good look inside), and also to make sure that no fragments of bone or splinters from the weapon itself were floating loose inside the wounds.

Agnes was obviously traumatised by the attack and was shaking violently from fear and shock. In order to get a good focus on the films, I was detailed to remain with her to prevent the x-ray plates from moving, so the radiographer handed me a lead jacket to wear. While holding numerous different-sized x-ray plates against her face, some of the dressings came loose and I was sickened by what I saw. There were a number of very deep gaping wounds on both sides of her face and her cheeks were split wide open enabling me to see her teeth, facial bones and tongue very clearly through the gashes. Although my heart was racing I kept talking to her to try and reassure her (and myself!) that she was in safe hands. It baffled me how anyone could do this to such a frail and helpless old lady. Agnes held on to my hand with a vice-like grip and wept pitifully while her x-rays were being taken. The films clearly showed that she had fractures of her skull, facial bones and right wrist, where she had tried to defend herself. Her deep lacerations would require many stitches. It was an absolute miracle she had survived.

The police arrived at the hospital after examining the scene to tell Agnes they had caught her attacker hiding in the outside lavatory, unable to escape because the backyard wall was too high to climb and was festooned with barbed wire. He was found cowering behind the door, still clutching the axe and covered in Agnes's blood. After a violent struggle, involving several police officers, he was eventually subdued, placed in custody and charged with armed robbery and attempted murder.

Once her x-rays were completed Agnes was taken back to Casualty, prior to being admitted to a surgical ward for observation and treatment. I never saw her again, but her story was in the local newspaper that same evening and I told my mum about my involvement in assisting her. I passed Agnes's little shop every day on my way to work and paid particular attention to see if it opened up again, but after two or three months it was boarded up and never reopened.

Slowly but surely I began to settle into the routine. As first-year cadets our duties were mainly office work, chaperoning, calling patients in and assisting those who were in wheelchairs or on stretchers. Sheila, Anne and I were becoming good friends, although we rarely actually worked together and only really saw each other at break times, but we shared our experiences and felt that we were doing fine. We were all reluctant to work in the room where the deep x-rays were taken, mainly because this was Mr Wilson's domain, but unfortunately we had no choice. Anne had already done a week in there and had hated it, but it was policy that each cadet should spend time in this room as it was so very different from the others. All x-rays taken in there were by pre-arranged appointment, usually following a referral from a GP who reported the patient's symptoms and requested some form of barium x-ray. (Barium is a white, radio-opaque solution, which means it will show up on x-ray.) With the help of a special fluorescent screen that is placed in front of the patient, the radiologist can see the bones clearly but only a vague outline of the organs, rather like looking at an ordinary x-ray. When barium is swallowed or inserted into the rectum, the organs become clear and any gastrointestinal abnormalities can be observed. X-rays are taken and reported on by the radiologist — all the findings of the investigations requested by a GP or a doctor within the hospital are recorded and a written report is sent to the doctor, who will then decide on an appropriate course of action.

Inevitably, some four weeks into my time as a cadet, I was moved to the deep x-ray room. I was forewarned by everyone to keep very quiet during the procedures and not to get in Mr Wilson's way, as he wasn't renowned for his patience. I had never been in the room before, which was dark and gloomy with a special kind of x-ray table in the centre. Thick electrical cables ran across the floor, a number of heavy lead jackets were hanging over a sturdy rail and in one corner was the screen which staff stood behind to protect themselves from radiation. There was a stool to assist the patient to climb on to the table, which was quite high, and a small dressing trolley carrying the equipment necessary for the various procedures. A small square door set in the wall at the back of the room opened up into a cupboard that had a second connecting door, which itself opened into an adjoining room. This cupboard was used to pass exposed x-ray plates through to the dark room where a member of staff was waiting to collect and process them. The two doors were never usually opened together during procedures, because any light could ruin the films (just like any other domestic camera film), so a primitive system of knocks was used to communicate, ensuring that lights were off and doors remained firmly closed until transfers had been complete.

On my first day working with Mr Wilson I felt sure that I would throw up because I was so nervous and I staggered around under the weight of my protective lead jacket. Hoping I would be inconspicuous, I backed into a corner and waited for the miserable old duffer to arrive. Two patients had already been asked to get changed and had been shown into cubicles where gowns were provided for them to change into. Patients usually put on two gowns, one that was similar to a nightdress that fastened with tapes down the back but invariably gaped wide open, and then a dressing gown to hide their blushes. They had to sit and wait inside their respective cubicles until called. I was relieved to find that a junior radiographer was also present, whose main function was to insert the films and set the required exposures. At least I wasn't going to be on my own with him.

The first patient was called in. He was asked to remove his dressing gown and climb on to the table. The deep x-ray room table was very different to the examination tables in the other rooms and the technical name for it was a Diagnostic Tilting Fluoroscopy Table. These tables could be manoeuvred electrically from a prone position into a vertical position at the push of a button, and a fluorescent screen was then swung around in front of the patient. This screen was attached to the metal frame of the table and could also be moved up and down manually on a wheeled drivepath, allowing the radiologist to examine the patient from neck to pelvis in one slow but easy pass. The table surface was black Bakelite, and was cold and uncomfortable, with a footrest at one end. As the first patient removed his dressing gown I felt myself go hot around the collar and didn't know where to look. He had put his hospital gown on back to front and was so obese that it barely covered him anyway, leaving absolutely nothing to the imagination. I had never seen a naked man before and my face must have said it all as the radiographer looked at me and smirked. I escorted the man back to his cubicle while he quickly reversed his attire, before returning to find Mr Wilson waiting impatiently, tapping his fingers and checking his watch.

'Lights,' he bellowed, and the room was immediately plunged into complete darkness. Initially it was so dark that I literally couldn't see my hand in front of my face and it took a couple of minutes before I was able to focus. Patient and table were manoeuvred into an upright position so that he was standing on the footrest on one end of the table with an illuminated x-ray plate in front of his chest. He was asked to stand as straight as possible and then given a beaker of barium to hold in his left hand. On Mr Wilson's instruction he took a mouthful of the white chalky liquid and held it there until told to swallow. When the screen moved up to his neck he swallowed on command, grimacing at the taste, and on the glowing fluorescent screen I could see the barium progress down his throat and into his stomach. Very interesting and very clever, I thought. Mr Wilson muttered something about a 'stricture' but at the time I didn't dare ask what it was.

'Lights,' he shouted again and then he left the room without uttering a word to the patient. Once again I had difficulty focussing. The patient was also rubbing his eyes but otherwise seemed fine. He was advised by the radiographer to see his GP in about ten days to get the results, and then he returned to his cubicle to change and go home.

I asked the junior radiographer to explain the findings and she told me that a stricture is a narrowing of a passage. In this man's case, it was possibly due to the cancer in his trachea (windpipe), which had been previously diagnosed, and was now pushing against the oesophagus (gullet). His prognosis was poor and he was likely to be facing some serious surgery in the not-too-distant future.

The next patient had a history of bowel problems, which had been fluctuating between the extremes of constipation and diarrhoea for several months and, according to the GP's referral, he had lost an alarming amount of weight over a short period of time. More worryingly he was bleeding from his rectum. He was scheduled to have a barium enema and on the previous evening he had been given medication to empty his bowels and had been instructed not to eat or drink anything after his evening meal. He was asked to lie on the table on his left-hand side with his knees drawn up to his chest. A funnel and tube were strategically placed on top of a trolley next to him, together with a quantity of barium enema.

'Lights,' shouted Mr Wilson and again there was instant total darkness. Mr Wilson briefly explained the procedure to the patient before inserting the end of the tube into the man's bottom. A considerable volume of gas was immediately released with a loud rumble and I felt quite embarrassed for the patient. Barium was then poured unceremoniously down the funnel, where it disappeared with a gurgling, slurping sound. Before I could blink, Mr Wilson was shouting at me to bring him some more barium, pointing in the direction of a large plastic bottle on the other side of the room. I edged my way around the room, avoiding the x-ray cables that snaked across the floor and carefully picked up the flask by its neck. Now how was I to know that the radiographer hadn't screwed the top on properly? I had barely taken two steps when the flask bounced out of my hands and on to the ground, cartwheeling across the floor and spewing out a sheet of thick liquid until it eventually came to rest, spinning slowly around, in a large pool of barium. My world turned a whiter shade of pale. The stuff was absolutely everywhere and everyone in the room was spattered. Floors, walls and x-ray equipment were soaking wet. My heart sank and I burst into tears, spluttering and apologising, then went rigid with fear as a ghostly Mr Wilson stood up and sighed loudly in disgust, removed the tube from the patient and stormed out. The lights came back on to reveal a winter wonderland of dripping white, rather reminiscent of a Christmas card scene. I was absolutely frantic but both the junior radiographer and the patient were howling with laughter. A mop and bucket arrived with a message from Mr Wilson to clear it up in five minutes or else! My shoes squelched with goo and my tights were sporting white polka dots. I felt such an idiot, apologised once more to anyone who was still listening and set about tidying up the mess. The fag-ridden monster returned precisely ten minutes later and inspected the scene without a word, although I was sure I saw him grin and wink at the patient.

★   ★   ★

The X-ray Department was very different to how I had first imagined it would be. Radiographers weren't just glorified photographers, they were highly trained professionals and worked quickly and efficiently, knowing precisely how to move and handle seriously ill and injured patients without causing them further pain or injury. New staff invariably had tricks played on them in almost every department, though. It was always very juvenile but seemed to be a ritual, as it was in most workplaces. I was asked by a senior radiographer to go to the sister in general theatre and enquire if X-ray could borrow a pack of fallopian tubes. I was sixteen, had never done biology at school and was naïve to the point of ignorance, but thought something was odd because I could hear staff giggling. When I rang the bell outside theatre, a male nurse appeared. He was dressed in mask and theatre clothes and asked what I wanted. I felt uneasy but relayed my request for fallopian tubes. He looked annoyed and told me to advise whoever had sent me that if they had nothing better to do he would find them some real work. On the way back I met a student nurse and asked her to explain what fallopian tubes were. She groaned and then smiled at my innocence, before explaining the female reproductive system to me. She advised me to ignore the radiographer's antics and simply carry on working as if nothing had happened.

Anne, in the meantime, had been sent all over the hospital for the legendary long stand, each department having been pre-warned that she was coming. She was left standing on the corridor for about half an hour everywhere she went, before finally realising that she was being teased and was quite distressed at having been made to look

44

a fool. Sheila, on the other hand, had observed the goings-on and decided to keep well out of the way. She was nobody's fool! We all laughed about it for a long time afterwards, especially when we heard from other cadets about being sent for equally ridiculous items, like a bucket of oxygen. I was going to miss X-ray, especially when I realised I was heading for CSSD.

★   ★   ★

Having seen the inside of CSSD during the initial hospital tour on that first day, I felt somewhat deflated knowing that this was where I was heading next; it had seemed to be so very hot and stuffy in there, but only time would tell. The manager, Mr Perry, took me around the department pointing out in detail the type of work that was expected of me. The first section was where all the dirty instruments from the theatres and wards were brought to be washed, scrubbed and sterilised. Nothing was ever thrown away or wasted and in 1966 few disposable instruments had been introduced. A large container full of bloodied instruments was wheeled in and the gentlemen working there began to open up each instrument, inspect every one meticulously, rinse them individually under a running tap before placing them into what at first looked like a standard stainless steel sink. Once the sink was reasonably full, he filled it with water, added a scoop of cleaning powder, pressed a button and a persistent vibration started up, showing as tiny ripples on the surface. This machine was ultra sonic and cleaned the instruments to perfection. At the end of the cycle, which ran for about twenty minutes or so, the instruments were removed and checked again to make sure they were thoroughly clean, after which they were handed over to the next group of staff who packed them and finally sterilised them, ready for redistribution around the hospital.

Moving into the next area I was introduced to four ladies, all dressed in white coats, who were sitting around large tables packing different types of dressings and theatre packs into paper bags. On one table was a pyramid of cotton wool balls, where a rather bored-looking young woman was counting out five balls at a time before putting them carefully into a white paper bag, which was then folded, taped and placed in a large metal tray ready for sterilising. At another table crêpe bandages of varying sizes were being rolled and packed. Someone else was putting different-sized kidney bowls in bags and the last lady had a larger table and was packing up special trays which were destined for theatre. Every pack had a number and the contents of each bag had to correspond precisely to the pre-agreed requirements. So, for example, an S11 had to contain five cotton wool balls; an S15 had to contain a small receiver and so on. The importance of this system was that when these packs were used in theatre, it was essential that each and every item was accounted for, so that at the end of the operation the number of items used could be reconciled to numbers at commencement. It was no good suddenly realising after the patient had left theatre that a swab was missing and they may have to be opened up again to ensure the missing item had not been left behind and sewn up inside the patient. So even though these jobs appeared to be monotonous, they were vital to the patients' well-being.

The third room was where the autoclaves were to be found that sterilised all the packs and instruments. It was the manager's job to make sure that these machines were maintained regularly, as a breakdown could well delay all operations and even bring the hospital to a grinding halt. A piece of special pale-coloured tape was used to seal the tops of each pack. If the autoclaves were working correctly and the process had been completed satisfactorily, then this tape changed colour to brown, thus ensuring that the packs were fit to use.

In the final room a middle-aged gentleman called Jack was responsible for the washing and sterilising of all the syringes. When I worked in this department, these were made of glass, and once a doctor or nurse had used a syringe it was carefully put back in its metal container, and placed in a large box ready to be collected along with everything else going back to CSSD. Jack's job was to separate the top from the bottom of each syringe, wash them thoroughly to remove any of the previous drug or blood, dry them and then pack them back into their cylindrical metal containers before inserting them into a machine which placed a foil seal on the end of the tube. From there they were put on a conveyor belt that slowly moved through a heating machine before they appeared out the other end fully sterilised and ready to use again. Just like the special autoclave tape on the packs, the tops on the cylinders changed colour when the process was complete.

Every ward and department ordered hundreds of sterile packs and syringes each week. Jack delivered the orders directly to the recipients in large brown panniers, removing the dirty items at the same time. The system ran like clockwork and my job was to work a week in rotation between the various rooms, where I certainly learned to appreciate the hard work that went into supplying the hospital with this necessary equipment. Despite so much equipment being regularly re-used, I quickly came to understand that the incidence of any infection spreading within a hospital is mainly down to a basic lack of cleanliness and good medical and nursing practice.

★   ★   ★

Three months later found me working in Medical Records. The hospital was not computerised so my main job was to gather the medical records of patients who had either been admitted on to the wards overnight and/or were attending clinics in the Out-patient Department. Records were always organised a day in advance of the clinic to ensure that they were ready for the consultants as and when they were needed. Each morning I was given several lists that contained the names and numbers of all the patients who had been given appointments to attend and all I had to do was find them, collect them together and put them in clinic order. While it may sound pretty straightforward, in reality it was quite a task because records were kept in several different places. There were two main records offices, each crammed from floor to ceiling with records, all in alphabetical order. In addition to these, doctors' secretaries often took them to write letters to GPs, and wards sometimes held on to them after the patient had been discharged.

There was a system in place that should have been fool-proof but people often didn't follow the rules and then things went wrong. If a set of notes were required, the person removing them was supposed to put a tracer card in its place recording who had moved them, what date they were removed and where they were being taken to. Unfortunately, staff were often in a hurry and weren't always able to find a tracer card to use or they were simply too lazy to be bothered. Thus when I came along, records were often missing and I then had to track them down by checking in all the usual likely places. I must have walked several miles each day but, on a positive note, at least I soon found my way around the hospital and met many very friendly and helpful people along the way.

One very important check I had to make once I'd actually found the notes, was to look carefully to see that they were, in fact, the correct ones. There were many patients with the same or similar name, but each person had a different hospital record number. It was very easy to pick up the wrong notes, unless both name and number were checked, and then the consultants would rant and rave at the poor Out-patient staff, having discussed a patient using the wrong records and sometimes given them false information.

An example of this happened to my own mum. She was an in-patient at the time and had been having investigations on the medical ward. I went to visit her one day and, before going in, was taken aside by the junior doctor. He took me into the ward office, sat me down and said that he had some rather bad news for me: Mum had undergone a liver biopsy and unfortunately it was malignant. I knew that she was really poorly but I had never expected this. I had to leave the ward to pull myself together and was seen by one of the ward sisters who came to ask me what was wrong. I told her the news the doctor had given to me and she looked at me as if I was mad.

'Who on earth told you that?' she said looking really angry and was absolutely livid when I told her, saying the information was completely untrue. It turned out that another patient had a very similar name to Mum and had been given similar tests. Mum's tests were normal, the other lady's weren't, and the doctor had not checked the case note number before giving me the awful news. It was an important lesson to learn and he was mortified at his mistake. Thankfully he hadn't told Mum and he apologised profusely to me. (Usually if there are two patients with the same or a similar name on a ward, a sticker is placed on the record cover warning of this. For whatever reason, that time it had been missed.)

By the end of my shift in Medical Records, if I had not been able to find every record (which happened on quite a number of occasions), I had to leave a note on the top of the pile of the appropriate clinic recording what was missing. It was then the cadet working in Out-patients who took over. When she came on duty the following day, she had to make a second check, since sometimes the people who had borrowed the notes, subsequently returned them later in the day. So, when I joined their ranks in Out-patients as my next move, I knew only too well what to expect.

★　★　★

Searching for records was only one of my new tasks — thankfully now I would also be coming in regular contact with real patients. Many of the nurses in Out-patients were middle-aged; they seemed to be a happy group of individuals and made me very welcome from my first day. The consultants changed each day, as did the type of clinic. One day there might be medical clinics for people having chest or heart problems, and another day might be Gynaecology or ENT (Ear, Nose and Throat). There was only one unit sister in charge and during my three months I got to work in every possible clinic.

The first job each day was to help to set up the different clinics. Equipment pertaining to each speciality had to be prepared and made ready for use as soon as we came on duty. For most clinics it was routine that patients had to be weighed on arrival and have their urine tested. I had never tested urine before, so for the first few patients, one of the staff nurses, a tall, slim lady called Margaret, showed me how to do it and then brought the patient's records to me so I could record the result before the patient saw the doctor. I would generally be allowed to listen in to the consultations if I was lucky, but it depended on the consultant. Some of them were not particularly forthcoming. In those days quite a number of the senior doctors could be downright rude and arrogant, even when dealing with their staff, and could be abrupt and outspoken, without any thought whatsoever for the feelings of the poor patient. (This was probably a throwback for many of them to the pre-NHS era, when they were treated as gods, especially if the patient wasn't being treated privately. Although a few of them never changed.) Many of them were kind and sympathetic, though, explaining to the patient why they were getting such symptoms and what tests were required.

To me the most interesting clinic was Orthopaedic. Patients had usually been operated on for broken bones sustained in an accident, or had routine elective surgery such as a hip replacement operation or cartilage removed from a knee. Once they were sent home they then attended clinic for a post-operative check and renewal of dressings, and I loved watching the nurses do this. I couldn't wait to start doing it myself but as a cadet, of course, I wasn't given the opportunity. I found it interesting to hear about their accidents or the reasons for their operations, though, and was fascinated to be shown their x-rays both before and after surgery, in order to appreciate the improvement. Many had been in hospital for months, others for only a few days, but I never once heard a complaint other than about the hospital food, which I have to admit was pretty grim even in the staff canteen.

★   ★   ★

During a surgical clinic one afternoon, an elderly lady was attending after first having seen her GP some six weeks previously complaining of persistent abdominal pain and severe weight loss. After her name had been called out at least three times, a stooped, rather frail-looking seventy-year-old lady stood up, shook her hearing aid and shuffled slowly into the clinic with the aid of two walking sticks. She flopped down heavily into the nearest chair, desperately trying to catch her breath. The doctor arrived and introduced himself as Dr Patel. She shook her hearing aid again, making it screech loudly with static, before eventually setting it at the correct volume. He asked her why she had been sent to the clinic. Being deaf and unfamiliar with his accent she looked at the nurse who was chaperoning, pulled her face in dismay and shouted at the top of her voice (as though it was everyone else who was deaf and not her): 'What? What did he say?' The question was repeated to her again but much louder (her hearing aid was already on maximum volume) and more slowly. She thought for a minute or two before looking at the nurse and saying: 'I've 'ad a bad belly ache for weeks an' I carn't stand it no more.'

Dr Patel hadn't grasped what she was saying so he looked at the beleaguered nurse, asking what a belly ache was. After she advised him that the lady was complaining of abdominal pain, he nodded seriously and, observing how thin the patient looked, asked her in a very heavy Asian accent if she had been losing weight.

At this question, she again fiddled with her hearing aid and began to shake it frantically, shouting as loud as she could: 'Carn't tha talk proper English, mon? I carn't understand a bloody word tha sez.'

The whole of the consultation carried on like this until eventually the story unfolded and this poor old soul was told that she would have to undergo a series of investigations, which she would receive appointments for as soon as possible.

Mind you, often there were communication problems even with the English doctors. On one occasion a lady came to see the gynaecologist after her GP had referred her because she was complaining of pelvic pain and offensive vaginal discharge. She was also in her seventies and stood no more than about five feet tall. The gynaecologist that day was a true gentleman who always liked to talk to his patients in his consulting room first before examining them. As the patient came in, it was soon apparent that she too was extremely deaf. Every question that he asked was answered at the top of her voice so that every patient in the clinic must have heard. He tried letting her read his lips which seemed to be a little better, then once she had told her story he asked her to go into the next room, get undressed and to lie on the bed for examination. She appeared to have heard and understood this request and toddled out dutifully with the attending staff nurse to take off her underwear.

Two minutes later, rather than waiting in her room she wandered back into the consulting room and, before anyone could say a word, hoisted up her skirt and got down on the floor. She raised her legs in the air, leaning her feet against the wall, and beckoned the shocked consultant to come and have a look. He was mortified as the staff nurse hastily hoisted her to her feet and managed to get her back into the examination room. When he did eventually manage to examine her he was dumbstruck and admitted to us later that he had never seen anything like it. This poor woman had at some point in her life had a vaginal ring inserted internally to support a prolapsed womb. These rings were supposed to be changed frequently but somehow this had not happened. After further questioning it appeared that this particular ring had been in place nearly ten years and the result was horrendous, to the least. The consultant asked the lady's allow us to see what had develo perfectly happy provided someb pared to do something about it, so lamp to give the staff nurse and m

Unbelievably the ring was now overgrown with vaginal tissue and had now literally become part of her body to the point of needing major surgery to remove it. Besides this, the whole area was also infected and oozed offensive smelling pus. The consultant left the room and sat in his chair completely lost for words as he honestly didn't know what he could do because any operation would be serious and involve drastic surgery. He couldn't understand how this had been neglected for so long. Old people always seemed very stoical when it came to doctors and hospitals; perhaps, in this case, she knew there was a problem but chose to ignore it until she was experiencing pain.

In the end, the patient was admitted to the ward to be put on an antibiotic drip to get rid of the severe infection first. Any decision beyond that would have to wait. (After the infection had cleared, the consultant eventually decided that he was not going to operate as he felt that she would not survive the anaesthetic. She already took a number of pills for a variety of medical problems and he decided to bring her back to the clinic every few months and keep a close eye on her.)

There was a Bank Holiday during my placement in the Out-patient Department and, while _____ say the _____ was closed, cadets _____ permission to _____ ped. She was _____ ay off. One of the _____ ody was pre- _____ that Matron had _____ he angled the _____ d the morning in _____ e a clear view. _____ observer. I was _____ wondering what

I was about to see. As I arrived outside theatre I was relieved to find another cadet called Barbara had been sent to join me. We looked at each other and squealed with excitement, but we were soon put in our place when a third-year student nurse arrived to take us to the changing rooms to put on theatre clothing. She wore a white scarf that completely covered her hair and a white cotton mask that hung loosely around her neck, a thin, pale blue cotton dress and a pair of white clogs which clomped as she walked along. Although only a student herself, she looked extremely officious as she eyed us up and down with obvious distaste before telling us with an air of authority how very lucky we were to be allowed to see an operation. She was most put out about it, grumbling that she had been in her second year of training before being permitted such an opportunity. She demanded that we behave ourselves, warned us not to get in the way of anyone or touch anything, and finally threatened to have us thrown out if we made a sound. She obviously wasn't thrilled to see us, which was more than a little intimidating, but we didn't care. We did, however, heed her warnings and kept very quiet as we quickly changed into theatre garb and masks, before being shown into the main operating theatre.

The first thing I noticed was the temperature: it was suffocating. Everything looked quite surreal; a rather large female patient lay on the table already anaesthetised, being carefully monitored by the anaesthetist. A number of people in masks, green gowns and surgical gloves were covering the patient with sterile green towels, leaving only a small area of flesh visible on her ample abdomen. There were three long narrow tables full of surgical instruments and two other staff (including the third-year student) were busy opening packs of sterile gauze and generally running around fetching and carrying. The surgeon looked at the anaesthetist for permission to start the operation and a quick nod of the head indicated that surgery could commence. Even though my fellow cadet Barbara and I didn't have a clue what was happening we were completely awestruck as the operation proceeded. The medical jargon went way above our heads and we couldn't really see an awful lot either from where we were standing, which was about eight feet away from the table, but just being there was totally fascinating and we knew this was bound to make all the other cadets green with envy. Every now and again, Sister (at least I presumed it was Sister, since it was hard to be sure with the mask — whoever she was, she was clearly in charge of the nurses) checked that we were okay; the surgeon on the other hand ignored us completely and was humming quietly to himself as he delved into the innards of this poor woman on the operating table. The surgery went well and took just over two hours to complete, after which the third-year nurse wasted no time in dismissing us from the theatre, again letting us know how fortunate we were.

Working in Out-patients gave me such an appetite to learn more. As a cadet, most of the time we could really only watch and listen, yet to me even the most minimal of patient contact was exciting. I learned a lot about patient's symptoms and illnesses, the tests they required and their eventual diagnosis and treatment. A whole year had flown by in the blink of an eye and now I was seventeen and could finally go on the wards. A new change list was due and I couldn't wait to see which ward I was heading for.

★ ★ ★

Blackburn Royal Infirmary (BRI) was one of two separate hospitals in the health authority to which I could expect to be posted as part of my formal training when I eventually reached the magic age of eighteen, Queens Park Hospital (QPH), another collection of Victorian buildings, was spread out over a much larger site about a mile from BRI. Occupying the top of a steep hill heading out on to the moors, this used to be the town workhouse and afforded uninterrupted views across virtually the whole of Blackburn. All maternity services for the area were centralised on the site, which also had extensive medical and surgical capabilities, some of which were contained within various tagged-on, inter-war, pre-fabricated or wooden structures which were already less than ideal. Park Lee Hospital came under the same Health Authority and was located half way between BRI and QPH but cadets and students were not sent to train there. A dedicated isolation unit, it was still known locally as the fever hospital and dealt with patients who had undiagnosed infections. Springfield Hospital was a geriatric ladies' convalescence and rehabilitation hospital, which was also part of the authority, and was based on Preston New Road. While students weren't posted to this particular location, cadets were and, to my consternation, I discovered that I was heading there next. Rumour had it that the Sister in Charge was a strict disciplinarian who ate cadets for breakfast. Lucky me! A second cadet called Linda, a very slight, shy, nervous-looking girl, was to accompany me.

Panic started to set in the night before I was due to report at my new placement. My mind was working overtime and I remembered hearing about two Springfield cadets who were thankful to get away after their three-month stint. Apparently, on their last day Sister had called the pair into her office and counselled them that they both had a long way to go and she didn't think either of them would make it through training. I hardly slept a wink that night in anticipation of what was to come and, as I met Linda on the bus the following morning, I could see that she was, if possible, feeling even worse than me. Although we were both nervous, as before any new placement, she was green around the gills and hardly spoke two words. We both looked like death warmed up, as my old mum used to say. We gingerly climbed the front steps of the hospital but, before we had even reached the front door, a chubby little woman clutching a mop and bucket greeted us with a toothless grin.

'Two more lambs to the slaughter,' she cackled as she all but dragged us inside.

3

Bridget, the cleaner, knocked hard on the office door and then unceremoniously pushed us into the room without waiting for a reply. The room was rather pokey and cluttered, smelt strongly of polish and disinfectant and the dreaded Sister White was sitting behind a large antiquated writing desk. With her tightly permed white hair and wrinkled face, I speculated that she must be at least seventy. She was wearing an immaculately pressed navy blue uniform with pristine white collar and cuffs, plus the usual starched apron and frilly white cap, and looked decidedly snooty as she inspected the pair of us through half-moon spectacles balanced delicately on the tip of her nose. Sister introduced herself then took us into a tiny locker room where we were to change into our uniforms (which we had brought with us from BRI), before telephoning upstairs to the staff nurse who was to supervise Linda. She materialised only seconds later, closely followed by a yapping little dog. This nurse and her pet dog apparently lived on the premises and the Jack Russell terrier 'entertained' the old ladies (although I was to discover that it also frequently did a wee on the furniture if it got the opportunity and occasionally ran off with a soiled incontinence sheet!). Staff Nurse, a plump jolly individual with thinning brown curly hair and a lop-sided cap, welcomed us warmly and took Linda away upstairs to work with her, while I was left alone with 'the dragon'.

The hospital had previously been a large Victorian private residence but now accommodated a maximum of thirty elderly ladies between two floors, serving the dual purpose of freeing up beds at BRI, while enabling the ladies to have physiotherapy and occupational therapy during their recovery process. As it was breakfast time, Sister White took me on a brief tour of the building. On the ground floor were two large, brightly decorated rooms with five or six beds in each, all occupied. I remember that there was no odour of age-related problems, so the staff obviously worked hard to maintain a high standard of cleanliness. Some ladies were sitting by their beds eating breakfast and others were being spoon-fed by a member of staff. There was a staff dining room, sluice, offices and, in the corner, an old-fashioned electric lift that I was warned was liable to break down. Upstairs were several more rooms for the residents, including a large dining room and a lounge. These other patients were much more ambulant and able to look after themselves than the ladies downstairs who needed extra nursing care.

Elsie was a stooped eighty-year-old who had recently suffered a second stroke and was tucked up in bed. She had been quite poorly and could do very little for herself, having lost the use of both her right arm and right leg. Two auxiliaries were in the room feeding other patients; each nodded a welcome as we walked in and unsuccessfully tried to stifle an ominous giggle.

Sister White thrust a bowl of porridge into my hands and asked me to try to get Elsie to eat some. I nervously introduced myself to her, pulled up a chair and sat down, placed a towel under her chin and spooned up a small amount of porridge. She watched my every move without a word, took the first mouthful perfectly happily and then, with great delight, laughed as she spat the next spoonful down the front of my uniform. The two auxiliaries joined in, laughing uproariously. I put a little less porridge on the spoon the next time as I offered it to her again, but this time she kept her mouth tightly shut like a petulant child, repeatedly refusing it and turning away. Finally she upended the spoon and threw it at me with her one good hand. This being my first task I was flustered but determined not to fail. I put some sugar on the porridge as Elsie now watched with interest.

'Right Elsie, let's try again.'

She opened her mouth like a ravenous baby bird, swallowed it and proceeded to eat the lot. A few minutes later, just as I was wiping her mouth, Sister White came back into the room, took one glance at the empty bowl and looked positively deflated. I learned later that Elsie was often used as a test case for new cadets.

For my next task I was instructed to change her nightdress and sit her in a chair, which was to prove slightly more challenging. I pulled the curtains around the bed to maintain her dignity and told her what I intended to do (not that she was taking a blind bit of notice!). Again she said nothing, but the moment I attempted to remove her nightdress she screamed blue murder, kicked out and even tried to bite me (a potentially nasty nip because she hadn't a tooth in her head!). For a tiny lady who was supposed to be sick and helpless she was incredibly strong-willed. The more the other staff laughed the more determined I became to tame this hellcat. With a little help from Sister White I eventually managed to get Elsie changed and sat her in a chair, although the effort left me completely exhausted. I was extremely relieved to find that the other patients were much easier to handle.

After breakfast all the patients were routinely taken to the toilet, regardless of whether they wanted to go or not. Those not able to walk unaided were assisted by staff using various walking aids or were taken on a sani-chair, which is basically a metal-framed wheelchair but with a toilet seat replacing the normal cushion. With the patient seated, it is wheeled into a toilet cubicle and the whole thing fits over the top of the lavatory bowl, the object being to give more privacy to the patient and involve less lifting for the nurses. However, one massive drawback is that the patient (especially the elderly and confused) often starts to 'go' before reaching the toilet cubicle and quite often a nurse will find herself sliding across the floor in a fairly unpleasant 'accident'. The road holding of my shoes was tested on many such occasions.

Most of the morning was taken up making beds, cleaning lockers, changing the water jugs and drinking glasses, and giving out warm drinks to patients. Some patients needed toileting regularly, with one bedridden patient in particular often needing a bedpan. This took some getting used to at first, as cleaning a bedpan or commode had not yet been demonstrated to me (like every other task, we were expected to learn on the job) and the hard, stainless-steel receptacles all had to be emptied, cleaned and sterilised without delay. Never having given a bedpan to a patient before, Sister took me through the procedure verbally and in stages: first, draw the curtains around the bed; next request the patient to lift their bottom; and then slide the bedpan underneath. Make sure that the patient is secure and will not fall off. Provide toilet tissue and leave them in private for a few minutes. On your return, remove the bedpan. Ensure that the patient is clean (assist, if necessary), take the pan to the sluice, rinse it clean and place it in the steriliser. Finally, provide warm soapy water to wash the patient's hands. It sounded pretty straightforward but I soon found out that there was a definite art to what seemed like a simple procedure. Not all patients were able to lift themselves up or help in any way; for example, some were too ill and others who had perhaps suffered strokes kept falling off the bedpan. One or two patients were so hugely overweight that it was difficult to get the pan in the correct spot and, occasionally, it was even more difficult to find or get a grip on it afterwards.

I was also less than confident on my first visit to the sluice. I wandered in to find Sister White changing the water in some flower vases at one of the small sinks. She was obviously in a good mood and singing happily as she laboured away. The bedpan I was carrying was fully laden and required both hands to support it. I smiled at Sister and tried to look confident without spilling the contents. Standing in front of the large sluice sink I was mesmerised by the various taps and levers that bristled from the tiled walls behind it. I tried to keep calm and concentrate on what I had been told; after all, I didn't want to look completely stupid. I talked myself slowly through each stage. First, empty the contents of the pan into the small bidet-type receptacle next to the main sink and flush. That part was easy. Next invert the empty bedpan over the central hole in the base of the main sink. So far; so good. I held on to the bedpan for dear life because I had been told that the water pressure was very powerful. Finally, after deliberating which of the four handles I had to use to turn on the water, I chose the nearest one, which seemed quite logical to me. WRONG! A split second after I turned it on there was a loud whoosh as a fierce jet of water shot skywards and ricocheted off the ceiling, drenching me from head to foot. I had mistakenly operated the adjacent water jet which was used to wash out urine bottles (not normally used in an all-female environment). In my shock I had totally forgotten about Sister White who was grimly standing there, also dripping wet, her starched white cap drooping limply over her forehead like a soggy pancake and one huge drip clinging tenaciously to the end of her nose like a large globule of snot. I desperately wanted to laugh but didn't dare, so I apologised instead. She snatched a towel, wiped her face, handed me a mop and bucket and stormed off without saying a word but looking absolutely furious. (I seemed to be permanently mopping up; perhaps I was really destined to become a cleaner?) Even after she had showered and changed, Sister never mentioned anything further about the incident. I was more unnerved by her silence than if she had bawled me out and wondered how my report would read: 'This cadet tried to drown me in the sluice!'

During my afternoon tea break, though, Bridget the cleaner confided to me that Sister had actually felt quite sorry for me when she saw my face and had laughed, admitting she should probably have physically demonstrated the correct use of the water jets to me. She also said that Sister White had been quite impressed by my handling of Elsie, because she was notoriously difficult to cope with, and this was a considerable boost for my confidence.

★ ★ ★

Mealtimes at Springfield could be a bit of a nightmare. On our first day Linda and I had sat down to lunch before Sister White came into the room. We realised, much too late, that everyone else, including Staff Nurse, was standing behind their chairs as she made her regal entrance. She said nothing but the scowl aimed in our direction had us instantly scrambling to our feet and standing to attention; it was worse than being at school. She marched in looking very

67

self-important, seating herself first before indi-
cating everyone else to follow her lead. She also
made a point of serving the food and, regardless
of any preferences or dislikes every member of
staff was given a small amount of each dish
provided. On the whole the meals were excellent,
although there were certain foods which I could
not and would not put in my mouth, such as
semolina or sprouts. The mere thought of being
in the same room as semolina made me gag.

One particular day, soon after I started work at
Springfield, I had the audacity to refuse the
semolina (which to my mind featured all too
regularly on the menu) and instead took a piece
of fruit from a bowl that was permanently on
display in the centre of the table. Before anyone
could stop me, I bit into the apple. At first I
didn't notice the reaction coming from the far
end of the table. Sister glared at me and turned
to a member of the permanent staff saying, 'Put
her straight please.' She then abruptly stood up
and left the room in a huff. The girls howled
with laughter but I hadn't a clue what was going
on. Apparently no one was allowed to touch the
forbidden fruit, which was for decoration
purposes only and belonged to Sister personally.
She occasionally gave a grape to a patient if she
was feeling generous but never the staff. Believe
me, I never touched it again.

* * *

A couple of months after I started at Springfield
we moved house. My grandmother (Dad's mum)

had come to live with us in Florence Street because she could no longer cope alone and was, of necessity, forced to share a bedroom with me and my sister Pat. Although the snoring was irritating and the habits and mannerisms of a deaf eighty-year-old were quite amusing to begin with, the situation eventually became unbearable for everyone and we were fortunate enough to be allocated a three bedroom local authority property.

Number 21, Lilac Road was a semi-detached prefab, a type of house which was only ever intended to be temporary and had been erected in large numbers after the war to re-house residents of the condemned terraced houses which were being rapidly demolished. Despite having a planned life of only 20–30 years, the house is still there today. To my family, though, it was a dream come true. A person who has never had to venture twenty yards down an unlit flagstone path in pouring rain or freezing cold in the dead of night just to 'spend a penny' cannot possibly appreciate the extent to which a fitted bathroom is sheer unadulterated luxury. Now they are simply taken for granted. Gardens front and back, a separate dining room and hot running water on tap were the icing on the cake. Catching the bus at the bottom of the road (and meeting Linda, my fellow cadet who also lived on the same bus route) I could hardly keep the smile from my face for weeks afterwards.

★ ★ ★

I gradually settled into the regular routine at Springfield and soon began to feel part of the team. Linda, however, was not happy; she became increasingly quiet and withdrawn and before long went off sick. She was admitted to hospital for tests and didn't return, so for a large part of my three-month stint at Springfield I was the only cadet there.

Sister and I crossed swords again when I managed to get myself stuck in the lift. At least I was carrying a tray of patients' meals with me at the time, so I knew that I wouldn't starve to death! There was no alarm bell in the lift, so it took nearly ten minutes before anyone heard my calls, but eventually Sister appeared and chewed my ear off for letting the dinners get cold.

If the weather was good I was expected to take one of the patients to the park or for a walk around the neighbouring streets. On my first outing I couldn't wait to get outside for some fresh air. The sun was hot and it was sweltering inside the hospital. Making beds and bathing patients made the heat seem even worse and everyone was listless and cranky. A number of the old ladies loved being taken out, so Sister White showed me down into the cellar where a couple of large, old-fashioned, cobweb-strewn bath chairs were stored. These were enormous antiques, reeked of damp and desperately needed an airing to get rid of the overpowering musty smell.

My first 'customer' was a lady called Stella. She was paralysed down her right side and unable to speak, which made her weepy and depressed.

70

Even though it was the height of summer, Sister insisted that Stella wore a thick woollen coat, fur hat and gloves, with a large plaid blanket wrapped around her knees. She resembled Miss Havisham from *Great Expectations* dressed as Nanook of the North. We managed to manoeuvre this relic (the chair I mean, not the patient) on to the path outside and, before too long, Stella and I were off on our travels. I was praying that no one I knew would see me in a mauve uniform several sizes too big, pushing a resurrected Dickensian character down the road in a relic from a museum. I decided to walk down Preston New Road, taking the first left, which led us into a beautiful, tree-lined street where the large houses were all surrounded by lovingly tended gardens. We had a peep through the imposing metal gates. I could never in my wildest dreams have imagined living in such splendour, which these homes certainly seemed when compared to the small terraced house where I was brought up.

It was a beautiful sunny day and we had only been out for around half an hour when I realised that Stella was sound asleep. I didn't want to go back too soon because I knew that Sister would find me some dirty job to do, so I walked on for a while, until Stella woke up and immediately began to cry. She pointed frantically to the ground and was desperately trying to tell me something but was unable to get the words out, which made her weep all the more out of sheer frustration. All she could manage to do was shake her head, point her finger and repeat, 'Yes,'

71

over and over again. It wasn't until we returned to the hospital that I finally discovered she had lost a shoe. Sister White demanded that I retrace my steps to find it and I scoured every blessed inch of every street we had walked down but to no avail; the missing footwear was nowhere to be found. Sister wasn't at all impressed.

Amazingly, two days later I was again trusted to go out. The same smelly old bath chair was unearthed but this time I took a different patient called Nora, who was dressed like a film extra in a period drama. She excitedly dabbed a touch of lavender water behind each ear and smeared her lips with scarlet red lipstick. This old girl was on the pull and was determined to look her best, just in case! The smell of mothballs was overpowering but Nora couldn't care less; she was going out and she couldn't wait.

This time I decided to go to the local park where Nora apparently delighted in being pushed around in her 'chariot', into which she clambered eagerly and she never stopped chattering. It wasn't long before she saw an ice cream van and looked at me in eager anticipation. I had a little money with me and asked her if she would like a cornet. She clapped her hands in glee and said, 'Oh yes please!' I bought her a large one with all the trimmings, which she devoured in record time, smacking her lips with satisfaction. I had barely started my own ice and wondered how she had managed to swallow hers so quickly. She chuckled with glee and told me that Sister White didn't let her have ice cream very often and when she did it certainly didn't have nuts, raspberry sauce and chocolate on the top because she was a diabetic! For a second or two my world stood still; granted, I didn't know an awful lot about diabetes but I knew that sugar intake had to be limited. I really didn't know what to think and looked at her wondering if she was going to drop dead any second. Nora's face creased with concern and she asked me if I would get into trouble for giving the treat to her. I couldn't answer at first; I felt like throttling her. She whispered conspiratorially that she wouldn't tell and said that she had eaten ice cream many times previously with no ill effects. On hearing her say this I began to relax a little, but should I tell Sister or not? I would have to make up my mind on the way back.

In the end, I am ashamed to say that I decided not to tell her, a decision which I now look back on with deep regret. I was seventeen, inexperienced and afraid of making mistakes and getting into trouble, but I should have said something. I hardly slept that night but, the next day, there was Nora, large as life, waving and laughing as if nothing had happened. It was such a relief! But the incident made me realise just how ignorant and immature my reaction had been. It was wrong to cover up something which could possibly have been a potential catastrophe for Nora. I was thinking about myself, not my patient and that was unforgivable. I had so much to learn.

Christine, who was becoming a good friend, was a very capable cadet in my group and had worked at Springfield before me. On one of our rare nights out, we were discussing Springfield and she told me a story about Beatrice, one of the old ladies who was recovering from a stroke and trying hard to regain her independence. After Christine had helped with meals, Beatrice asked to be taken to the toilet. Christine assisted Beatrice to her feet, helped her walk to the toilet using her tripod frame, squeezed her into a cubicle and sat her on the toilet, promising to come back in a few minutes to help her back to her room. When she went back Beatrice was in tears and in an awful mess. She had tried to clean herself up using her one good hand but only succeeded in spreading faeces everywhere. Walls, floor and toilet roll were covered in the stuff. She was distraught, but Christine assured her that everything was OK and she bent down to remove the poor dear's saturated stockings. Trying to be helpful, Beatrice stood up by placing her hand on Christine's head. (Oh yes, a hand covered in 'you know what'.) Despite realising what she had done, Christine simply took Beatrice to the bathroom to wash and change her, before asking permission from Sister White to go and sort herself out. Thankfully possessing a great sense of humour, Christine was eventually able to see the funny side of the situation and took great delight in recounting the details, particularly the colour of the water when she washed the subtle brown highlights from her own hair. What really impressed me was her patience and kindness in ensuring that Beatrice wasn't made to feel in any way more upset or embarrassed about the situation than she already was. She demonstrated what real nursing is about — care and compassion, without displaying personal distaste or inconvenience no matter what the circumstances.

My three months at Springfield flew by and I was truly sad to leave, but was also desperately eager to learn more about nursing. It had been a good grounding on which to build for my first 'proper' ward, since a lot of the skills I had learned at Springfield were sure to come in handy back at BRI. On my final day Sister White thanked me for my hard work, shook my hand and said that I would make a good nurse if I studied and worked hard when I commenced my formal three-year training at eighteen. Coming from her that was praise indeed! Despite my inexperience, I came to appreciate during my time at Springfield that Sister White was strict and demanding simply because she cared passionately for her patients and had high standards. She educated me in caring for the infirm and the dying, and she taught me to respect the elderly regardless of mental infirmity and, most importantly, to allow them always to retain their dignity. To me she was a shining example of what nursing should be all about.

★   ★   ★

After my initiation into patient care at Springfield, my next move was to Ward 11 (women's medical) which was on the second floor of the old wing back at BRI. I had arrived early as usual and a second cadet from my group, Kathleen, arrived a few minutes late out of breath with rushing but still smiling and she was going to be on the opposite ward, Ward 12 (which was the male equivalent of Ward 11). When Miss Hanlon had taken us on to Ward 11 during our original tour, we had met the red-haired Sister Frew and several members of her permanent staff. This morning the junior sister was also on duty and she introduced herself as Sister Thompson. Like Sister Frew, she was about thirty years old and looked very efficient, although the heavy, black-framed spectacles she wore made her look much older. Immaculately dressed in navy blue uniform, she had her long, black hair taken severely back off her face and pulled up into a bun tucked neatly underneath a white cap. She gave us a big welcoming smile and wished us good morning.

We were then introduced to John, a young doctor who had been on duty for the last three days without a break, which his appearance confirmed. Yawning a greeting, he smiled weakly and wandered off to bed. John was the House Officer, the most junior doctor on the ward. Typically house officers were in their first year after qualifying; they would be given all the basic routine jobs to carry out and were usually in post for only six months before moving on to gain more experience. Next rung up the ladder was the Senior House Officer, usually referred to as the SHO, who had at least one year's work experience in two different specialities and was not now expected to carry out quite as many mundane tasks, but was still looking to gain more experience. Moving up once again was the position of Registrar. This was the first role where a doctor has made a decision as to which branch of medicine they would like to specialise in. Charged with organising and implementing the treatments decided by the consultants in charge of the ward, the registrars assumed daily responsibility for the patients and supervised the junior doctors. As there were always two consultants in charge of each speciality, occasionally with conflicting ideas on how best to treat a certain illness or condition, the registrar had to be very careful to comply with each consultant's different requirements. As their skills and specialist knowledge increased, the doctor then progressed through appointment to Senior Registrar and finally becoming a consultant themselves.

Most admissions to both wards were for acute conditions such as coronary thrombosis, stroke, acute asthma, diabetic coma and chest infections, including pneumonia, while others came in for investigations or even for terminal care. All admissions came directly on to the wards because specialist coronary care and high-dependency units weren't yet established, so at any given time there could well be a high proportion of seriously ill patients.

Duties, as at Springfield, started with breakfasts. Large heated stainless-steel containers called hot locks were brought to the ward by the porters and nurses distributed the meals. Any patient unable to feed themselves had to be assisted and Sister Frew always made her presence evident at this time in ensuring that the duty was carried out. Liquid diets would be provided for those unable to manage solid food or, alternatively and as a last resort, intravenous drips were in situ for any patient unable to swallow. Fluid intake and urine output were routinely recorded so that all patients' needs and progress could be seen at a glance. After breakfast the crockery was removed and put back in the containers and then nurses began to give bed baths to patients and get them up wherever possible.

My first tasks were to collect, wash and refill the water jugs and drinking glasses, clean lockers and renew flower water. Metal sputum containers had to be collected from patients' lockers then cleaned and replaced by yours truly (there were no disposables in those days unfortunately). These were assembled on a small trolley and taken to the sluice where each one had to be emptied, scrubbed clean and sterilised. It was a horrible job because the glutinous congealed contents clung stubbornly to the pots, seemingly welded to them, until they were finally dislodged by holding them under the running hot-water tap, and would plop rather satisfyingly into the sluice sink and slide away down the drain. I was gagging! I decided straight away that I didn't like spit, but managed to complete my task without actually throwing up. On one memorable occasion I recall pushing a trolley fully laden with overflowing sputum pots towards the sluice when a student nurse came rushing in the opposite direction and we collided head on. All the pots were launched into orbit and, of course, 'Sod's Law' meant that they virtually all fell upside down, emptying and spreading their contents across the floor. Any guesses who had to scoop it all up? I can honestly say that it was one of the worst tasks I have ever had the misfortune to carry out.

Once the sputum pots were cleaned, my next job was to clean the false teeth of anyone who wasn't able to do their own. I sincerely hoped there wouldn't be too many, but, as usual, was to be disappointed. I took them one set at a time, scrubbed and cleaned them and, although some were quite lively and tried to escape, managed to return them all to their rightful owners without breaking any, thank goodness. I was told about a previous cadet who had the really bright idea of collecting all the false teeth together in one bowl for cleaning, with resulting chaos!

My first morning was going reasonably well until I was asked by Sister Frew to remove the water jug and glass from a bed which had the curtains drawn around it. The patient's name was Rose, she was dying and wasn't expected to survive the day. All the staff had been made aware of her condition and nurses carried out their work with a minimum of noise, no loud voices and certainly no laughter. I was feeling more than a little apprehensive as I quietly tiptoed behind the screen to retrieve the items from her locker. The patient was lying on her side facing me, her eyes were closed and her skin appeared as waxy as a Tussaud's model. I edged a little closer and stared in fascination, seeing for the very first time someone who was dying, and then I nervously whispered to advise her what I was doing, not having the faintest idea whether she could hear me or not.

I'm not sure what I expected but there was no response whatsoever, not even a flicker when I stroked her forehead, and I was really startled to discover how cold she felt. Without warning she suddenly began to groan, foam at the mouth and her whole body started to convulse. I shot out of there like sugar off a shovel. With no nurse in sight I flew to find Sister Frew and, in my panic-stricken rush, nearly knocked her over as she was coming out of the office. She grasped my shoulders firmly, instructed me to calm down and tell her what was wrong. I could barely breathe, let alone speak. Once I had managed to control myself and told her about Rose, a knowing look appeared on her face and she walked slowly back to the bed with me, gripping on to the back of my uniform to prevent me from running.

Rose lay quiet and still. Sister checked for a pulse. There was nothing. Producing a stethoscope from her pocket she listened to her chest. Again, nothing. Rose was dead. Not for the first time my young heart was working overtime but Sister's quiet calm helped me to retain my self-control. She was professional and understanding, checking that I was okay before asking if I would help her to make Rose look presentable. I would have done anything for her at that point but I still felt very nervous. Together we rolled Rose on to her back, combed her hair and made her look as respectable as possible. Why had I been so scared? Perhaps it was fear of the unknown, I really don't know. Sister asked me to clean Rose's teeth and put them back into her mouth, while she went to her office to ring the house officer but, try as I may, her mouth refused to open fully and she had begun to feel increasingly rigid. I was beginning to worry that Sister would consider me useless, when she reappeared and took the dentures from me. She was very gentle and respectful as she attempted to insert them herself but was equally unsuccessful, which made me feel a whole lot better. She explained that this sometimes happened and that Rose's body had been shutting down for several days, although she didn't explain to me about rigor mortis until later. Sister put the teeth into an envelope with Rose's name on and said that the mortuary attendant or undertaker would put them in later. The question passed fleetingly through my mind as to how he would manage to do it if the two of us couldn't.

The house officer arrived after having been dragged out of his bed, to check and certify that Rose was, in fact, dead. He appeared totally unconcerned, listened to her chest, shone a light in her eyes and grumbled that her death meant more work for him now that there was another bed to fill. To my inexperienced ears his remarks sounded callous and uncaring, but I suppose after a while death does indeed become commonplace in hospital. Rose's family arrived a little later but didn't stay very long as they had been expecting the news and shed few tears. In truth they seemed more interested in her possessions, so Sister and I emptied her locker, recording every item in a property book, asked Rose's daughter to sign it and packed everything into a large brown paper bag. The daughter insisted on taking the wedding ring from her mother's finger, which again had to be witnessed and signed for. 'One yellow metal ring' was added to the property sheet which I witnessed and countersigned before handing it to the daughter. After the family had gone I asked Sister why she had not written 'gold' ring. I was amazed to be told that it was not uncommon for a family to try and sue the hospital, demanding the gold ring that had been clearly entered into the property book when it had, in fact, been cheap metal, obliging the hospital to pay compensation. It disgusted me how mercenary and dishonest some people could be, even at times such as these.

Now it was time to lay the body out before dispatching Rose to the mortuary. Sister Frew asked if I wanted to help her and I agreed to help without hesitation, even though I hadn't a clue what this involved. As it turned out the whole process was very similar to a bed bath. We washed Rose from head to toe, packed cotton wool into every available orifice, cut and cleaned her nails and combed her hair. We straightened out her arms and legs (bandaging her big toes and ankles together to keep them straight and in place) and put her into a shroud, wrapping her like an Egyptian mummy within a white sheet, which was then taped down. Labels stating identity, date of birth, date of death, case note number, ward number and attending doctor were attached to the sheet, and her admission wristband was checked and left in situ as a duplicate identity check. Once we had finished this part of the task we closed the screens around the other patients' beds so they would not be upset by seeing the body removed. Sister had already contacted the porters, who arrived promptly with the mortuary trolley. Afterwards, all the screens were drawn back, except the one around the now empty bed, which was stripped, scrubbed and remade. The bedside locker was also thoroughly cleaned, together with the thermometer which was kept in a container behind the bed; everything was now ready for the next admission. That first day had seen my first death, yet when my three months were concluded Ward 11 had chalked up sixty such sad events, and every one of them was given the same meticulous attention and respect by Sister Frew and her staff. Standards were never allowed to slip.

All bed-ridden patients had to have their pressure areas (any bony prominence) massaged with surgical spirit in order to prevent bedsores developing. This was considered to be an essential part of basic patient care, as was cleaning and lubricating a patient's mouth if they were not able to eat or drink for themselves (mouths will crack and become very painful if the salivary glands are not stimulated through normal mastication). Every patient needing oral hygiene had a mouth tray left permanently on top of their lockers for the nurses to use, containing a sodium bicarbonate solution to cleanse, a mouthwash to freshen, and a mixture of glycerine and lemon to encourage saliva in order to moisten the tongue, teeth and lips. Another major worry for patients was their bowels. Oh, how they were preoccupied with their bowels! Each ward had a bowel book and a member of staff had to record all movement or non-movement of patients' bowels every single day. Sister would carefully scan the book on each shift and supply pre-prescribed aperients, suppositories or enemas as required. I learned volumes about bowels on Ward 11. Every specimen collected was examined for abnormalities, like blood or mucous.

I especially recall one patient who was admitted with a tapeworm (usually acquired by eating undercooked meat) whose every stool had to be collected, put in special containers and sent to the laboratory for examination. It was absolutely essential to find the head of the tapeworm, as until this was expelled and identified it would continue to reproduce itself indefinitely. The patient was given special medication to purge the intruding beast, so that some unhappy 'prospector' in the laboratory could trawl through every last vestige of specimen trying to find it. I had visions of this anonymous person, masked and gloved, searching diligently day after day for the head of the tapeworm. What a revolting way to earn a living!

Patients confined to bed obviously had

insufficient exercise, which in turn affected normal bodily functions. Hospital food, change of diet or lack of fluids all had the potential to cause problems, hence the need for the bowel book. One particular student nurse was asked to give a foreign patient two glycerine suppositories. She simply handed them to the patient and told her that they were for her bowels. The patient looked puzzled but smiled, thanked her and promptly swallowed them with water. The student nurse was horrified, but it was already too late. She had not unreasonably assumed that the patient knew what suppositories were and what to do with them. Sister was distinctly unamused, but fortunately the patient suffered no more than a little nausea and was otherwise unharmed.

Ward 11 taught me many things and dealing with incontinence was one of them. My initiation was with a lady in her sixties called Dawn. A severe stroke had left her with paralysis down one side of her body (hemiplegia) and loss of speech; she also had difficulty swallowing and was doubly incontinent. Mentally Dawn was fine, she understood exactly what was going on around her and would moan and wave her good arm frantically at staff in order to gain their attention but she wasn't able to put her thoughts into words. It was extremely frustrating for her because by the time she had made herself seen and understood it was often too late and had already been incontinent, but she was always eternally grateful for assistance.

I had been on the ward for about two weeks

and was going around doing my routine chores when I noticed Dawn waving at me urgently. As I approached her bed there was a distinctive odour of what nurses lovingly call 'tish' (which is slightly less indelicate than calling it sh** all day long!). Dawn grunted, trying her best to make herself understood, smiled and grasped hold of my arm. Her hand, and now my arm, were both liberally covered in the unmentionable, and I soon realised it was also in her hair and, horror of horrors, even in her mouth. Basically 'it' was everywhere, a situation to which she appeared blissfully unconcerned. I went for a nurse who came back with me and we pulled the screens around the bed to investigate further. When we turned back the bedcovers there was 'tish' everywhere and the smell was enough to make anyone's hair curl. Poor Dawn; she hadn't been like this long because she had only just had her breakfast and was fine then, but the nurse asked me if I could face the clean-up process and, although I wasn't too sure, I dubiously nodded in agreement. After first scrubbing my own arm I brought a washing trolley to the bedside, ensuring that we had gallons of hot water and plenty of bed linen. The nurse and I donned gloves and gowns to protect our uniforms and proceeded to strip the bed, leaving the patient covered with a sheet, although the hot water sickeningly seemed to intensify the smell. It took ages to clean up, Dawn's mouth proving to be the most difficult. Thankfully she was totally cooperative and only too willing to help, almost seeming to enjoy the novel flavours and the amount of attention she was receiving. For the rest of the day the smell lingered, following me around to such an extent that I found myself constantly checking my uniform and regularly washing my arms and hands.

As a cadet I found that cleaning an incontinent patient was embarrassing at first, especially for the patient, and to see faeces spread around the bed and clothing was stomach churning. It took me quite a while to get used to it, although it eventually became routine and simply another essential job. Most nurses have one particular pet hate, mine was and still is sputum, but faeces comes a close second.

★   ★   ★

Kathleen and I rarely ever saw each other during ward work, we were too busy, but during breaks and ward rounds we took the opportunity to have a laugh and catch up on what was happening on the wards. Consultant rounds were something else, and the first one Kathleen and I came across was an eye-opener. Nurses were scurrying around beforehand making sure that patients (and lockers) were spotless, hospital corners on the counterpanes were perfect and anyone not expected to be on the round (which meant all the students, cadets and auxiliaries) was warned to disappear from sight when 'His Lordship' arrived. This suited me and Kathleen fine, because we could hide in the kitchen with some of the junior nurses and have a crafty cuppa. We heard the consultant arrive and Sister welcome him as 'Sir'. Junior doctors were frantically checking scrunched up pieces of paper from their pockets on which they had scribbled notes to themselves about the various patients. A trolley full of patient records and test results was set up, ready to be ceremoniously pushed along as the procession moved from bed to bed, reviewing the treatment and progress of each patient. The consultant would question his junior staff as he went round and often used the opportunity to continue their training. What a performance. You would have thought that the Queen herself was in attendance. Once the round was completed the doctors and Sister retired to the office for refreshments, while we 'underlings' came out of our hidey-holes and carried on with the work.

My three months on Ward 11 had gone by too quickly, but I had learned a great deal about basic general nursing care and I also had come to realise that cadets were pretty much at the bottom of the pile within the very distinct hierarchy among nurses. When on duty anyone senior could tell you what to do; and believe me there was no argument, you simply did as you were instructed without question. Etiquette was fierce. Juniors were expected to open doors for senior staff, always standing back and letting them through first. It was also frowned upon for anyone to address you by anything other than your rank, especially in front of patients. Familiarity was totally unacceptable. Personally, I found that most of the nurses were always helpful and eager to guide me through the daily routines and procedures, though. During my time on the ward, I had seen patients being admitted at death's door only to be lovingly nursed back to health and I had watched others die despite every best effort. There had been numerous cardiac arrests (which, of course, we as cadets weren't involved with); some patients had been successfully resuscitated and others sadly had not. Importantly, I had at last begun to learn how to care for unconscious and critically ill patients. Of course my input had been limited to basic care and assisting the nurses, but now, all too soon I had to move on again and I really didn't want to leave. My next move was to be a surgical ward; I could only hope that it would be as organised and as interesting as Ward 11.

★　★　★

Ward 3 was situated at ground level in the new tower block of the hospital. Patients in this ward were admitted either as acute surgical emergencies or for pre-arranged operations. The senior of the two sisters in charge of the ward was Sister Nancy Adams, renowned within the hospital for her efficiency and professionalism. She never raised her voice, commanded attention at a glance and was highly respected by her peers. She worked hard, set high standards and never asked her staff to do anything that she wasn't prepared to do herself. Sister Adams was also a very good tutor and wasted no time in teaching new staff the basic nursing techniques needed on a surgical ward. The junior sister was also efficient and worked hard, although I found her to be less than helpful at times and she made it quite plain that she had no time for cadets. Although as cadets we were not allowed to carry out 'hands on' nursing duties unaccompanied, we did do many routine basic tasks like changing water jugs, cleaning lockers, giving out meals and feeding patients who couldn't manage by themselves, helping to give bed baths to patients, making beds and cleaning false teeth — most wards were glad of the extra pair of hands. For some unknown reason, though, this particular sister couldn't be bothered with such junior staff. Thankfully this was not the usual reaction.

It soon became very apparent that there was a vast difference between working on a medical ward and a surgical ward; operation schedules required precise instructions regarding theatre preparation, with specialised attention to both pre- and post-operative patients. Extra care had to be taken with patients due to go to theatre because food and drink were strictly forbidden. 'Nil by mouth' notices were a feature on Ward 3 and it was essential that every member of staff adhered strictly to their instruction. I was required to have total awareness of patient operation status and it was essential to avoid disturbing the many drips and tubes that commonly festooned the patients' beds, particularly post-operatively. Sister put me to work with a very experienced auxiliary, Hazel, and we carried out the routine tasks between us. While she collected breakfast trays, I collected, washed and refilled water jugs and beakers, working my way through the men's side first, introducing myself as I went along.

In the end cubicle I found a very overweight old gent called Alf, who had only just been allowed to sit in a chair for the first time since his operation. He looked absolutely panic-stricken and was gripping his abdomen, begging hysterically for help. I walked around the bed towards him and saw fluid around his feet which I initially thought was urine. When I looked again I could see why he was holding his huge girth with both arms: his stitches had pulled through his skin and his abdomen had burst wide open! I could clearly see the coils of his bowel, an experience which left me feeling distinctly queasy, so I quickly drew the curtains around him and went for help. Sister Adams saw my alarmed expression, followed me back to the cubicle and immediately took control of the situation. I helped to put the old man on to his bed, feeling terrified that his guts would ooze out all over me at any second. There were few staff on duty so I was asked to stay with Alf and keep him immobile, which I agreed to do, albeit with a mixture of terror and fascination. While I was talking to and trying to reassure him, Hazel popped her head around the curtain to see how I was coping. She took a quick look at the patient and a much longer look at me, asked if I was OK and swiftly disappeared with a huge grin on her face.

Fortunately Sister came back fairly quickly. She had already informed both the doctors and the operating theatre and had brought with her a dressing called a 'many tailed bandage'. After first applying sterile saline pads over the gaping abdomen she secured the bandage completely around his girth like a corset, pulling the tails as firmly as was comfortable in order to hold everything in place. The junior doctor arrived and put a drip in the patient's arm and then, without further delay, Alf was taken back to theatre for re-suturing. Sister was my heroine and she did my confidence a power of good by thanking me for helping her so professionally, although I had done no more than follow her precise instructions while trying to prevent myself from panicking or throwing up. After all the excitement had died down Sister asked me to mop the floor, strip the bed and remove the blood-soaked sheets for laundering. I could really have done with a lie down and a cup of tea, and wondered if I would ever be able to keep calm and cope in such a situation, but I was certainly an expert with a mop and bucket by now. What a start! Ward 11 now seemed positively sedate by comparison, although I was assured by Sister that this sort of thing very rarely happened. Alf was particularly obese and was therefore much more at risk than most other patients. His massive body weight caused extra strain around the stitches when he moved, until eventually they had actually torn through the skin thus opening up the whole wound which had not yet started to heal.

Once Alf was on his way to theatre, Sister carried on with her own routine work as if nothing had happened. I finished off the water jugs in a world of my own as other members of staff were kept busy rushing backwards and forwards to theatre, checking drips and tubes and attending to patients coming round from anaesthetics. Alf returned to the ward about an hour later, made a full recovery and eventually went home a couple of weeks later.

The next few weeks went by routinely, Hazel helped me to settle in and worked alongside me. We were forever cleaning beds (including the wheels) and lockers, even mopping floors if there had been spillages of blood or urine. Patients had to be fed and nurses asked us to help them change incontinent patients or do bed baths; there was certainly plenty of work to keep me occupied. One afternoon, Casualty alerted the ward about an admission. Ray, a young man in his twenties, had suffered serious head injuries at work. He was unconscious and critically ill and, as we didn't have an Intensive Care Unit, Sister ensured that his bed was positioned so that he could be clearly seen from the nurses' station. We didn't know what to expect until he arrived accompanied by a doctor, a staff nurse from Casualty and two porters (his large frame completely filling the stretcher), followed by his distraught family. Both his badly bruised eyes were closed and very swollen, blood trickled ominously from his ears and his head was swathed in bandages.

Initially he was monitored by the nurses every few minutes for temperature, pulse, blood pressure, pupil reactions and consciousness level. Fragments of bone and brain tissue could be seen through gaps in the hastily applied bandages. As soon as he was stable he was taken to theatre to have the bone fragments removed and for a metal plate to be inserted into his skull to protect his brain tissue. As a cadet there was little that I could do other than to make sure his family had drinks and were comfortable. I didn't sleep very much that night as my adrenaline levels were still sky high after watching the nurses prepare him for surgery; shaking their heads, not believing that he could possibly survive. I couldn't stop thinking about him.

The next day Ray was deeply unconscious and not responding in any way. A nurse told me that he wasn't expected to live, or would be seriously brain damaged if he did survive. His family had been allowed to stay with him overnight and had tried to get some sleep in the day room. Despite looking utterly exhausted they refused to go home. The junior sister was in charge that morning but, unlike Sister Adams who tried to involve me in most cases, refused to allow me anywhere near the patient and told me to keep out of the way. Although she was very abrupt and, for some reason appeared to have taken an instant dislike to me, I had to accept the discipline without question and carry on with my routine duties. Ray made little or no progress during the remainder of my time as a cadet on the ward; he was completely unresponsive and critically ill and I felt a great sympathy for his family who had virtually taken up residence on the ward. It was going to be a long struggle.

Many patients came in for routine operations

and went home having experienced a totally uneventful stay, but the moment I set eyes on Jack I knew that he would be unforgettable. Admitted via Casualty the previous night suffering from pneumonia, he was in a side ward on the surgical unit because of a lack of vacant medical beds in the hospital. I was in the process of distributing breakfasts when I went into his room with a tray and there he was — Neanderthal man! His grimy, leathery brown face was framed by a shock of matted dark hair, large wiry tufts sprouted from his nostrils and ears and I very much doubted he could see anything from behind long, bushy eyebrows. The rotted black stumps of his teeth were just visible through the tangled undergrowth of facial hair, which could have concealed a platoon of Japanese snipers. He was extremely emaciated, absolutely filthy and in desperate need of some TLC. As he lay there with an oxygen mask perched drunkenly on top of his head, I placed the tray in front of him and watched as his eyes grew ever wider and I heard his mouth water in anticipation of this veritable feast. Out of the corner of my eye I noticed his drinking glass was full of what appeared to be Lucozade, although on closer inspection I realised that Jack needed educating about asking for assistance in order to use the toilet. I quickly whisked away the evidence and replaced his glass, leaving him a urine bottle and a buzzer to call a nurse, for use in the future. Grinning to myself I left him to get on with it, wondering just what we were in for. When I collected his tray after breakfast, I was impressed to find that his

95

plates were literally licked clean. It was only some time later that I noticed the porridge and scrambled egg oozing out of his locker and dripping on to the floor. Jack had decided to hoard any uneaten food in case of emergency! Having lived on the streets for many years he couldn't bring himself to waste anything and looked on anxiously as I scraped his leftovers into a bin bag.

In addition to his pneumonia, we soon discovered that Jack had gangrene in both feet (which was due to bad circulation). When I helped the nurses remove his socks to give him a bed bath, a haircut and a shave, a couple of his toes had dropped off. Over the following weeks, we often found the odd lump of crispy black flesh between the sheets and wondered which bit would be next. Some poor, unsuspecting nurse always had the dubious pleasure of retrieving and disposing of these little mementoes. It quickly became apparent that as soon as the pneumonia cleared up he faced having both his lower legs amputated.

My favourite patient never did quite get the hang of using a urine bottle because his drinking glass was always a little too convenient. I walked in on him one day when he was having a wee in the washbasin and was horrified at what I was seeing; not that he was relieving himself, but that he was capable of supporting himself while doing so. Jack had lost all feeling in his feet because of the gangrene and, as he stood there, one of his rotting feet was twisted around through 180 degrees but he still managed to shuffle back to his bed unaided. The image was totally grotesque.

The surgeons came to see him one day to discuss his feet and to explain all the available options. Jack was told that he needed surgery to have both legs amputated because of the gangrene and that without this operation he would die. I could only imagine the dilemma he must have been in and he initially refused to contemplate such an operation. However, he had a change of heart after speaking with the hospital social worker (known as the almoner) who reassured him that he would be found accommodation and would be cared for, for the rest of his life. On hearing this news he willingly agreed to the operation and speedily signed his consent form. After having led such an independent existence he was going to be looked after twenty-four hours a day and the attraction of this idea greatly outweighed any other considerations. Amazingly, he made a fantastic recovery and learned very quickly how to use his electric wheelchair; soon he was zooming along the corridors and ready to be discharged. We were told by the rest home to which he was sent that he still stashed his food in his cupboard and utilised any available container when the need arose, but was now healthier and cleaner than he had been for many years. He was deliriously happy.

★   ★   ★

Megan, a lady in her late seventies, was admitted for abdominal surgery to remove a blockage in her bowel. When first brought into Ward 3 she was in agony, her abdomen was distended and

97

she was vomiting profusely. After having had blood tests and x-rays it was decided to take her to theatre. The nurses had put a tube up through her nose and into her stomach (a Ryle's tube) so that the contents of her stomach could be kept to a minimum to prevent her from vomiting. She was terrified; more so because she no longer had her beloved husband Charlie to comfort her. They had been married for forty years and he had died the previous year from a heart attack. Not having any close family left, this is where I came in. I held her hand and tried to reassure her that she would be well looked after. She filled with tears and nodded, and I promised to be round to see her when she woke up afterwards. She smiled and squeezed my hand tightly before I left her, as the theatre orderly came to take her down for the operation.

She was in theatre for over two hours but the operation was a complete success and before long she was recovering well. She loved being on the ward, often remarking how grateful she was to be there. Having lived alone for a year she was enjoying enormously the care and the companionship of her fellow patients, as well as the nursing staff and I made time to speak to her as often as I could because she had few visitors. This sweet old lady was making such good progress that within a week she was due to be transferred to a convalescent unit at Queen's Park Hospital. On hearing this news she was absolutely distraught because Megan remembered QPH as being the old town workhouse when she was young. She desperately begged and pleaded with us not to send her there, becoming almost hysterical. Although I tried hard to reassure her that it was no longer an institution she simply refused to believe me, crying and pushing me away, saying that I didn't care about her. I was heartbroken on her behalf, but what could I do?

When the ambulance arrived the next day to make the transfer she sobbed uncontrollably and refused to even look at me. I cried with her and stupidly felt as though it was somehow my fault. Sister Adams took me into her office and talked to me firmly about becoming too involved with a patient. All that I had done was spend time with her and listen to her concerns, but we bonded immediately and she had trusted me to look out for her. Sister reassured me that Megan would soon settle once she got to QPH; after all, she was going to a brand new, state of the art convalescent ward, and Sister promised to check on her progress the following week. True to her word, enquiries a week later established that Megan had progressed so well she had already been discharged and returned home.

★   ★   ★

Two years working in and around the hospital had left me in no doubt whatsoever that I wanted to be a nurse. The cadet system was ideal for helping young people to decide if nursing was the career for them; similar to an apprenticeship, you familiarised yourself with the unique sights and sounds of hospital life. Two or three cadets who started at the same time as me had already resigned but the majority of us were going forward to student nurse training. After passing our NHS preliminary exams, Matron summoned all the cadets to her office to confirm our results. But, before we had the opportunity to congratulate ourselves, she brought us down to earth with a bump. She told us that while we had done well so far, we actually still knew very little; that it would take several more years of hard work and dedication to become a good nurse and she wasn't convinced that everyone would make it. I left Matron's office completely deflated but now more determined than ever to show her just what I could do.

★　★　★

Coming up to 1968 (and student training), things were changing rapidly in hospitals. A key development came in the form of the Salmon Report, which recommended a drastic alteration in the nursing structure and heralded the end of the old-fashioned matron system. It was recommended that each hospital appoint a Chief Nursing Officer who would report to the hospital management and reside over a whole new hierarchy of Principal Nursing Officers, Senior Nursing Officers, Nursing Officers and Ward Sisters or Charge Nurses. Although many resisted the abolition of the matron post, the Salmon Report assured doubters that the profile of the profession would be raised and nursing staff would have a greater say in management.

The counter argument against these changes was based on the fact that there would no longer be one individual person who was in charge of nursing standards and patient care. Some new recruits were now being educated to degree standard at university, rather than practically on the job and, at the time, it was feared that this system would begin to attract candidates far more interested in becoming administrators rather than hands-on carers. And so it was in the 1960s that these first graduate nurses began to trickle in.

Of course things had to change because medical advances were being made in leaps and bounds. Treatments were improving rapidly with better medication, more effective vaccines were developed and dialysis for chronic renal failure had been introduced, as well as chemotherapy treatments for some cancers. Specialist coronary care units and intensive care units were being created in many hospitals. It was truly an exciting time and we who were just about to start our nurse training were in the thick of it.

As far as the nurses themselves were concerned, though, some changes were very welcome indeed, including the ending of regular split shifts. (Split shifts were horrendous and usually meant going on duty from 7.30am — 12pm, then going home for a few hours only to return about tea-time for the late shift.) It was soul destroying, especially when, like me, getting to and from work meant having to catch two buses each way. (It was some time, however, before these changes came into effect.) Part-time shifts were also introduced, which some hospital authorities had always refused, and for staff who were married with young children this was a major step forward. Sisters and senior nurses were now able to get married and start a family, if they so wished, without postponing or abandoning their career, which in turn opened up the opportunity for promotion to a much wider number of people.

In Blackburn, like many other hospitals, changes were only very gradual, though, so when it was time to commence my training, Matron was still very much in evidence. Often strict and demanding, Matron was greatly respected by nurses, doctors and patients alike and, in my opinion, when the matrons were replaced the whole concept of nursing standards changed forever. I didn't much care for the strict discipline and at times I felt very much on edge in case I made a mistake or stepped out of line but, to my mind, as far as the patients' welfare was concerned the system could not be bettered.

4

Having completed two years as a cadet the time had now come to start my nurse training proper and I couldn't wait. All new students were required to study in Preliminary Training School (PTS) for twelve weeks, where we would be taught the basics of nursing care before being allowed to continue our training on the wards. I recognised several fellow cadets who had started with me in 1966 and there were also some new faces in the group, who had either just joined us after studying A levels or who had perhaps tried other jobs first, but we were all buzzing with enthusiasm and keen to get started.

Miss Frankland, a tiny mouse of a woman, was our main tutor. She was rather eccentric and spent much of the time fiddling with her grubby spectacles or gazing out of the window, but was an extremely knowledgeable and capable teacher. The Principal Tutor was Mr Winterburn, a superb lecturer, an absolute gentleman and a real sweetheart.

Those of us who had started as cadets naturally felt infinitely superior to the newcomers and were, after all, already familiar with many of the basics, such as bed making, feeding patients, bed bathing and assisting nurses with a number of routine daily procedures. Here in training school we were also taught the practical subjects in depth, such as how and where to give injections, correct lifting techniques (which were intended to protect our backs and avoid causing unnecessary injuries to patients), how to set up different trolleys for drips, catheters and nasal gastric tubes, and how to carry out the many varied dressing techniques, while minimising the risk of infection. In addition to learning about practical procedures, there were also more formal studies such as human biology, including anatomy and physiology.

Our breaks were more often than not spent laughing and chatting about our experiences as cadets, with one girl named Judith recalling the first time she was asked to clean the ward thermometers. She had unwittingly put them all into a bowl of boiling water and all thirty immediately burst, exploding globules of mercury over the floor and sink, whereupon Sister apparently went berserk and threatened that the cost of replacing them would come out of her wages. My contribution was to tell the girls about drowning Sister White in the sluice. Everyone who knew her was hysterical with laughter and couldn't believe that I hadn't been thrown out, especially in view of her fearsome reputation. The stories went on and on and it was greatly reassuring to realise that I wasn't the only one to make mistakes.

After lunch on most days, the various consultants would come in to lecture us about their specialities. Mr Brun, a consultant surgeon who had an incredible talent and ability to illustrate the human body, talked about the type of operations he carried out in theatre and drew magnificent, detailed, coloured diagrams of individual human organs to help in explaining their function. It seemed a sacrilege to destroy these works of art afterwards because they were so perfect. Someone mentioned that art was his hobby and some of his paintings and drawings had even been exhibited in a local gallery.

Another consultant, a lady dermatologist called Miss Maguire, was talking to us about body lice and numerous other creepy crawlies that can infest the human body, such as bed bugs and scabies, when she suddenly burst out laughing in the middle of her presentation. Looking around the room, she remarked that nearly every single one of us was squirming in our seats and scratching energetically.

Despite almost continuous lectures and instruction, the experience wasn't at all like ordinary school lessons, which I had hated, and I absolutely loved the sessions in training school because it was so refreshing to be studying subjects that actually interested me, while at the same time getting to know the other cadets a little better. In the school was a large room full of medical equipment and it was here where we practised taking each other's blood pressures, temperatures and pulses, at the same time learning how to distinguish the normal from what was considered to be abnormal. We were shown how and where to give intramuscular injections and practised on an orange. By this time the hospital had started to use the new sterile disposable needles and syringes which were an absolute boon as they were used only once before being discarded. We were observed making beds in the correct manner (sometimes with the 'patient' still in it) as well as being taught the correct way to give a bed bath. Every single day was interesting and different, but this was still only the beginning of our education and much more would have to be experienced on the ward.

There was not a formal examination at the end of PTS, although we were regularly tested to make sure that we had been listening and absorbing the information. I really enjoyed every second of these twelve weeks and even my social life improved when I started going out with some of the girls to clubs in and around Blackburn. We all had one week off before recommencing our training and I felt my life was definitely on an upward trend.

Before being issued with our student uniforms, we were measured so that our starched aprons, blue dresses and white starched caps actually fit. I thought I looked fantastic, especially in my outdoor coat and navy blue pillbox hat, and I imagined that everyone must surely be looking at me. I felt ever so important and couldn't wait to show Mum my new uniform. The list of placements for our first three months as student nurses went up on the notice board, with my name rostered for Ward 5 (Orthopaedics) along with Christine (of poo-in-her-hair fame).

★　★　★

On that first day, I arrived on the ward feeling very excited, despite being a little apprehensive because of my new responsibilities, and I was relieved to have Christine with me. I had got to know her well as a cadet and as a friend, and I knew that she cared passionately for her patients, worked hard and had a great sense of humour. Ward 5 was in the new tower block and, like all wards on the New Wing, had sixteen male beds and sixteen female. The first procedure at the beginning of every shift change was the ward report. Usually taken in Sister's office, the nurses going off duty were required to give a report on every patient, regardless of any change in their condition during the shift. There was only one sister on this ward at the time, (the junior sister having been promoted and not yet replaced) who took the opportunity to introduce me and Christine to the rest of the staff on shift, which that morning included two staff nurses, one enrolled nurse, a second-year student, a third-year student, two auxiliaries and one second-year cadet. Christine and I were not allowed to work together, but were each allocated a more senior nurse who would work with us and 'show us the ropes'. A third-year student, Carol, was to work with me for the day on the female side. Christine was working with the second-year student, Alison, on the male side. It seemed quite strange watching the cadet and the auxiliaries dealing with breakfasts and somehow I felt that I should be helping them, but I had of course moved on and therefore had other different jobs to do, starting with preparing designated patients for surgery.

As was the usual practice, the night staff had already placed large 'nil by mouth' signs on the appropriate beds and removed the water jugs and drinking glasses from their lockers, ensuring that they wouldn't be given anything to eat or drink (which may make them vomit under anaesthetic and could ultimately prove fatal). Each patient had to have a bath prior to surgery (if they were ambulant they could bath themselves, otherwise the nurses gave them a bed bath). The night staff had got the ball rolling before we came on duty and the first two patients on the theatre list had already been sorted out and were changed into theatre gowns, long, white, knee-length socks and a paper hat which covered their hair. Their beds had been stripped and remade with freshly laundered sheets, on top of which was placed a special canvas sheet, the purpose of which was to (when necessary) allow the theatre porters to insert wooden poles down either side to lift the patient on to the theatre trolley. The patient would then be asked to lie on top of a cotton sheet covering the canvas before being made comfortable with blankets to await their turn for theatre.

On theatre day, general nursing duties were always combined with preparing patients for surgery. The anaesthetist would usually have already visited the designated patients the previous evening, when he would have examined them to ensure that they were fit for anaesthesia and acquired their consent to be given the anaesthetic. Pre-meds were also prescribed at this time; these were medications which helped to relax the patient and dry up excess secretions, as anaesthetics rendered them unable to swallow. The pre-med was meant to be given an hour or so before surgery by injection, although the well-rehearsed procedure didn't always go smoothly. Sometimes theatre staff became preoccupied and forgot to contact the ward in time for the next patient to have their pre-med, and the theatre orderly would arrive to collect the patient only to find that they weren't ready. A delay would inevitably occur and sparks would fly, as anaesthetists in particular weren't renowned for their patience (especially the consultants, who could often be downright offensive if they had to wait around due to what they considered incompetence). It wasn't just a case of giving a quick injection either, because before the patient left the ward pre-operative checks had to be carefully carried out by two nurses. These checks included the removal of anything that wasn't fixed, such as false teeth, false eyes or prosthetic limbs. Jewellery was banned, apart from wedding rings; which had to be taped to prevent patients scratching themselves. Make-up (particularly nail varnish) wasn't allowed and had to be removed before theatre. But most importantly, hospital identity wristbands were always double-checked to ensure that the correct patient was being anaesthetised, the appropriate limb having already been marked with an indelible pen to ensure as far as possible that the correct appendage was being 'lopped off' or operated on.

It was a heavy workload on Orthopaedics. Many patients were bedridden because they were on traction with broken legs and the female side appeared to be permanently full of elderly ladies with fractured femurs. In pain and reluctant to move, it was an endless daily battle to ensure they didn't develop bedsores, which always reflected badly on the ward and disgraced the staff. The only way to prevent them (certainly in those days) was to ensure good nourishment, smooth bedding, regular changes of position and gentle but deep massaging combined with the application of barrier creams or surgical spirit to bony areas. Although the use of 'old-fashioned' surgical spirit was discontinued some years later due to the fire risk, in my opinion, when used correctly it was extremely effective in preventing bedsores. The ladies seemed more complex than the men because they were often much older and more infirm, while the male side tended to be full of young men who had sustained sports injuries, been involved in road accidents (motorbike accidents were common) or were suffering from an industrial injury.

Carol, the third-year student, was an enthusiastic teacher, showing me how to prepare patients for theatre and also showing me the correct procedure when going to collect them afterwards, which was not as simple as it sounds. In those days there was no recovery area in theatre like there is today so, as soon as the operation was finished, the patient was sent back to the ward. A nurse was dispatched from the ward to accompany the patient on their way back and it was the nurse's responsibility to ensure that the patient had a clear airway at all times throughout the journey.

Carol explained that each patient coming back from theatre usually had an airway in their mouth, which looked rather like a baby's dummy but was made of black rubber and had a hole through the middle. However, this airway was curved and went all the way down to the back of the throat; its purpose being to keep the patient's tongue from slipping back and choking them. Carol demonstrated how to tilt the patient's jaw upwards on either side, allowing them to breathe freely through the tube. Although I had seen this done as a cadet, as I wasn't allowed to do it myself, I had never really taken too much notice. Today it was my turn and, after watching Carol several times, she supervised me while I had a go. I was really proud to be 'hands on' and felt very grown up. The one thing Carol made absolutely clear was that any patient with an airway in place was especially vulnerable and, if left alone, they could dislodge it and choke. So until the patient actually spat it out themselves (which usually occurred as soon as they were coming round) a nurse had to stay with them to make sure that they were breathing.

Throughout the day we were constantly on the go, bed bathing and giving out medicines, making beds and assisting patients with their meals. Carol was very confident in her own abilities and I found it difficult to believe for one minute that I would ever get to that stage myself.

My first day had passed so quickly that I was

surprised when Sister told the morning staff to go home. We had worked from 7.30am–3.30pm, although it felt much less than that. I had only chatted briefly with Christine during our lunch break, but as we were leaving the ward to go home she couldn't wait to tell me what sort of a day she had had. There were quite a number of young men on the ward and, knowing that it was Christine's first day, they had (shall we say) not exactly been gentlemen.

Christine was asked by one of these charming young men for help to visit the toilet. He had both arms and one leg in plaster and was in a wheelchair. She pushed him into the toilet, where he was able to stand on his good leg and lean against the wall. Holding his broken arms aloft, feigning total innocence, he apologised and asked for her assistance, explaining that he urgently needed to pass urine but needed a helping hand (so to speak!). Deeply embarrassed, but determined to be professional and carry out her duties, she gave him the requested 'support', rearranged his trouser area and pushed him back to the ward. When they came out of the toilet a cheer went up; the lads in his cubicle had put bets on that she wouldn't do it. Christine blushed furiously when she saw him give the thumbs up to his mates but managed to laugh it off. Personally I thought this so-called 'joke' was completely unnecessary and I'm not sure that I would have accepted it with the good grace that she did. She didn't even mention the incident to anyone else, mainly because she was too embarrassed and didn't want to look foolish.

This young man was perfectly able to cope, of course, and had his request been genuine then a male nurse or orderly (had one been available), would have helped him, although any nurse would obviously assist if absolutely necessary.

Male orthopaedic patients were renowned for being mischievous but sometimes they could be a downright pain in the backside. Usually young, with a leg in plaster or on traction, they weren't really ill, just bored and looking for mischief. They would regularly tease new nurses mercilessly, be offensive and suggestive, swear and tell dirty jokes, often groping female staff at every opportunity if they thought they could get away with it. After only a week or so, I was working over on the male side and trying my best to ignore their antics but it wasn't always easy, as I was still a painfully shy, impressionable young girl with little knowledge of men. As a cadet I had not really had much experience dealing with such young patients; so far they had tended to be much older than myself and not quite as unrestrained. My parents would have been mortified if they could have seen and heard what I had to contend with on a daily basis.

Christine was helping one of the other nurses to tidy the ward in preparation for the consultant's round one day when she passed a bedridden Asian patient in a side ward who shouted that he wanted to go to the toilet, so she went to get him a urine bottle. His command of the English language was limited, but after looking at the bottle somewhat dubiously he nodded to her. The consultant and his accompanying entourage of doctors worked their way around the ward, eventually arriving at the side ward of this patient, who promptly handed the urine bottle to the consultant; protruding from the top of which was an enormous faecal stool. The consultant accepted it graciously, turned and handed it to Christine as though presenting her with a bunch of flowers: 'For you I believe.' Everyone burst out laughing, but I was relieved that it wasn't passed to me.

One little joke the patients played on me occurred a week later, just after breakfasts had been cleared. Patients who could get out of bed were being assisted where necessary and I was due to give a young male patient his bath. Daniel was a young motorcyclist who had somersaulted over the handlebars of his bike after colliding with a car, and slid along the road at speed on his backside.

I was happily filling the bath that morning for his daily wash when two other young male patients rushed into the bathroom, lifted me up bodily and dropped me into the water. I was soaked from head to foot, my starched cap and apron hanging limp as a wet dishcloth. Before I could move, Christine rushed into the bathroom. Having heard the commotion she came to warn me to be quiet because Matron had literally just walked on to the ward. The two culprits were mortified but, being the gallant gentlemen that they were, ran off. Totally panic-stricken, I started to climb out of the bath. I was in deep trouble and would doubtless have been blamed for 'encouraging' the young patients, even

114

though I had done no such thing.

Daniel, recognising my dilemma, limped in as fast as he could and locked the door. He told me not to worry and, before I could say anything, promptly jumped into the bath where he began singing and splashing loudly. I heard Miss Donavan enquire where I was and one of the lads who had tried to drown me told her I was helping a patient in the bathroom. The dignity of the patient being paramount in those days ensured that Matron wouldn't dream of entering the bathroom without a very good reason; so instead she knocked on the door to ask who I had in the bath. After having a brief conversation through the door she wished him well and carried on with her rounds. I was standing there with an ever-growing puddle around my feet, shivering with fear and scarcely daring to breathe, wondering what on earth I should do. Christine kindly volunteered to sneak back to the locker room and brought me a clean, dry uniform, plus cap and apron, although I had to wear paper theatre knickers and squelch around in wet shoes for the rest of the day. The two lads had been afraid that I would be sacked and apologised profusely, so for their cheek I thrust a mop and bucket in their direction and vowed to get my own back.

At around the same time, there was a middle-aged married man on the ward who had broken his leg and bruised a kidney in a road traffic accident. He was even worse than the young lads and behaved quite appallingly for much of the time, constantly showing off and making crude suggestions while 'touching up' any female in close proximity. Because of the kidney injury his urine had to be checked on a daily basis. He would push his way into the sluice in his wheelchair and, regardless who was in there, would openly urinate into a bottle. I was mortified at his behaviour but, even though I asked him to use the toilet cubicle in future, he just sniggered and said, 'You're a nurse aren't you? What's your problem?' After having put up with his innuendo and crudeness for long enough, and knowing that all the nurses had also had enough of him, I relayed my concerns to the ward sister, who suggested I was being prudish (which I probably was), even insinuating that I must have incited his behaviour and refused to do anything about it. But the story was very different when, soon after this incident, the patient grabbed her and fondled her bottom. She was absolutely livid and within the hour had summoned the consultant on to the ward. There were a rather uncomfortable few moments when the doctor arrived as he spoke up for *his* nurses and told the patient in no uncertain terms that this type of insulting behaviour would not be tolerated. After looking carefully at the man's medical records he decided that the rest of his treatment could be adequately completed as an out-patient and he was unceremoniously dis-charged. Thankfully, I gradually became virtually immune to this type of behaviour and, over time, ceased to blush or react in any way when it was encountered.

Many orthopaedic patients were on the ward

for weeks on end, some of them for several months, especially the road traffic accidents and the fractured femurs, so it was no surprise that after working on the same ward for three months, the nurses got to know them pretty well. Although fraternising was never openly permitted there was plenty of flirting going on, and sometimes this was the only thing stopping these young patients dying of extreme boredom.

★　★　★

Christmas Eve in BRI was always special, with a choir of hospital staff, all in uniform and carrying lanterns, calling into each darkened ward in turn to sing carols. The atmosphere was quite magical and I remember sitting on a chair next to the bed of an elderly lady on Ward 5 who had a fractured femur and was on traction. The choir sang 'Silent Night' and a lump came to my throat as I saw tears run down her cheeks. She whispered, 'I'm so glad to be here. My husband used to love carols and I do miss him. He died last year and I was dreading Christmas, I'd have been alone at home and missed all this.' I couldn't speak, but held her hand as the choir gave a loud rendition of 'Ding Dong Merrily on High' and wondered how many more people were out there who had no one with whom to celebrate Christmas.

Each year there was great rivalry between the wards at Christmas, when a prize was presented to the ward which produced the best festive display. A number of local shopkeepers kindly donated real Christmas trees and the wards were festooned with balloons, tinsel, mistletoe and decorations. Nurses and patients on Ward 5 constructed a large framework from cardboard made to resemble the outside of a house, and several of the bored young patients spent many hours painting bricks and windows to make it look authentic. Inside, seen through a plastic window, was a complete room scene including a Christmas tree strung with lights and hung with presents, Father Christmas with his legs dangling from the chimney, greeting cards above the fireplace and a tray on a small table laden with (cardboard) drinks and mince pies. We didn't win on that occasion but it kept the lads occupied and was fun to do.

All bedridden patients had their beds and lockers 'trimmed up' whether they liked it or not, though very few ever objected, and patients on traction had happy faces drawn on their toes while having to lie there completely powerless to do anything about it. Patients' visitors were asked to bring in presents on Christmas Eve so that Father Christmas could distribute them on Christmas morning. Some of them sneaked in illicit booze, which was quickly and quietly stashed in lockers to be consumed under cover of darkness, so on Christmas morning the ward smelled like a brewery and the only response to my cheery 'Merry Christmas!' was loud snoring.

Matron enjoyed the festive season and encouraged patients to have a good time, but she would have gone berserk about the alcohol, especially had she realised that the sister who was unlucky enough to be on duty that year was a bit 'happy' herself from the night before and had turned a blind eye to their illicit consumption. All the nurses had mistletoe and tinsel hanging from their caps, inviting boozy comments and the odd sloppy kiss, and at breakfast time a rather bedraggled Father Christmas arrived on a huge wheelchair 'sled' surrounded by sacks of presents. His 'Ho! Ho! Ho!' was repeated with surprisingly little enthusiasm as he went from bed to bed. One of the off-duty doctors had been railroaded into doing the job, despite suffering the effects of substantial amounts of alcohol the previous evening. With his bloodshot eyes and raging hangover he looked dreadful but managed to shake hands with the men and kiss the ladies (getting it right most of the time) as he doled out their presents. Our greatest fear was that he might fall off his 'sled', but with some assistance he completed his rounds without major mishap before being pushed into the linen closet to sleep it off.

★　★　★

My first surgical experience as a trainee nurse was to be back on Ward 3. Having already spent some time on this ward as a second-year cadet, and knowing the way Sister Adams worked, I was not quite as nervous as usual. When I arrived on my first early morning shift I recognised a few familiar faces among the permanent staff and, to my relief, another student from my PTS called Susan. Unfortunately the junior sister was still the same; but I hoped she would be a little friendlier this time around now that I was a student. Going back to this ward as a student nurse was going to be very different to having worked there as a cadet, as I was now to be much more directly involved with patient care and would be expected to put into practice some of the skills I had acquired in the meantime.

Sister Adams welcomed Susan and me to the ward, and together with the other staff I listened intently to her morning report on the patients. I was completely surprised to hear that Ray (admitted with very serious head injuries some six months earlier during my previous stint on the ward) was still a patient and now no longer in danger of losing his life, although he had made very little progress and his doctors doubted that he would ever be able to speak or walk again. His parents still visited faithfully every day, helping to feed and stimulate him, but he never showed any sign of recognition or flicker of understanding. Sister continued her report, detailing which patients were going home that day and those who had to be prepared for theatre.

As usual, being new I wasn't allowed to 'fly solo' at first and had to relearn the routine of a surgical ward from a different perspective, especially the necessity to check and double-check. It was standard training procedure and considered essential to learn from and be guided by someone more experienced and I was allocated to work for the duration of the shift with a third-year student nurse called Joyce, while Susan was to work with a second-year student called Laura (this varied on a daily basis). I liked the look of Joyce very much, I had seen her laughing and joking in the hospital canteen on many occasions, and the staff and patients all seemed very fond of her. From all accounts she was a star student and expected to pass with flying colours when she took her finals in a few weeks' time.

Susan and I both began by taking routine observations, she was on the female side and I was on the male. Taking blood pressures, temperatures and pulses was not exactly rocket science and anyone could do it, but the important factor was recognising the variations between the readings and, even more importantly, understanding their significance. For example, a high pulse rate and a drop in blood pressure following an operation could herald internal bleeding; a high temperature could mean post-operative infection. If there was any doubt at all it was charted and reported to whoever was in charge of the ward at the time.

Having Joyce as my mentor really helped me to relax, knowing that I could ask her anything at any time. When I eventually came to Ray's bedside, his mum was busy feeding him but paused when she recognised me. After giving her a twirl to show off my new uniform she welcomed me back with a big hug. Ray clearly didn't appreciate the interruption and grunted for more food. It was tragic to see this once active and healthy young man dribbling porridge down his chin like a baby, yet despite the expressionless face and blank eyes his mum radiated with optimism as he opened his mouth like a fledgling to accept the food she offered. Regular sessions with physiotherapists, intended to prevent his muscles wasting, were fairly futile because he objected loudly whenever they attempted to bend and stretch his limbs, struggling and resisting their efforts with all the strength of his burly physique.

When I first spoke to Ray there was no response and I wasn't even sure that he could hear me, but as soon as I took hold of his arm to put on the cuff to take his blood pressure he pushed me away determinedly. His mum apologised and tried to calm him, while I did my utmost to proceed as gently as possible, but it was no easy task trying to straighten one arm while he was bashing me over the head with the other. He was a big lad with a hefty punch and this procedure had to be repeated every four hours.

A couple of weeks later I was carrying out my routine checks and chatting away to him as usual when suddenly, for the very first time since the day he was admitted, he slowly and deliberately raised his head, looked straight at me and appeared to be trying to focus his gaze. His eyes continued to follow me around the bed and then he coughed and spluttered as if trying to say something. Of course, he hadn't even attempted to speak for several months and was obviously having difficulty getting any words out. Screwing his face up in a mixture of frustration and concentration he made one supreme effort and bawled out: 'Who are you?'

At first I couldn't believe my ears and thought I must be dreaming, then beaming from ear to ear I replied that I was one of the nurses looking after him. I was hopping up and down like a lunatic and absolutely thrilled to bits. The other patients in the cubicle surrounding his bed were grinning like Cheshire cats, all trying to speak to him at the same time. I called Susan, Laura and Joyce over and before long Ray had an audience around his bed making a din that could have wakened the dead. By this time Sister Adams had heard the commotion and had come to investigate what was happening, bringing one of the doctors with her. Everyone was laughing and crying in amazement and when Ray's mum arrived a few minutes later he immediately recognised her, gave her a huge grin and whispered, 'Hi Mum.'

The look on her face will remain in my memory forever. There was not a dry eye in the house and even the doctor had to blow his nose a few times. Ray, on the other hand, was totally bewildered and not sure what all the fuss was about. He couldn't remember a thing about the accident or being brought to hospital, refusing to believe his mum when she told him how long he had been there.

His recovery was slow, but now benefited from the help and support of the physiotherapist who worked with him each day and gave him numerous tasks to complete. For example, to improve his grip he would be given a soft ball to squeeze, which would help strengthen his fingers. When this became too easy she would give him more difficult tasks such as picking up a spoon or a fork and asking him to use it at mealtimes without spilling any food. Getting food on to a spoon was difficult enough, but then trying to coordinate the journey to his mouth was exasperating, and if he didn't get it right first time he regularly threw the spoon on to the floor in disgust. Rather like a stroke victim learning to do the simplest tasks, it was a hard slog but Ray had age on his side and was determined to get better, forcing himself a little further every single day.

His legs were particularly weak and emaciated from lack of use, so the physiotherapist had the unenviable task of building up his leg muscles. She worked him hard, at first manually pushing and pulling his legs until he shouted out his objections. Then she made him bend and stretch them himself, encouraging him to wiggle his toes and flex and extend his feet backwards and forwards, or to raise his legs in the air and try to keep them up for as long as possible. It was tough but eventually he gained sufficient strength to be able to stand up and bear his own weight.

The most frustrating problem for Ray was his slurred speech. He found it embarrassing that he knew exactly what he wanted to say but his brain seemed to be in slow motion and it took ages for him to get out even the simplest of words. This is where the speech therapist came in. She visited him several times a week and before too long had him forming his words perfectly, albeit a little slowly. The occupational therapist gave him games and puzzles to increase his concentration and he was soon a cheerful young man again who rarely stopped talking.

When he was discharged some months later he could wash and feed himself and take a few steps unaided. Although he suffered an occasional fit, these were well controlled by medication and, about a year later, we heard that he had even returned to work. This was a totally unexpected but fantastic outcome for him and for his family, which ultimately made all the hard work by so many staff truly worthwhile.

★   ★   ★

Not all cases had happy endings though. A young man named Oliver, a tall, handsome blond individual, was a regular patient on the ward. He seemed pleasant and friendly to me, although the permanent staff were sick of seeing him. He suffered from Munchausen Syndrome (which basically meant that he feigned illnesses because he craved medical attention) and he also self-harmed. His hospital notes were extensive and covered his innumerable visits to BRI: mainly to remove objects he had swallowed. It was easy to get annoyed with him for tying up acute beds with self-inflicted problems, but he was a lonely individual with a flawed personality. He wasted many hours of valuable time and resources and in earlier years would probably have been confined to a secure psychiatric unit for his own safety, because sadly there was no medication that could help. In his favour, I have to say that he was never aggressive, yet he found being the centre of attention addictive. Even when a member of staff told him off he would laugh and say, 'But you still love me, though, don't you?'

One of the staff nurses, who had seen Oliver several times before, warned him that one day he would go too far and kill himself. He seemed not to know or care how dangerous his actions were; they gained him attention, which was what he desired more than anything else.

On this particular occasion he had swallowed a table fork and x-rays showed that the prongs were in a very dangerous position. Any jolt or sudden movement could cause the perforation of a vital organ, so we had to be very careful not to bend or twist his torso. On all his previous admissions a quick anaesthetic and a non-invasive removal of the offending object had been sufficient, but this time it was thought to be potentially more serious. Fortunately, while under anaesthetic and using x-ray equipment to highlight the position of the fork, the surgeon managed to manipulate it into a more accessible position. This, in turn, enabled him to get a good grip on the prongs of the fork using long thin forceps and to remove it without causing any damage (much to Oliver's disappointment, because this meant he would be allowed home the next day).

I was to see Oliver only once more, several

months later, after I had left Ward 3. During a break in training school I went to visit a friend who was a patient on Ward 4 and as I passed the first bay I saw one of the other patients who seemed familiar. It was only when I looked at his nameplate that I realised it was Oliver. His swollen, shaved head was deeply scarred, heavily bruised and covered with stitches. There was a tracheotomy tube in his throat and a drip in each arm. A catheter was draining into a bag fixed to his bed and he looked desperately ill. His breathing was shallow and rasping, his eyes open but unseeing. A staff nurse from the ward asked if I knew him.

'I nursed him on Ward 3 after he had swallowed a fork,' I said without taking my eyes off him. She spoke sympathetically and told me that this time he had been found unconscious at the foot of a multi-storey car park in the town centre. No one knew if he had jumped or been pushed. Poor Oliver, I squeezed his hand and talked to him for a few minutes, but there was no reaction whatsoever and, when I returned to classes later, I found it impossible to concentrate. I knew he could be a real nuisance at times but he wasn't a bad person, he was simply crying out for someone to love and care for him. He died peacefully shortly afterwards.

★ ★ ★

One day while I was on duty, a rather upper-crust and awfully well-spoken middle-aged lady was admitted for urgent surgery. It was very obvious that she would normally have expected to be treated as a private patient in a side ward but, to her disgust, a shortage of beds and the urgency of her admission meant that she had to be placed on the general ward. Her superior attitude and constant petty demands quickly alienated the nursing staff on the busy unit. To her utter dismay the adjoining bed was occupied by an elderly female vagrant who was dying. The 'posh lady' was taken down to theatre and very soon afterwards the 'bag lady' died. Sister instructed two student nurses to prepare the old lady's body for the mortuary and to clear out her locker. Several hours later when the toffee-nosed patient was coming round from her anaesthetic following successful surgery, her first request was for her dentures, which had been put away inside her locker prior to the operation. When the nurse looked in the locker she was rather puzzled to find only a sliver of cheap hospital soap, a moth-eaten rag which had been used as a facecloth and a set of very old, discoloured false teeth which clearly didn't belong to this patient. Realisation swiftly dawned that the nurses had inadvertently cleared out the wrong locker so, making a quick excuse, one of the nurses went in search of the missing choppers. Sister had to be informed, of course, and was furious, especially when the mortuary assistant told her that the 'lady of the road' was now lying in state, sporting a broad smile and displaying a gleaming array of expensive dentistry. Unfortunately rigor mortis made it impossible to remove the teeth without breaking her jaw. Perhaps they would try later? The recovering patient had thankfully fallen asleep while all this was going on and was surprisingly grateful when she was eventually reunited with her missing dentures, although she must have been a little disconcerted over the next few days when the nursing staff had to choke back laughter on the rare occasions she smiled at them.

* * *

Wards were always expected to provide a nurse to accompany each patient back from theatre after surgery. On one particular busy day Sister Adams asked me to carry out this task. When I arrived in theatre the consultant anaesthetist looked at me, saw my plain cap (which denoted that I was a first year student nurse) and asked me how often I had acted as escort. When I told him that I had only been to theatre three or four times, he refused to let me accompany the patient back to the ward and demanded a more senior nurse. On my return to the ward I relayed this message to Sister, who said that her only senior nurse was busy elsewhere and couldn't be spared, so she rang Matron for assistance. Sister looked shocked as she put down the receiver and said that Matron had decided to go for the patient herself. This was simply unheard of.

Matron presented herself to the anaesthetist. 'Will I do?' she asked in a very supercilious voice. 'Am I senior enough for you?'

A few harsh words were exchanged between

129

them and Matron set off back to the ward accompanied by the theatre orderly. Unfortunately the patient was restless, agitated and confused as he regained consciousness and attempted to climb over the trolley sides. Matron did her best to subdue him, but seconds later he had clambered over the side and fallen on to the floor, ripping out his drip and sustaining a broken arm in the process. The anaesthetist was furious and Matron would never live it down. It was good of her to take the trouble to assist the ward at the time and I felt sorry for her embarrassment, but it just goes to show that no nurse is immune to this sort of accident happening, regardless of how much experience they have had and how much care they may take.

I still found the junior sister difficult to work for, as she was constantly trying to show her authority at every opportunity. On one very busy morning half the nurses on Ward 3 were off sick with flu, which left just two student nurses and an enrolled nurse to do all the work. The workload was completely manic and it took us until after lunch to finish getting everyone up who could do so and bathing all the bedridden patients. There were thirty-two beds to make, medicines to dispense, drips and catheters to check, observations to do, bedpans to give out, etc. etc. By the time the next shift arrived we were exhausted. The junior ward sister came on to the ward for her late shift and walked up and down the length of the ward, checking the patients and looking in all the rooms. Minutes later she called us into the office and gave us a good telling off. She was fuming and accused us of being grossly untidy. Her main concern, believe it or not, was that the beds didn't have perfect hospital corners! She demanded that the three of us go back on to the ward and strip every single bed before remaking them properly, warning us that she would come and inspect them later. I can't adequately express how I felt at the time, although murderous is probably quite near the mark. I could have ripped her head off! We were all totally shattered and I clearly remember going into the sluice with the other two and breaking down in tears. It didn't matter how well we had coped with so few staff, she had to have things perfect and nothing else would do. During my time on the ward I disliked her intensely and considered her something of a control freak, but given the choice I would much rather someone be meticulous and disciplined than otherwise; she did her best for the patients and that was what we were all there to do.

★　★　★

An old lady living alone had opened her door to a late-night caller, only to be roughly pushed back inside her living room by a man demanding food and money. Terrified, she gave him her purse, which had little in it, and hastily provided him with something to eat. Ada was in her late seventies, only five feet four in height and weighed no more than six stone. Her attacker, on the other hand, was a big, stocky man about forty years of age, who tied her up and gagged her. He systematically ransacked every room in the house but found little of value. As it was late he decided to stay the night and violently dragged Ada upstairs, forced her to undress and pushed her on to the bed where he raped her several times. He punched her viciously in the face when she cried out and showed no mercy to the frail old lady, even forcing her to perform oral sex. He made his escape early next morning, leaving her injured, terrified and in pain.

I was on duty in the ward when she was brought into hospital after being discovered by her home help. Detectives accompanied her, desperately wanting to question her as soon as possible; they were obviously anxious to find this coward quickly but she wasn't in any fit state to be interrogated. We put Ada into a side ward opposite the nurses' station in order to keep a close eye on her because she was in a very distressed state, covered in blood, bruised all over her body, rambling and confused. She had sustained several broken ribs and her eyes were almost closed from bruising and swelling. The hardened officers who stayed at the hospital with her were visibly upset.

Trying to be as gentle as possible, I helped to undress her and put her in a warm nightdress, although she winced with pain at each small movement. All at once she gripped my arm tightly, pointing in terror to the window, crying out that the man had come back again, although it was simply the reflection of one of the detectives. I reassured her that she was completely safe, but she kept repeating, 'He put it in my mouth. He put it in my mouth', then she would retch and vomit. A police photographer came to the ward later that day to photograph her injuries for evidence. Ada was so terrified by his presence (she thought every man was her attacker) that we decided to move her on to the main ward so that she wouldn't feel quite so isolated. All the other patients had heard about her ordeal and, without exception, made a determined effort to look out for her and keep her company. The lowlife responsible for this dreadful crime was caught and sent to prison, although Ada never got over her ordeal and spent the rest of her life in a nursing home, too afraid to return to her own home.

Every day was different on Ward 3 and I learned a great deal. I was becoming proficient at passing urinary catheters and Ryle's tubes, and had learned to cope with the many drips, drains and injections like a veteran. Like me, Susan loved the work and we soon became quite good friends, sharing many moments together over the next couple of years comparing the rapidly expanding repertoire of our newly acquired skills and experiences. The senior student nurses who had mentored us on Ward 3 had been marvellous and their comprehensive training was greatly appreciated by us both. It came as a huge shock to everyone on the ward when Joyce failed to pass her written final exams at the first attempt. She was acknowledged as one of the brightest, most capable students in the hospital and thankfully sailed through the second time around. In the space of just a few months and seeing life at its most raw, I was growing up and maturing fast. I felt more confident every day and was becoming a much stronger person, which was just as well because my next move was to Casualty.

★ ★ ★

My first impression of the Casualty Department was sheer chaos, but on meeting one of the two sisters who were on duty she reassured me that, to begin with, I was expected only to observe. She introduced me to some of the other nurses on duty (I didn't know any of them) and showed me around, starting with reception, where every patient had to be manually checked in (the hospital wasn't yet computerised and all the records were still handwritten). If it was difficult to identify a patient for any reason, e.g. a multiple trauma victim or an unconscious person without accessible identification, the staff had to search their clothing for wallets or identifying paperwork in order to contact relatives. If nothing could be found then they were given a number, and a brief description of their appearance was entered on a record card. The admission system in reception wasn't the best in the world and with only one receptionist on duty at any given time the job was sometimes almost impossible. The receptionist was variously expected to file record cards, answer telephones and register new patients, while trying to answer enquiries and pacify disgruntled patients (and staff) at the same time. The triage system wasn't yet in operation, so the receptionist was also expected to draw the attention of the nursing staff to anyone in the waiting room who was bleeding profusely or looked particularly unwell. There was a minor injuries section for the walking wounded, where staff attended to patients with non-urgent injuries and ailments, and a major trauma section that dealt with acute emergencies.

After showing me around, Sister left me in reception with Heather (the receptionist of the day) to watch and learn, and that first day was a real eye-opener. The stream of patients was usually headed by the regulars. They wanted good seats, one with a view, and would then sit there reading a newspaper or discussing their ailments with anyone who cared to listen. The receptionist worked non-stop, noise levels gradually rising around her as the day progressed; more grumbles, increasing complaints and uncontrollable children running around screaming their heads off. The regulars often greeted the receptionist by her first name as though they were a friend or relative.

The first telephone call of the morning was from a butcher to say that his apprentice was on his way to Casualty as a matter of urgency; while cutting up a carcass of beef he had missed and chopped his fingers instead. The butcher sounded very distressed, emphasising that the injury was serious and begging that someone see him as soon as he arrived. A short time later a young fair-haired lad in a striped apron wandered in holding a bloodied towel around his hand and he gave his details. Looking remarkably relaxed, if not a little pale, he repeated the story to us in a very matter-of-fact manner. Bearing in mind what his boss had already told us, I took him into a small cubicle in the minor injuries section, where a third-year student nurse called Sylvia checked to see just how serious the injuries actually were. She agreed to let me observe and I was sickened to find that he had virtually severed all four fingers, and they now dangled precariously down the back of his hand. Thankfully his thumb was undamaged.

'Hell's bells! You don't do things by halves,' I said to him. I knew that I shouldn't have been in there but I simply had to have a look and, as a result, very quickly began to feel light-headed and experienced a peculiar stirring sensation in the pit of my stomach. I realised that I was about to pass out when, without warning, the patient beat me to it and fainted, which brought me back to reality pretty quickly. Sylvia asked me to get Sister and within seconds he was virtually mobbed by senior staff, who placed him on to a trolley and wheeled him into the major trauma area with me tagging along behind. A doctor examining the lad's hand unexpectedly asked me to fetch a bowl. All the fingers were literally hanging by a thread of skin and the doctor swiftly snipped off each one in turn with a pair of sterile scissors, dropped them into the bowl and handed it to me. I vividly remember looking at four very white, very dead chubby fingers lying helplessly in the bowl and wondering what on earth I was supposed to do with them. Thankfully Sister quickly took the bowl from me, grinning at my horrified face. Sadly there was no prospect of saving the fingers by sewing them back on because microsurgery was very much in its infancy at the time and very few doctors had the ability to use it successfully. I was sent back to reception not knowing what was to happen to him and felt distinctly unsettled for the rest of the day. I had recurring visions of those four lifeless digits, wondering how on earth I would cope if something even more gruesome came in. Only time would tell.

That first day saw a great variety of medical problems, from nosebleeds to strokes, cut fingers to multiple major injuries and the time absolutely flew by. It was brilliant but I was desperate to have a go at dealing with some of the wounds myself and couldn't wait to get my hands on them. When I arrived home and told my mum about 'the fingers' she pulled a face and asked if I fancied fish fingers for tea. She always did have a warped sense of humour!

The next day I had to shadow and observe Sylvia in the minor injuries unit. She had already completed two stints in Casualty and hoped to become a staff nurse in the department after passing her finals. The procedure for dealing with minor injuries was unsophisticated but designed to make efficient use of the doctor's time. After check-in, patient cards were put into order by time of arrival and placed in a box on the wall just outside the minor injuries area. With four cubicles at her disposal, the nurse took the first four cards and called a patient into each cubicle, then went into each one in turn and established the patient's reason for attending and carried out the initial preparatory work for the doctor's examination. A patient with a foot injury, for instance, would be asked to take off their shoes and socks, while an open wound would need cleaning thoroughly in order to establish how deep it was and to assess the extent of the damage. If someone had a nosebleed, ice packs would be provided for the patient to apply to the bridge of their nose and their blood pressure was taken and recorded. All this saved precious time, so that when the doctor arrived he could check each patient with minimum delay. The doctor would then detail any recommended treatment on the patient's casualty card, leaving the nurse to comply with the instructions once the examination had been completed. The nurse who actually carried out the treatments then had to countersign the bottom of the card. Accountability for your own actions was drummed into us from the very beginning of training.

The list of requirements and different procedures seemed endless. Crutches and splints had to be supplied, a wide variety of bandages and dressings applied, appointment cards made out for x-rays and fracture clinics, and innumerable injections administered. I thrived on the variety and involvement, especially when I was allowed to call the patients in myself and prepare them for the doctor, in addition to carrying out many of the treatments. Before very long my repertoire was extensive.

The one procedure that I did find fiddly at

first was packing a patient's nose with gauze in order to stop a persistent nosebleed. The first patient I dealt with had been bleeding on and off for about two hours with no sign of stopping. His blood pressure was normal and the senior house officer had examined him and suggested a nose pack. This was the second patient that morning with the same problem so I asked the other student if I could have a go. First of all I sat the patient upright and put a cover around his neck to avoid any blood spoiling his clothes. I told him that I was going to put a pack of gauze into each nostril, that would form a firm pressure on the bleeding point and thus, hopefully, stop the bleeding. Opening a pre-sterilised kidney bowl, I asked him to hold it under his nose to catch any drips. A long strip of ribbon gauze that had been covered in liquid paraffin was then slowly and carefully fed into each nostril, pushing it as far back as it would go until the patient's eyes watered. There was a definite art to packing the gauze in firmly and if you didn't put enough in then the patient would simply carry on bleeding. It was not a comfortable procedure to have carried out and the patient would obviously have to breathe continuously through their mouth for a period of anything up to twenty-four hours or more. If packing failed to stop the bleeding then it would have to be cauterised on the ENT ward. I felt rather nervous as I continued but the patient gave me the thumbs up, which I took to mean he was feeling OK. The student watched me carry out the packing and seemed satisfied with the result so, after taping a small gauze pad underneath his nostrils to prevent everything from falling out, the patient was allowed home with instructions to remove the pack himself the following day.

In addition to understanding some of the medical jargon, the biggest difficulty I encountered was trying to decipher the doctors' handwriting, and I found myself constantly asking questions, but recognised that both these unfamiliar aspects of the job would take time to learn. In the meantime, I was ready to try my hand at anything.

After a couple of weeks, and once I had become familiar with most of the basic procedures, I was then allowed to work on the major trauma side. This was the big stuff and I was apprehensive because it was usually the domain of the sisters and senior nurses. Junior staff needed to have their wits about them and not get in the way. In those early days my nerves were stretched like piano wire but I soon learned to cope.

Infestations were a pet hate of mine and, unfortunately, most of these were more often than not to be found on people who had been found collapsed somewhere and been brought in unconscious or very seriously ill. The first I can recall was a vagrant who was brought in by ambulance after being found unconscious in a derelict building. As was fairly common in such cases, he was filthy, with long, dirty, unkempt hair and whiskers, had rotten teeth and reeked of urine. The stench filled the room and two of us were 'volunteered' army-style to get him undressed,

140

cleaned up and into a hospital gown ready for examination. First of all we donned gowns and rubber gloves for protection and sprayed perfume on to a facemask to mask the smell. Undressing him was like peeling an onion. He wore multiple layers of crusty, smelly clothes which were mainly holes connected by bits of material; a jacket, two jumpers, three vests and a T-shirt, which had probably never been taken off since the day he acquired it. I left the cubicle to get a trolley to wash him, but hadn't gone very far before I heard a piercing scream from my fellow conscript. Rushing back to the cubicle I found her standing on a chair clutching her uniform tightly around her legs.

'A bloody rat!' she cried. 'It came out of his trouser leg when I tried to take them off.' Like her, I instinctively took a firm grip on my uniform to prevent any unexpected rodent intrusion and looked around with a shiver but couldn't see Roland anywhere. Seconds later when someone came through the main doors, the offending animal emerged from his hiding place and bolted outside. We started to breathe a little easier but still had to get on with undressing the tramp, a task which we now continued with extreme care, especially since we could clearly see where the rat had been gnawing at his leg.

The doctor arrived to assess the man's level of consciousness and first of all checked for his response to sound by calling to him loudly and watching for a reaction. There was none. Slowly and meticulously he proceeded to examine the

141

patient from head to toe, checking his reflexes and looking for any sign of movement, but sadly there was absolutely nothing. The old man was freezing cold and his pulse was barely palpable; he was already close to death and an hour or so later he passed away without having regained consciousness. No one knew who he was, there was no identification on him and I don't believe his name was ever established. He simply became a 'John Doe', similar to a number of others brought in dead (B.I.D.). One slightly unsatisfactory aspect about Casualty was that we rarely heard whether the police had ever traced any relatives or friends in such situations.

There were many incidents that I remember from those impressionable early days, although one particularly sad case was a cot death. A hysterical young mother came rushing in clutching her baby, which had turned very blue, screaming at me to make him breathe as she thrust the tiny body into my arms. I shouted for the doctor and almost immediately several senior staff surrounded the baby, administering CPR and starting well-rehearsed resuscitation procedures. It was the first collapsed baby I had ever seen in my life and I could feel the adrenaline pumping through my body. I was terrified and could only observe helplessly from the sidelines. Everyone was willing and begging the child to breathe, but to no avail. He was eventually pronounced dead after about thirty minutes of what seemed more like hours of desperate but ultimately futile efforts to resuscitate him. I stood and watched as all the needles and tubes were gently removed from the baby's body, which was then lovingly cleaned and his hair neatly combed. Sister propped him up on a pillow as though he was asleep and arranged a sheet over him so that only his tiny head was visible. Everyone was too emotional to speak although someone still had to break the news to the mother. Her screams silenced the whole department. It was truly heartbreaking as she pounded her fists on the doctor's chest in grief and despair, blaming the staff for not trying hard enough to save her baby. I had to take myself off into the toilets where I sobbed uncontrollably.

Casualty definitely isn't all gloom and doom, though; it can be equally gratifying and amusing. A perfect illustration of this was when a middle-aged man was brought into Casualty by ambulance following a road traffic accident. He was very pale, incoherent and covered in blood. We undressed him and checked his observations: all were normal. He gradually 'came to' and gave us his name and address. Despite the large amount of blood we could find no obvious sign of serious injury, other than bleeding down one nostril, so the doctor questioned him to establish exactly what had happened. The man blushed and lowered his head, unwilling to answer. Only when the questions were repeated did he tell his tale of woe. He had been stationary in his car at red traffic lights, and was picking his nose when suddenly he had been shunted by the vehicle behind. The impact jerked his head forward so violently that he rammed his finger up his nostril, bursting his nose. When he saw the amount of blood he fainted and was found in this condition by the other motorist, who had come to apologise for what he thought was just a minor bump but he ended up having to ring for an ambulance!

A girl aged about nineteen was brought in by her parents one day with severe abdominal pain. They were convinced she had appendicitis. I took her into a cubicle while a staff nurse, Connie, escorted the parents to register her details at reception. The girl undressed quickly and put on a gown, but only seconds later was again doubled up in agony. Connie returned and helped me to get her on to a trolley where she continued to writhe around in pain. Her observations seemed fairly normal considering the amount of discomfort she was apparently suffering, so Connie lifted her gown and asked her to indicate where the pain was coming from. She immediately saw a tiny foot on the end of a tiny leg.

'Oh God!' shouted Connie. 'She's in labour and the baby is coming the wrong way!' Connie had completed her midwifery training and clearly knew what she was doing but I was totally gobsmacked. We pushed the trolley into a bigger cubicle, Connie instructing the girl in no uncertain terms NOT to bear down. A quick telephone call produced two doctors from Gynaecology who rapidly took charge (BRI didn't have an obstetric unit), while Connie remained on guard with her gloved hand preventing the unexpected small patient from emerging any further. One of the doctors skilfully manipulated the child and only minutes later out popped one tiny, scraggy blue mess, barely two pounds in weight and not breathing. Frantic efforts were made to assist the baby and within a few moments, which seemed like hours, a kitten-like squeal thankfully heralded the new arrival. A quick dash by ambulance to the premature baby unit at QPH confirmed that all was well. Mum was kept in Casualty until the afterbirth was expelled and then she, too, was transferred to be with her baby. For now, though, she had the problem of telling her parents. The doctor first congratulated Connie on her quick action, he had no doubts that the baby would not have survived but for her, and then he went along with Sister to break the news to the new grandparents. Connie and I listened at the door.

Doctor: 'Your daughter has been transferred to another hospital and I have some news that may surprise and shock you.'

Mum: 'Oh no, is there something seriously wrong?'

Doctor: 'It really depends on your point of view. I have to tell you that you are now grandparents to a little girl.'

Dad: 'I'll kill the bastard!'

Mum: 'Are they both all right?'

Sister: 'Your daughter is fine. The baby is premature and is very tiny, but she has been sent to the premature baby unit in an incubator and will be well looked after.'

All the staff in Casualty were thrilled about this happy outcome, which was one of the main topics of conversation for several weeks afterwards. I would have loved to have been a fly on the wall when granddad had a few words with the new father.

★ ★ ★

Unlike current student nurses, who now spend a great deal of their training in a mainly theoretical classroom situation studying for a degree-level qualification, students in the 1960s had to work virtually full-time in a practical situation. We were never given a choice of which wards we would like to work on, but were expected to gain experience in all medical and surgical specialities. The children's ward, where I was sent next, had two sisters, along with two staff nurses, two enrolled nurses and several students. Being on this ward was my personal nightmare because I couldn't bear to see sick children, and still can't. My first stint there scared me to death.

Tiny babies could be perfectly happy one minute and fighting for life the next. They could literally deteriorate before your eyes and I hated it. I also found the noise level on the ward too much at times. The sound of eight or more tiny babies all demanding to be fed at the same time was ear splitting, and even putting cotton wool plugs in my ears didn't help. I lived on paracetamol for my tension headaches. The hospital rules at that time didn't exactly help either, as the parents weren't allowed to stay with their children overnight and had to be off the ward by 8pm. Imagine being one of only two untrained students, who were the people normally on duty at night, trying to feed umpteen babies in addition to trying to pacify a dozen or so crying toddlers, all poorly and wanting their mums. If we were fortunate and the sisters covering nights on the other units had some time to spare they would usually help us, otherwise we had to struggle through as best we could.

We had three toddlers on the ward at the same time, two boys and a girl, all critically ill. The beautiful little girl, Joanne, was born to parents who had been trying desperately for a baby all their married life, more than ten years. They had been so happy when she was born, but she had contracted viral meningitis and was now very poorly. Viral meningitis is generally much milder than bacterial meningitis and is contracted through everyday viruses such as mumps, chicken pox and herpes simplex (cold sores). As people get older they usually build up an immunity to these viruses, but babies and toddlers have not always yet developed the immunity. From previously being a lively, happy youngster, Joanne had become a helpless tragedy and, although she survived the original infection, she was left both physically and mentally disabled, unable even to sit up unsupported. Her parents rarely left her side and insisted on feeding her themselves. They washed and changed her and, quite honestly, the only input the nurses had was administering her medication and changing her intravenous infusion (drip).

In the next cubicle was a baby boy, Ben, whose case was almost identical. He, too, like the little girl, was suffering from viral meningitis and was also permanently brain-damaged. His mother stayed with him as much as possible and became close friends with Joanne's parents. Both cases were extremely tragic, yet they amazingly seemed to gain support from each other and often spent time together chatting and comparing their children's progress. The little boy also survived but would similarly need twenty-four-hour care for the rest of his life. Antibiotics were not an option, as viruses don't respond to them, so the only care that nurses were able to give was good general hygiene, assisting with feeding, and giving an abundance of support to the families.

The third child, about ten months old and born with hydrocephalus (water on the brain), was in another cubicle and critically ill. He had been abandoned by his parents who hadn't been in to visit him since birth. We never knew whether they simply didn't care or if they couldn't bear to see him suffer and die. It wasn't our place to judge. Most of the time he was receiving sedation for his pain but he rarely moved or made a sound until he was hungry, when he became increasingly restless. Feeding him was a major undertaking because his head was hugely swollen and heavy with fluid. He was so weak that even sucking exhausted him and it took an hour to get him to take barely two ounces of feed. I used to find a firm surface, put down two pillows to support my arm and let him lie there, trying my best not to jerk his head as I fed him. He needed feeding little and often so all the nurses took turns to fuss over him, even though there was little response. We kept him as comfortable as we possibly could until he died a few weeks later. I was in pieces and even went to Matron to beg for a transfer. I had anxiety feelings, couldn't sleep and felt like running away. My request was refused, of course, although Matron was very kind and sympathetic. She pointed out that part of the training to be a registered nurse included working on a children's ward, so if I wanted to complete my training I had to persevere.

There were obviously days when the children's ward could be fun, and it was fantastic to see the children come in poorly and then go home laughing and smiling. Being a children's nurse is very special and needs a certain sort of person to be able to deal with sick children day in and day out. I am just not one of them. Trying to feed tiny babies who could hardly breathe and caring for terminally ill children left me a wreck, but the experience certainly helped when my own son was born a few years later.

There was one wonderful and moving story from the children's ward that brought several staff to tears. A policeman named Alan was on duty on Christmas Eve and had called into Casualty earlier in the evening to see his wife who was a sister on nights. She told him about a three-year-old boy on the children's ward who she had heard about because his parents hadn't been to visit him since he was admitted, and she felt particularly sorry for him. Like in the other wards, family had been asked to bring in their children's presents on Christmas Eve ready to be distributed on Christmas morning. Not a single present had been provided for this particular youngster so she asked Alan if he could help. Despite the late hour he went around to all the officers on duty, and rang some others who weren't, to ask if they would each provide one present for this little boy. By midnight on Christmas Eve he had collected two sacks of gifts, either purchased by a quick whip-round at the police station or 'borrowed' from the individual officers' own children's presents. Alan wanted to see the child's face when he opened them on Christmas morning so 'had his arm twisted' to dress up as Santa and distribute all the children's presents.

Arriving at 8am in full red outfit and fluffy white beard, he distributed parcels and gifts to all the other children on the ward. Coming to the little boy last of all, he carefully emptied the treasure trove of presents on to the child's bed and watched the youngster's little face light up. Being a father of three teenagers himself, Alan couldn't begin to understand the parents' callous behaviour towards the child, so he stayed to help him open all his parcels. The boy had a great day, even though his parents didn't even bother to visit, and the nurses made damn sure he had a fantastic time. Even now, some forty years later, the memory of that big, tough copper dressed in an ill-fitting Santa suit, tears streaming down his cheeks as he shared a magical moment with a lonely three-year-old child brings a warm glow. I was glad when the new list went up and I found I was going to ENT, but I will always remember that little boy with affection.

5

It was 1969 when American astronaut Neil
Armstrong took his first tentative steps on the
surface of the moon. At around the same time I
was beginning my second year as a student nurse
and taking my own faltering steps into the brave
new world of the ENT (Ear, Nose and Throat)
Ward. Not quite an ideal comparison, but to me
it was just as important; we were both venturing
into the unknown. I remember chatting to an
elderly patient the morning after the moon
landing and telling him about this historic event.
The look on his face said it all; he clearly
thought I was making the whole thing up.

'Eeh, you young uns, you'll tell us owt,' he said
with a big knowing smile.

ENT had the largest turnover of patients
within the hospital. This was due to the
operations being of a mainly minor nature. Most
were admitted for elective procedures such as
tonsillectomies, ear operations and sinus wash-
outs. The more serious cases that were dealt with
tended to be related to facial surgery following
trauma injuries or for cancer patients. ENT
Wards 9 and 10 were identical in layout to Wards
11 and 12 — all were traditional Nightingale
wards in the old wing, the only difference being
that the ENT theatre divided the two wards.
Apart from the cancer patients, most of the
others were admitted and discharged so speedily

that the nurses barely got to know them, and because of the high turnover it was always frantically busy.

It was a bright, cheery ward, with many of the otherwise perfectly healthy younger people only spending the actual day of their operation in bed, the rest of the time found them wandering around socialising or playing cards or dominoes in the day room (no daytime television then). This made the routine work much quicker and easier for the nurses.

Sister Taylor was the only sister on this ward during the time I was working there because her junior sister had been promoted and had moved away to another hospital. Although a very gentle person, she was strikingly professional and, like most of the sisters at that time, was strict and precise in everything she did. To help her manage the ward, a senior staff nurse, Alison, was 'acting' sister until a permanent replacement could be appointed.

About a week after starting on the ward I was asked to work a night shift on the men's ward (there was an acute shortage of staff) and Sister had said in her report that all was quiet with only routine matters arising, so once the day staff had gone home I started to go around the ward familiarising myself with the patients. Many of them were fully mobile and often took themselves off down the corridor to stretch their legs or to sit in the day room watching television, so it was difficult to establish precisely where they all were at any one time. At one empty bed I enquired if anyone knew where the patient had gone, because it surprised me that the young man was fit enough to be wandering around. He had been admitted only the previous day with serious facial injuries sustained in a fight and had undergone an operation to wire his fractured jaw. None of the patients seemed to know where he was and I couldn't find him anywhere so, presuming that he was walking around the hospital, I decided to carry on with the medicine round hoping he would reappear by the time I had finished. When he still hadn't shown up, I enquired again, but other than a few guilty looks got no response. I strongly suspected that someone knew exactly where he was but for some reason they weren't admitting it, so I went over to check the female ward, thinking that he might have been chatting to someone over there. There was no sign of him.

On my return, a middle-aged patient quietly took me aside to tell me that Peter had left the ward with his visitors earlier that afternoon. He had told some of the other young patients that he intended going to watch Blackburn Rovers play that evening at Ewood Park, their home ground only about a mile away from the hospital. I was both worried and angry and couldn't believe his stupidity, since he'd undergone massive facial surgery only twelve hours earlier, and I couldn't understand why the day staff hadn't missed him. I was absolutely furious and reported my concerns to the night sister (who was busy in Casualty) and I told her that I would let her know when he returned. Back on the ward I decided to move Peter's bed and locker into the side ward, swapping the young man from in there back on to the main ward in the now empty space. Some of the patients obviously wondered what I was doing, so I announced to the curious: 'It looks like Peter has taken his own discharge so I'm changing the beds around. The side ward can take an emergency if necessary without disturbing you all.' They looked worried but stubbornly still said nothing.

At around 11pm, when most of the patients were in bed, a scruffy, greasy-haired youth sloped in looking very smug and pleased with himself. His face was badly swollen and still black and blue from the assault and the surgery. He breezed nonchalantly past my desk in the centre of the ward and headed back to where his bed had been, but soon lost his grin when he saw another patient occupying his space. Having followed him down the ward I asked him who he was. Rather sheepishly he told me his name and asked where his bed was. I feigned surprise and told him that I presumed he had taken his own discharge because I had been informed that he had left the ward with his visitors. I then went on to say that his bed was about to be used for an emergency who was waiting in Casualty. He visibly wilted and didn't know what to say. He looked uncomfortable and was no doubt in considerable pain. He repeatedly apologised and simply hadn't a clue what to do next. I could smell alcohol on his breath, which made me even more annoyed because he was on strong analgesics to relieve his pain in addition to antibiotics, both of which meant that alcohol was forbidden.

For a minute or so I left him in limbo wondering where he was going to sleep that night, before asking him to follow me to Sister's office where I read him the riot act and spelt out the dangers to which he had exposed himself. I rang Sister who arrived two minutes later and also give him a stern warning that any repeat behaviour would not be tolerated, and she then wrote a report of the incident in his records. I eventually had to admit that no new patient was expected, but informed him that for the rest of his stay he would be confined to the side ward. He trudged off to his bed looking completely dejected but didn't dare protest. He assured us that he had only consumed one glass of beer so Sister grudgingly gave permission for him to have his night medication, and I never heard a peep out of him for the rest of the night. I had begun to feel a little sorry for him by then, but had already learned not to let this sort of behaviour get out of hand.

Back on days I became acquainted with a lovely lady in her seventies called Trudy who was having problems swallowing. After numerous scans and investigations her results showed extensive throat cancer that required major surgery. Although she was obviously frightened, her trust in the doctors and staff was absolute. In the absence of an intensive care unit she was to be nursed in a side ward following her surgery and have a 'special' nurse based in the room. This meant exclusive individual nursing and I was chosen to do the first shift. When she left the ward for theatre she gripped my hand and confessed that she was scared to death. I gave her a big hug and tried to reassure her, but deep down wondered if she would even survive the surgery. She was in theatre for such a long time that I had gone off shift before she returned. I was convinced that she hadn't made it but, when I came back on duty the following morning, Sister's report told us that she had come through the operation and was in a critical condition after being in theatre for almost six hours. She had required extensive surgery involving the removal of her larynx (voice box) and part of one lung. Unfortunately, the surgeon had only been able to remove part of her tumour, which had spread to many other areas of her throat and chest. A tracheotomy tube was inserted to help her breathe more easily but her prognosis wasn't good.

Sister took me into Trudy's room to give detailed and specific instructions of the nursing procedures I was to carry out while she was in my care. I had only just started my second year as a student and I have to admit to feeling terrified when I first saw her. She looked and sounded terribly ill, her breathing was loud and torturous and she was sweating profusely. Her tracheotomy scared me witless because it hissed and rattled and sounded revolting, but Trudy was so heavily sedated that she had no real awareness of anything around her. She had drips, drains and catheters everywhere, but good basic general nursing was all that I was able to provide to make her comfortable. Thankfully, as the days went by Trudy started to show signs of gradual improvement.

As part of our training, one of the compulsory practical assessments for the state finals involved monitoring the total care of one individual patient. The examiners decided to ask Trudy for her consent to be that person and, even though she was still rather poorly and in some discomfort, she willingly agreed. Susan, another student who was also working on ENT and from my PTS, and I were to take the assessment together. This was a little less demanding than working alone, although we were still both very nervous, not only because everything that we did was going to be scrutinised but also due to the extent of the care Trudy needed. She still had her intravenous drip, chest drain, tracheotomy tube and urinary catheter festooned around her body, but the complex care she needed was carried out routinely on the ward every day; the big difference was that we were going to be watched by two examiners.

We purposely took our time with Trudy, chatting to her and trying to make her feel at ease as we bed bathed her and massaged her pressure areas, at the same time changing her bed linen while trying desperately not to disturb any of her tubes. Once she was clean we put on her nightdress and sat her up while we dealt with her tracheotomy tube. This had to be suctioned out and cleared of any secretions to enable her to breathe properly and, when this was completed, fresh sterile gauze was placed around the tubing to cushion her neck where the tube had a tendency to rub. Her drip was checked next, as was her chest-drain; and thankfully both were working well. Finally, we cleaned her mouth and dentures, before propping her up as high as possible on her pillows to help her breathe easier, before providing her with a drink of fresh juice and the daily newspaper. At this point, the examiners moved into Sister's office to discuss our performance. Susan and I had a quick chat as we tidied everything away and felt quite confident that we had done well, so it was an absolute blow when we were advised that we had both failed. The only reason given was that we were far too slow; there was absolutely nothing else wrong. To say we were gutted was putting it mildly.

That afternoon when Sister Taylor came on duty for the late shift and found out what had happened she was furious. She went to check on Trudy who was still smiling and quite happy, and then, without further ado, took herself off to Matron to complain. After explaining to her how complex a patient Trudy was, she soon returned to give us the news that the result had been overturned and we had indeed passed the assessment. We could have kissed her, but instead thanked her for her support; now feeling completely vindicated and knowing that we had done our best. Matron had, of course, already met Trudy on several occasions during her ward rounds and was fully aware of her case. She had undoubtedly been fair in her ruling, for which Susan and I were eternally grateful.

We told Trudy that we had passed and she was elated. We thanked her for her support and felt humbled that this lady remained so stoical regardless of what life had thrown at her. She hardly ever complained, grateful for everything that was done for her and, although she couldn't speak, simply squeezed my hand or nodded her head if she was okay. As she slowly began to improve she was given a notepad so that she could write messages to the nurses, which she thought was a brilliant idea. The only thing she really found difficult to deal with was the tracheotomy; it distressed her the most because it often needed to be sucked out by machine. To break up the secretions and enable good suction a product called Bisolvon had to be inserted into the tracheotomy tube. This made her cough violently and gasp for breath (rather like someone who inhales a crumb) but she accepted the procedure as worthwhile because she knew that it eased her discomfort for a couple of hours afterwards. I hated having to carry out this process because it seemed so harsh, but Trudy simply smiled to reassure me and put both her thumbs up to show approval. She was a star. I admired her bravery and doubted that I would be so patient and uncomplaining in a similar situation.

Over the next two weeks we were gradually able to remove her drips and drains but, unfortunately, the tracheotomy tube was now a permanent fixture and she had to learn to live with it. One day she scribbled a note asking me if it was possible to go back on the main ward because she was bored and needed company. At first Sister wasn't too keen on the move because of the unsettling noises made by the suction machine, but after discussing the idea with the other patients and gaining their approval she decided to give it a try. There was an immediate improvement and Trudy looked much happier. She made slow but steady progress and before too long was able to get out of bed for short periods.

The nurses were all made aware that there was a potential for her to haemorrhage because the remaining part of the tumour was close to an artery and already causing discomfort. There was one scare when she coughed up blood through her tracheotomy tube, but it quickly settled and thankfully didn't recur. All the nurses were shown how to clamp an artery in the event of such an emergency, although most of us secretly prayed hard that it would never happen. Thankfully it didn't and she was soon ready to go home.

The day Trudy was discharged she produced chocolates and a thank you card for the nurses. I was blubbering as usual and, as she held me tight, I realised that I would probably never see her again. Several weeks later we heard from her daughter that she had died peacefully in her sleep at home. She was a real gem and I have truly never forgotten her.

The nurses who worked on ENT sometimes had to assist in the Out-patient ENT Clinic, where patients were initially assessed and tested before being admitted to the ward. The only other speciality that did this was the Eye Ward, who also insisted on using their own ward nurses in the clinic, the reason being that ENT and Eye Ward used specialised instruments and carried out particular procedures. The consultants were used to getting whatever equipment they asked for immediately from their nurses, who were completely familiar with their own speciality, so it obviously saved time and prevented temper tantrums to use their own.

One of the ENT consultants was a character it would be difficult to forget. Built like a rugby player, he had a reputation for being abrupt and outspoken to both staff and patients alike. I had the dubious pleasure of assisting him during one particular clinic and found his manner quite alarming on the one hand and comical on the other. A very quietly spoken staff nurse was also working with him (as he always insisted on never being alone with a patient), who confided to me that she hated working with this man intensely because of his downright rudeness.

I got the gist of her concerns after only the first minute of the clinic. The doctor was sitting in his swivel chair with a head torch encircling his head (rather like a miner's lamp) and in walks mum, hand in hand with her five-year-old son. Doctor told mum to get her big backside sat down on a chair and beckoned the child towards him. After adjusting his head light and taking a quick look at the child's records, he bellowed at the little boy to tell him what the problem was. Before the child could respond, his mum began to answer but was quickly stopped by the doctor. He commanded her to shut up and let her son speak. The staff nurse and I looked at each other with raised eyebrows. The mother initially looked concerned, then upset and angry, but said nothing. The child was asked again, and quietly whispered that he had a sore throat.

'Right then,' the doctor bawled. 'Open your big, fat gob and let me have a look.' The child opened his mouth wide, looking terrified. 'Mmm, I see. OK. Shut it now, there's a train coming.' He scribbled a few sentences in the records and without looking at the child's mother muttered that he would be put on a waiting list to have his tonsils out. 'Ta, ta,' he then said to no one in particular and shouted for me to bring in the next patient.

The staff nurse told me later that she spent half her life trying to pacify patients after they had come out of his clinic and was fed up with apologising for his unacceptable behaviour.

The next patient was a very well-spoken middle-aged lady who came in a little sheepishly after overhearing the previous patient's mother complaining. The doctor was similarly abrupt, asked her name and enquired what her problem was. The lady explained that she was having hearing problems. Without further ado he dragged her chair towards him and roared, 'Get that bloody great suitcase on the floor!'

At first she hadn't a clue what he was referring to and desperately looked from one to the other of us to explain. Staff Nurse politely asked her to put her handbag underneath her chair. He then checked both of the patient's ears, told her that she needed to have her 'lugs cleared out' and sent her into the next room, where a registrar was waiting to syringe her ears. The consultant smirked and gave me a cheeky wink. The old devil was enjoying winding everyone up, especially Staff Nurse, who he had got successfully tied in knots. He was a bit of a bully, if the truth be known, but I soon came to understand his eccentricities and learned to cope with his offhand behaviour. The answer was basically to play him at his own game and give him back as much as he gave out or, alternatively, to completely ignore him.

Soon after working on ENT, we were due to go back into training school for a week. I found these study days and lectures really enjoyable, more so because my group were such a great bunch of individuals, and time at the school helped us become reacquainted; we rarely saw each other on the job. One or two of the original girls had already resigned but the majority loved the work. Even Anne the redhead, who had been steered into nursing somewhat against her will, was still hanging in there, still not entirely convinced about the job but deserving full marks for perseverance.

After lunch on our first day, the discussion was about the two main uses of a Ryle's tube. One use was to feed a sick patient via the tube and the other to aspirate the stomach contents both pre- and post-operatively in order to prevent vomiting. The tube was usually inserted into a nostril (although it was occasionally passed directly through the mouth if the nose was injured or diseased) and gently pushed into the stomach. This distressed some patients, although others seemed to accept the procedure without a problem. The tutor asked how many in the group had inserted a Ryle's tube into an actual patient and a couple of us raised our hands. I had passed two when working on Ward 3, although I had been supervised both times. I was asked to describe the procedure to the other students and the tutor asked for a volunteer to have one passed into her stomach. Christine, my masochistic friend from Orthopaedics, volunteered because she thought it would be a big laugh. Personally, I thought she must be completely and utterly barmy, especially as she had just eaten a huge lunch. I would never volunteer to have a tube inserted into any part of my anatomy for a mere demonstration, not even if I was offered vast amounts of cash! My only concern now was that she might throw up all over me. Even with my limited experience I knew that patients having Ryle's tubes inserted were quite liable to vomit, despite having eaten very little, and I wondered if I would have to get out the old mop and bucket yet again!

Sitting my volunteer on a chair in front of the class I asked if she had a preference about which nostril to use and she chose the left. I gave her a plastic cape to put around her neck in case of accidents and insisted on giving her a vomit bowl. I then explained the procedure to her (as I would if she were a real patient). Placing the tube into her nostril made Christine's nose wrinkle and her eyes water. Then, just as I was about to instruct her to swallow, she gave an almighty sneeze and the tube shot out together with copious amounts of nasal secretions. As usual, my 'patient' was hysterical with laughter, as was the whole class, while I was gagging and trying to wipe off several large slimy green blobs of mucous which were sliding down the front of my blouse.

At the second attempt the tube went up her nose and, on my command, she swallowed hard and I quickly pushed the tube all the way in. Christine was cooperating superbly and, ludicrously, still laughing. To confirm that it was in her stomach correctly it was necessary to aspirate the tube, which entailed fixing a syringe to the end of the tube and withdrawing some of the stomach contents. The secretions were then tested with litmus paper — it would change colour in the presence of stomach acid. The test confirmed that the tube was correctly in place and everyone groaned at the graphic description which Christine gave of the emerging beef casserole being sucked up the tube. They expressed their distaste even louder when she asked me to return it because she had paid for it only half an hour earlier and she didn't want it to be wasted! Strangely enough, there were no further volunteers.

Throughout training, the nurse tutors would come and work on the wards with each individual student at one time or another, in order to monitor our ongoing progress and competence. This didn't happen often, perhaps only twice a year, but when they came they often turned up unannounced (although they always had to ask the ward sister's permission first). When they arrived they would work with us, acting as an extra pair of hands for the day; checking that the procedures we had been taught were being carried out correctly and seeing how we interacted with our patients. I always felt uncomfortable when I was being observed in these sessions, but they were an essential part of our training and were a good preparation for our periodic formal practical assessments so had to be endured.

A vivid illustration of the training regime and high standards expected arose when I had just finished scrubbing down a bed after a patient had been discharged. Every inch of the bed framework had to be thoroughly cleaned with a bacteria-killing solution called Stericol. The mattress had to have a new cover fitted and even the patient's locker had to be scrubbed. Miss Yates, our main practical tutor, came on to the ward to work with me just as I was about to move on to my next job. She asked me what I had been doing and then, without further comment, knelt down on her hands and knees and crawled along the floor underneath the bed. At first I wondered what on earth she was doing, then watched as she ran a gloved finger under the bed frame and found a trace of dust. She brandished the 'evidence' directly under my nose and said loudly in front of several patients, 'I am surprised at you, Nurse. I expected better from you. Now go and scrub the whole frame again.'

I was so embarrassed I could have smacked

her, but she was right and I couldn't argue. I seriously doubt that anyone even contemplates crawling under a bed to inspect the cleanliness these days — it would, no doubt, contravene Health and Safety guidelines anyway without a prior risk assessment being carried out and forms filled out in triplicate . . .

★　★　★

Every student nurse was obliged to work several weeks each year on night duty. Day staff on the ward would give a report on each patient, especially the ones who had been to theatre or needed special attention. If it was that particular ward's night for emergency admissions, then bed availability was reported and, finally, if patients were due for theatre or special tests the following morning, instructions were given as to who needed to be 'nil by mouth' or required special preparations.

Once the day shift had gone off duty, in addition to carrying out all the usual observations, particular attention was given to ensure that all drips, tubes and drains were operating correctly before the patients settled down for the night. Drips could be a nuisance, often stopping for no obvious reason and refusing to restart despite all our efforts. Nurses weren't allowed to clear them by using a syringe, due to the risk of causing an embolism (clot), so a doctor always had to be summoned to correct any blockage or to re-site a new drip. Ryle's tubes had to be regularly aspirated throughout the night and all catheters and drains were monitored. Keeping on top of all these procedures (and many more) sometimes felt like a juggling act; crashes were liable to follow if any of them were neglected.

It is a complete misconception that nurses sit around at night doing nothing except drink tea; sometimes we were extremely lucky to get even a single tea break. It is a similar myth that patients sleep at night; in my experience this is the time when night-sedated gremlins wander the wards in a drug-induced stupor or hurl themselves head first out of their beds. We had to fill out more accident forms on nights than at any other time.

Wards always had a minimum number of staff on duty at night and in BRI this usually meant one student nurse on the male side and one on the female. With luck we also had a nursing auxiliary to share between the two of us. These auxiliaries were generally indispensable because they really knew everything about the normal routine, most of them having worked on their particular ward for years. Naturally there was always the occasional one who thought she knew better than Matron, although this was pretty rare. Family commitments quite often didn't allow some of them to train and qualify as nurses, but they were usually a priceless asset on any ward.

With so few trained staff actually stationed on the wards at night, each individual unit only had one registered nurse in charge, armed with a bleeper in case of emergency, covering from two to four wards. I was terrified at first, knowing that I was solely responsible for observing and reporting any sudden deterioration in any of my patients, and remember feeling physically sick before going on duty, so much so that I almost turned around and went home. However, after two or three sessions of nights my confidence grew and I even began to enjoy the buzz. Although without some marvellous auxiliaries I would have been totally lost. I will be forever grateful to these unsung but indispensable staff who supported me so much in those early days. Nights certainly made you grow up quickly.

Miss Donavan, the matron at BRI in the 1960s, was very stern but always fair and often chose to do her rounds at irregular times. She was liable to appear unexpectedly, even during the night, and question the staff about their patients; which certainly kept everyone on their toes, including the sisters. In those days, a nurse was expected to know every patient on their ward by name, in addition to their diagnosis, treatment/operation to date, and what stage of recovery they were at. Miss Donavan's memory for detail was unnerving; give her an incorrect answer and you were very quickly made aware of her displeasure. She was able to remember surprising amounts of detail for virtually every single patient in the hospital, together with the names of all her staff. She was an amazing lady but never permitted familiarity from anyone, always insisting on being addressed as Matron, never by her first name. Anyone found incorrectly dressed or behaving inappropriately would be severely reprimanded, and her mere presence was enough to guarantee the highest standards. She rarely raised her voice because she never needed to and her decision was always final. The respect afforded to her was total, from cadet nurse to senior consultant.

One night shift, around 11.30pm, when most of the patients had been settled down, we decided to have an unofficial break at the nurses' station. We were sitting quietly having tea and biscuits when the ward doors creaked open and a patient's voice was clearly heard to say something which included the magic word 'Matron'. Tea and biscuits disappeared from view in a flash and by the time Miss Donavan appeared at our station we were angelically writing in the nurses' record books. We immediately stood up, as was expected in Matron's presence and spluttered our 'Good evenings', to which she only nodded in reply.

Being the most junior student on the ward at that time, I was chosen to do the rounds with her and was quaking in anticipation of the imminent inquisition, knowing her fierce reputation for detail. She asked for the name and diagnosis of each patient, moving on without comment if I was correct, but standing stock still with a quizzical look on her face at the end of the bed if I got it wrong. Several times she found it necessary to furnish me with the correct information, but overall she seemed reasonably happy with my first efforts. She didn't waste words but warned me that next time she expected a faultless report. On the point of leaving, she stopped abruptly in front of the nurses' station, walked around the desk and rapidly pulled open several drawers, spilling the 'hidden' cups of lukewarm tea over the contents. Her parting shot was to warn us all that if she caught us out again there would be trouble! We looked at each other in embarrassment and, as soon as she had gone, frantically rang one or two friends on the other wards to warn them that she was on the prowl, before starting to clean up the soggy paperwork in the drawers.

By 11pm most patients had usually been given their medication and evening drink and had settled down for sleep; punctuating the long night hours with grunts, groans and snores from one end and noisy grumbles from the other. Sorry chaps, but you were by far the worst offenders. How anyone ever slept in hospital was a mystery to me; with the constant chorus of buzzers and the squeaky pacing shoes of nurses and doctors (and yes, the chatting), it sometimes added up to mass insomnia. When you are ill and exhausted it is the last thing you need. It was around this time when disposable bedpans, urinals and vomit bowls were introduced to the wards. They were a complete godsend, not only for the patients who didn't get woken up quite as frequently by clattering bedpans, but also for the nurses who no longer needed to clean and sterilise them; they were simply emptied and stacked in a macerator (which was essentially a large paper shredder) never to be seen again.

Andrea, one of the nurses who lived in the Nurses Home, was off duty but couldn't sleep. She decided to sneak down the fire escape

171

(which was often used for furtive visits) to have a chat to a friend who was working on the ward with me, despite the fact that a strict rule required that no one 'living in' who was off duty was allowed to visit the wards at night. Everything was deathly quiet and we had just sat down with the forbidden cuppa when we heard the main doors open. We suspected that it was Miss Donavan because Sister had already done her rounds but, with no time to reach the fire escape, Andrea decided to dive under the nearest bed instead. Unfortunately, the patient, an elderly lady who was only dozing, saw her disappear and immediately became distressed. Matron appeared and made a beeline for the lady's bed. I just beat her to it and was already there trying to calm the patient.

'There's someone under my bed,' the old lady cried. I tried desperately to quieten her down and to reassure her that she must have been dreaming. She was having none of it, insisting that she had definitely seen someone and refused to be pacified. Bending down, I pretended to search for the phantom intruder and came face to face with Andrea, who was looking terrified but half-laughing at the same time. I repeated to the patient that there was no one there, praying desperately that Matron wouldn't take it into her head to look for herself. She didn't, she simply asked if someone could make the old lady a warm milky drink, and then moved on. It was incredibly lucky since Andrea's nocturnal visit would have been considered a serious 'offence' and such a breach of discipline could well have resulted in her dismissal. Discipline had to be total!

Some nights passed without incident but others could be hell, and I remember my worst one ever was on women's medical. We were short-staffed, yet again, so I was completely on my own. There were sixteen beds on the ward and three of those were empty. Day staff had reported two patients, Sally and Emily, to be very poorly and it was our turn to accept emergencies. Somehow I just knew it would be busy, so I rushed through routine procedures in case I started receiving admissions. Most patients seemed settled, apart from the two mentioned. Sally wasn't expected to last the night. Her blood pressure and pulse were virtually non-existent but I made sure that she was clean and comfortable. Her relatives, who lived quite a distance away, were already aware of her condition so there was little else I could do. Night Sister made a brief appearance on the ward, apologised for not being able to give me an auxiliary, then five minutes later rushed off to help in Casualty. Her parting words were, 'Ring me if you need me.'

About half an hour later Casualty telephoned to say that I was to receive a patient who had taken an overdose. Bernice was a rather rotund, middle-aged lady who had swallowed dozens of paracetamol tablets. Her stomach had been washed out in Casualty and she had been put on a drip. Fortunately, she had vomited up most of the tablets soon after taking them so had absorbed less amounts of the drug into her system. Her blood levels were raised but not dangerously so. Bernice arrived on a trolley looking exhausted and drawn. After the porters put her on the bed, a staff nurse gave me her notes and suggested that she would need her blood pressure and pulse checked every half hour. Her drip was running well so I checked her over and introduced myself, but she was so distraught that she simply turned her back to me and sobbed. Minutes later the house officer who was on call came in to see her. He looked worse than she did, having worked all day non-stop and was now first on call for the night shift. He had just finished examining Bernice when his bleeper went off with an urgent recall to Casualty, so he dashed off leaving me to settle her down for the night. I quickly checked the critically ill patients and was about to sit down when the telephone rang informing me that another admission was on its way. This time it was an elderly lady called Lucy, who had suffered a massive stroke and wasn't expected to survive. Her relatives were aware of how serious her condition was, but weren't with her. After putting the telephone down I decided to put the new patient in the same cubicle with the two other critically ill ladies so that I could keep an eye on them all at the same time. I prepared oxygen and suction for her and hunted around for cot sides to attach to her bed in case she became restless.

Just as Lucy arrived Bernice began to retch (although there was little left in her stomach to bring up after having had it washed out), screaming with every spasm and waking the whole ward. I asked Bernice to stay calm and assured her that I would be back to help her as soon as I could. The porters and the accompanying nurse introduced me to Lucy, who was deeply unconscious and oblivious to the world, as they put her in bed and left the ward. She looked as poorly as the others and it was a toss-up who would go first. I doubted that any one of them would see morning. By the time I returned to Bernice she had yanked the drip out from her hand and was bleeding all over the bed. Fluid from the now open and flowing drip poured freely on to the floor and spread rapidly around her bed and locker. Where to begin? Put gauze firmly on to bleeding vein and apply pressure for a couple of minutes. Yes, it stopped. Now get the mop and bucket. One crispy clean newly made bed and sparkling floor later, I needed to speak to Sister about the doctor re-siting the drip. No student nurse was allowed to ring the doctor directly because, in the past, some students had been ringing them inappropriately at all times of night and the doctors had complained to Matron. Now, even though I was certain that a doctor was needed, a sister or staff nurse had to make the call after first assessing the situation. I set up a new drip trolley in readiness for the doctor and then checked my three critical ladies again. Sally was dead. I pulled the curtains around the bed and checked again for a pulse, but there was nothing. I placed the lady on her back, arms by her sides, washed her face and combed her hair. She had no dentures that I could find so I left her as though sleeping, and then rang to inform Sister and ask if I should contact the relatives, but she told me to do nothing until she had seen the body.

When the doctor arrived to re-site Bernice's drip, Sister had already informed him about the death, so I asked him to check the old lady first. He certified that she had definitely departed and then went to Bernice. He put up another drip as she continued to sulk and was less than cooperative. Sister came to tell me that the relatives had been informed of the death but weren't coming to the hospital. At this point we took a five-minute breather and had a quick drink. Refreshed, I set about laying out the old lady's body by myself because both Sister and the doctor had been recalled to Casualty. Not easy, but I just had to get on with it. After the porters had removed the body I did a quick round of the other patients, checked blood pressures and drips before scrubbing the bed down ready for the next patient.

Lucy didn't look good; her pulse was barely present and there was no response whatsoever. Ten minutes later she died. I rang Sister again, who in turn telephoned the doctor and they both arrived together. Once again the doctor certified the death, Sister rang the relatives (who weren't coming), and while I was itemising the belongings in Lucy's locker Sister was called back to Casualty. Again I had a body to sort out on my own. It was now 3am. The doctor was sitting in the office, pen in hand, nodding off and looking completely worn out. How were these doctors supposed to function? Was it any wonder

176

that mistakes were made? By this time most of the ward was awake so I went round with drinks, hoping they would settle. Porters came and took away the second body of the night while making derogatory comments about my nursing skills, commenting that they hoped none of their relatives ever ended up in my care. At the time I was too busy to respond, although sticking my tongue out seemed sufficient and sent them off laughing, while I set about scrubbing the bed down in readiness for any further admission. I prayed for quiet, but it just wasn't to be.

Another patient was admitted in a mad rush, escorted by a staff nurse who helped to get her on to a bed. Stella, an enormously overweight eighty-year-old patient, was desperately ill from heart failure and, because of a lack of oxygen her whole body was tinged blue. She was dripping with sweat and desperately fighting for every breath, thwarting all efforts to keep her oxygen mask in place, groaning and gasping as she listlessly dragged it off her face. Her notes said she had gross left ventricular failure, basically meaning that her heart wasn't pumping adequately, and she was literally drowning in her own body fluids. The cocktail of drugs she had been given to relieve the fluid build-up and control her heart weren't working. Very little was draining from her catheter, her body was simply giving up and I was alone with her. All I could do was sponge her down, moisten her dry mouth and ensure the oxygen supply was flowing. Doctor came on to the ward an hour or so later, examined her chest and shook his head; she wasn't going to last much longer. He tried giving her further drugs, before going into the office to try and sleep, as there was little point in him even trying to go to bed yet. About fifteen minutes later Stella died despite receiving the additional treatment. The doctor went back to the office to write his notes and was so exhausted he looked close to tears. I rang Sister for the umpteenth time; she moaned and asked me if I was on piecework. On her return she realised that I hadn't been relieved for my meal break, which should have been at midnight but by this time I was past caring. Anyway, I had another body to sort out, although this time Sister helped me. I was grateful beyond belief because Stella was a big woman and I had been wondering how the hell I was going to lay her out without assistance.

It was dawn by the time the third body was removed. The doctor was sound asleep in the office so I switched the light off and left him in peace; he would be on duty again all day and I doubted he would get through it. The ward lights would soon be switched on and patients would need their drinks and medicines. Sister thankfully managed to find time to come back to the ward to sort out the medicines, which then gave me the opportunity to do the observations, give out morning drinks and check drips and tubes (also ensuring that no one else had sneakily popped their clogs when I hadn't been looking!). The remaining critically ill patient remained unchanged and I prayed that she would remain so, at least until I got home. I went into the office to write the final reports. The doctor had disappeared; presumably gone to bed, as I knew Casualty was now much quieter. I made myself comfortable and attempted to write an accurate report on each patient. Minutes later the day staff arrived bright and breezy, asking if I had had a quiet night. Where could I start? Sister's mouth dropped open when I told her about my three deaths. I begged her not to ring the doctor unless it was absolutely necessary as he was dead on his feet, and gave her a full and unadulterated account of everyone still breathing. I believe that was my most difficult night ever, made much worse because I was on my own, but I was really proud of the way I coped.

I always smile when I remember a small group of mental health nurses who came to work at BRI. They were all qualified as Registered Mental Nurses and were previously in quite senior posts at the local psychiatric hospital but had opted to commence general nurse training. Two of the group were charge nurses (the male equivalent of sisters) when working in the psychiatric hospital, but here at BRI they were students again and were obviously expected to follow the rules like everyone else. One of the new faces named Hughie asked me, quite seriously, where the nurses slept when on night duty. He thought I was joking when I told him that to be caught sleeping on duty would mean instant dismissal and that he would be lucky to get even a break let alone some sleep! Several nights later he looked an absolute wreck and clearly couldn't wait to get back to the psychiatric environment, which he said was much more sedate.

Glyn Webster had worked as an auxiliary on the medical ward in the late 1960s and enjoyed the work so much that he decided to do his nurse training. He hadn't been working at the hospital for very long, but very quickly earned himself a reputation as a practical joker. One particularly quiet night at about 2.30am he decided it would be a good laugh if he pretended to be a dead body. In order to play a trick on the night porters he persuaded his colleagues to wrap him in a sheet and prepare the normal paperwork that usually accompanied a deceased person to the mortuary. One of the other nurses rang the porters to ask them if they would come and remove 'the body'. Everyone heard the mortuary trolley arrive (it wasn't made to Rolls Royce standards and squeaked and rattled along the corridor). Constructed of heavy, unpainted metal it looked like a deep coffin, which in effect is exactly what it was. During transport to and from the mortuary the porters always covered the trolley with a large sheet in order to disguise its appearance (not that it worked because everyone who has ever been inside a hospital knows precisely what it is).

The porters were shown into the side ward where Glyn, the recently departed patient, was lying silent and perfectly still. They checked that all the correct paperwork was present and lifted the 'deceased' into the trolley. The lid was closed and off they trundled, heading for the mortuary. But first of all they had to take the lift to get back down to the ground floor. Glyn knew exactly where he was and waited until the lift doors closed. The two porters were chatting to each other when Glyn decided to make his presence felt by gently tapping on the sides of the trolley. One of the porters went very quiet before asking his colleague if he had heard a noise. Glyn heard the comment and stopped tapping. The other porter listened intently, then laughed and they carried on with their previous conversation. Glyn remained silent until the lift stopped, the doors opened and he knew they were on the main corridor. To get to the mortuary, the trolley would have to be pushed the full length of the corridor, out through the hospital entrance, across the forecourt and through the staff car park. He stayed quiet until he was sure they were outside and then, when he felt the temperature drop and the path become uneven, he decided to make his 'resurrection'. The time was now 2.45am.

'Don't take me in there,' he shouted, as he knocked loudly on the 'coffin' lid. The two porters freaked out and ran away! Not for help — they simply abandoned him, leaving the trolley in the middle of the car park.

The nurses on the ward (where he was supposed to be on duty) were getting worried; he had been missing for over half an hour and there was no sign of him. Thankfully the ward was quiet, but Sister was due to make her rounds and they didn't know what to do for the best. Where was he? Strangely enough, he was still trying to get out of the trolley! Eventually, after another thirty minutes or so, one of the nurses plucked up the courage to ring the porters to ask where he was. They were less than impressed when they were told who was in the trolley but they went back to find him, only to see him haring down the corridor heading back to his ward as though pursued by the devil himself. The porters didn't report him because they themselves had been wrong to run away as they did (and were probably too embarrassed to admit it) so Glyn got away with it on that occasion. He played many tricks on unsuspecting staff during his time at the hospital and on more than one other occasion wasn't always so fortunate. Glyn went on to pass his nursing finals but he then left the profession to become ordained in the Church of England. Now the Reverend Canon Webster holds the position of Residentiary Canon-Chancellor of York Minster; although, I am assured by his long-suffering staff that even today he is not averse to the occasional schoolboy prank.

When we had a few quiet moments, the auxiliaries who worked on permanent night shift took great delight in trying to unsettle the students by telling scary stories, although I personally experienced a very spooky episode one night on the surgical ward. Returning from my midnight break, I entered the ward and saw a little old lady at the far end of the ward walking around in a long nightdress. She appeared to have come out of the bottom four-bedded cubicle. She walked past the nurses' station and then into a side ward which was empty at the time. I didn't recognise her and wondered if she was OK. When I reached the side ward I looked through the window but the room was empty. I scanned the four-bedded cubicle and all the beds were occupied and the patients were asleep. I returned to the side ward and opened the door, half expecting to find that the old lady had fallen on the floor. A blast of cold air met me and I felt goose pimples spring up all over my body. The room was definitely empty and it was freezing cold. I checked the heating; the radiators were full on and all the windows were closed. To say I exited the room quickly is a bit of an understatement. When I told the others of my experience, a knowing look came over the auxiliary's face.

'I bet that was Martha,' she said, and went on to tell us about an elderly female patient who had died in that room some weeks before. Several different people had supposedly seen this figure whose description exactly fitted the lady I had seen. I went back into the room five minutes later and it was warm and cosy.

* * *

Around the time I came off nights, if we weren't on duty, my social life at weekends centred mainly on clubbing with my friend Denise Ashcroft, one of my fellow students from PTS. Coming up to Christmas we were at the Cavendish Club (the place to party in Blackburn at the time) where we met and paired up with a couple of reasonably good-looking young men. After getting a lift home at the end of the night, I made a date with Bill and started seeing him as regularly as my off duty would permit.

By early 1971 and some nine months before my finals I had worked my way through almost every ward and department in the hospital (some of them twice), from orthopaedic and surgical wards, to medical wards, ENT and Casualty, and, except for my time on the children's ward, I had loved every second. My social life was virtually non-existent but Bill, my (by then) long-suffering boyfriend, was very supportive and understanding, even helping to test me with questions from my medical textbooks. Unlike some of the other students, I always found examinations difficult, so to get through my finals I knew that I would have to become a near recluse and needed to keep studying at every opportunity. My greatest worry was the practical examination. Left alone I could cope very well, but I found that having a tutor or examiner scrutinising my every move still made me nervous.

The format of the practical exams had been revised during the previous two or three years and students were now allowed to be assessed on certain practical procedures as soon as they themselves felt capable (provided they had completed a minimum of two years training), a change which replaced the previous requirement to take all the exams at the end of the three-year course. I clearly remember the examiners coming on to the ward to observe me doing a dressing, then following me around the ward with a clipboard making notes as I gave out medicines. The final assessment saw me in charge of a ward for a day. Each of these tasks had to be completed satisfactorily before I was allowed to take the final practical. I passed all of the assessments and got them out of the way; thankfully, well before the end of my third year. I still had a further stint of nights to do, as well as Gynaecology and theatre experience to complete.

★   ★   ★

Ward 20 was a very busy and efficient gynaecological ward and, at that time, a senior staff nurse was in charge of the ward, pending the appointment of a new sister. Based in the old wing, it was only a small ward with a maximum of sixteen patients, who were generally admitted for prearranged gynaecological operations, some minor procedures, such as D&Cs (Dilatation and Curettage, also known as a 'scrape'), terminations, and other major ones, like hysterectomies and vaginal repairs, all of which created a daily 'conveyer belt' to and from theatre.

Up until 1967, abortion was only legal if two doctors agreed that there was a serious physical risk to the health of either mother or child. (So-called 'back-street' abortions by unqualified practitioners in unhygienic conditions led to higher death rates for pregnant women, due to infection or haemorrhage.) Subsequent to The Abortion Act 1967, though, termination of a pregnancy was also permitted if there was considered to be any risk to the mental wellbeing of the mother. This led to a large increase in these operations, not all of which could strictly be defined as falling within the new criteria.

On Ward 20 we had two gynaecology consultants; one of them was far from happy but was prepared to carry out terminations that were strictly within the new amended legal guidelines, while the other was vehemently opposed on religious grounds and refused outright to perform any such procedures. A mother, who had three children already, was admitted for a termination on the basis that to continue with the pregnancy would affect her mental well-being. She was laughing and joking with the other patients from the minute she arrived and so a number of staff were not entirely convinced about her motivation, but two doctors had independently agreed in writing and the operation was completed routinely. When the consultant surgeon carried out his ward round the following day she made a point of asking him what sex the baby had been. I had never seen the consultant so angry. With barely concealed distaste he asked the woman why on earth she cared, before storming off the ward. The rather poignant part of all this was that in the next bed to her was a young woman who was having investigations for infertility.

The nursing procedures were virtually the same as on any other standard surgical ward: caring for patients who had been to theatre, ensuring drips and catheters were not blocked, bathing, changing dressings and checking their observations. But the best word I can think of to describe the atmosphere on the ward was 'hormonal', by which I mean that not a day went by without at least one patient having a quiet weep for no apparent reason. Even when questioned, the patients invariably didn't have a clue why they were crying, so the cause was always put down to their fluctuating hormone levels.

The most common phrase heard on Ward 20 was: 'Try and relax.' Easy enough to say when you're not the one on the receiving end of some spotty adolescent male doctor, barely out of short trousers, whose clumsy attempt at carrying out an internal examination has you retreating frantically up the bed, gripping tightly on to the backrest, while at the same time involuntarily clamping his head between your knees. Mind you, some of the female doctors were little better, with their frequently gung-ho attitude and insensitive manner. One stroppy madam was notorious for her 'navvy-like' touch and every patient in the ward dreaded her being on duty. She rapidly changed her approach after being admitted herself and being on the receiving end for once. Back at work she was transformed into a gentle, caring, sympathetic young doctor. I firmly believe that some medical procedures have to be experienced personally before one truly appreciates how painful, uncomfortable or simply embarrassing they can be, which means that it's a great pity that no male doctor will ever have the pleasure of an internal!

Patients obviously come in all shapes and sizes; some are able to relax easily while others are tense and difficult to handle. One potentially difficult patient with a lengthy history of problems weighed in at an incredible thirty stones. She had unfortunately been on the receiving end of far too many inexperienced and uncomfortable examinations, to the point that she was as taut as a coiled spring. It needed two nurses to simply hold back the rolls of fat while the doctor tried in vain to carry out an internal. It proved impossible, which caused the lady to become even more stressed, so eventually the registrar was called in. Even though he was a senior surgeon, he was the comedian of the ward. After taking one look at her from the office he stood up, rubbed his hands together and said, 'Right then, I want three nurses. One on either side to support the flab, and one to hold on to my legs in case I fall in!' As totally insensitive and callous as that may sound, this type of humour was only too common throughout the hospital. It often helped to relieve the tension in many potentially unpleasant or embarrassing situations. The patient was obviously unaware of what had been said and everyone was completely professional and supportive while completing the examination.

Ward 20 certainly left me with a much greater appreciation and understanding of how to cope with the yo-yoing emotions involved in 'women's problems'. My experience on Gynaecology seemed to pass in the blink of an eye, leaving only my general theatre placement to complete.

★ ★ ★

The superintendent in charge of the general theatres was Sister Bunion, a bespectacled, slim, quietly spoken, middle-aged lady who had worked in there for many years. On my first day she showed me into the female changing room where I had to change from my normal uniform into theatre blues, before giving me a quick tour of the department and a comprehensive list of instructions which were the 'house rules' for students in theatre:

- Never touch or go near anything green.
- Never leave theatre still wearing theatre clothes.
- Never enter the department wearing out-door shoes.
- Always wear a mask on entering theatre if an operation is in progress.
- Always leave the theatre instantly if you start to feel faint.
- Be quiet and alert at all times.

Working in theatre was like working on another planet; so many faces were almost totally obscured by surgical masks that it took some time to get to know which name belonged to which set of eyes. Name badges weren't allowed because of the risk of infection, so at first it was difficult to distinguish nurses from doctors. And the heat was more often than not almost unbearable.

As a student nurse, my main job was to be a runner, in other words fetching and carrying. It wasn't anywhere near as boring as it sounds and much of what I observed I found genuinely fascinating. My first experience of watching an operation as a cadet had been exciting, even though I took no part in the actual operation and hadn't a clue what was going on. Now I would get closer to the action and perhaps eventually be allowed to scrub up myself. Even watching the doctors and nursing staff scrubbing up and donning sterile green gowns before an operation was impressive, the whole process precise and even artistic.

Once scrubbed and gowned, staff had to cover the patient in sterile green towels, leaving only the operation area visible. The anaesthetist would give the okay to start and the skin was cleaned and prepared for incision. I hated watching that first incision and even today it gives me the creeps when I think about it. I used to have to turn away every time the initial cut was made, yet was absolutely fine afterwards. My knowledge of human anatomy improved a hundredfold after just a few weeks in theatre, with some consultants taking great pleasure in showing any new staff each layer of skin and every internal organ, chatting merrily as they went along. It almost persuaded me to become a vegetarian.

When Sister asked for swabs or any other item of equipment, it was the runner's job to get them. There was a special way of opening the packs without contaminating everything in sight, which had been demonstrated on my first day, but executing it wasn't always as easy as it looked, and the first time I tried to do it everything went pear-shaped. I was trying to shake out some cotton wool balls from a bag on to the instrument table but one or two of them had become stuck in the creases of the bag and, instead of getting a new bag, I persevered in shaking the one I already had in my hand as hard as I could. Then, horror of horrors, the stupid thing slipped from my grasp and the unsterile outer bag landed smack in the middle of all the sterile instruments. I felt sick, but all I could say was, 'Oh!'

The consultant went ballistic and the operation had to stop while I removed everything for re-sterilisation. Sister was remarkably tolerant. Without going overboard she reprimanded me but then set about replacing all the equipment at impressive speed, packing the contaminated instruments into the autoclave to sterilise them. Everyone else just stood around making small talk while they waited with folded arms and barely concealed smouldering tempers. I tried very hard not to repeat my mistake, though before my time in theatre was completed I saw a number of other staff, trained and otherwise, do exactly the same thing and even the sisters got it wrong sometimes. I suppose that was why Sister hadn't reacted too harshly.

I did actually come close to fainting once during a major operation, on a man who had been hit by a train, suffering massive internal and external injuries. One team of surgeons worked on his shattered legs and pelvis while another team worked on his abdomen. I was asked to scrub up as the surgeon needed an extra pair of hands to hold up the inside of the patient's ribcage. I had been shown how to scrub up once or twice previously, but actually doing it was something else. However, once I was ready I shuffled towards the operating table, hands held aloft and already feeling very, very warm. The room temperature had hit 100 degrees and rising, due to the numbers of additional staff called in. The consultant showed me where he wanted me to place my hands and — oh Lord, everything looked so red and raw and the patient's heart was literally beating against the back of my hand! This entirely unique sensation felt really weird, yet I was instructed not to move under any circumstances. I can't remember how long I stood there but it felt like a lifetime, although in reality it was probably about an hour, and I began to feel almost unbearably uncomfortable. Sister enquired if I was OK and I nodded, although probably not very convincingly. A few minutes later she glanced at me again and immediately ordered me to leave the table. The colour must have drained from my face and that was the closest I have ever come to fainting. I am still convinced the cause was the heat, not the sight or feel of the open chest and beating heart, but I will very definitely never forget the experience.

One lingering memory of theatre was of a doctor amputating a gangrenous leg. Normally he would have passed it to an orderly for incineration. But the orderly wasn't around so, without further ado, he tossed it vaguely in my direction with a casual instruction to put it in a bin bag. I cannot begin to describe how I felt when the severed leg landed with a soggy splat on the tiled floor at my feet; there was no way I could even touch it let alone catch it. I wouldn't have picked it up for a thousand pounds and was extremely relieved when the orderly returned at that precise moment, picked up the rotting object and limped away pretending to be Rolf Harris singing 'Jake the Peg'.

I didn't find too much to laugh about in theatre, but there was one instance when I couldn't help myself. The patient was on the operating table and had been anaesthetised. He was about to be circumcised and the only part of his body visible among the layers of green towels was his penis, which lay there looking rather shrivelled and lonely. Along came the surgeon who grasped the organ in his left hand and cleaned every nook and cranny with antiseptic. He wasn't gentle. He then attached forceps on to the foreskin and lopped it off with one swift cut. That wasn't the funny part; it was observing the reactions of the three male staff present that really amused me. A male nurse, an orderly and a junior male doctor all grimaced as though experiencing the pain themselves. One was holding on to his lunch box like a footballer standing in front of a free kick and the other two were standing cross-legged. I started sniggering and Sister looked at me sternly, so I just nodded in their direction. She started laughing and so did the surgeon. Stitches were then whacked unceremoniously into the prepuce, bringing even more tears to their eyes. You really had to be there to appreciate it. I wonder where that naïve sixteen-year-old schoolgirl disappeared to?

When my boyfriend Bill had been admitted for surgery some three months earlier to remove impacted wisdom teeth, he was expected to be in for only two days. Because I had told him so many stories about pranks which had been played on the family of staff members when admitted for minor surgery he begged me not to tell anyone on the ward that we were an item. Theatre staff had sometimes been known to cheer themselves up while the patient was under anaesthetic by painting a smiley face on a nipple with gentian violet (a washable purple dye/antiseptic that was used for cleaning wounds), or to decorate a penis with ribbons. I laugh even now when he tells people how the very first thing he did when coming round, still groggy from the anaesthetic, was to check out his nether regions.

★ ★ ★

The morning of my practical finals dawned all too soon. It was the most important examination of my life, which I was to take at Burnley General Hospital some fifteen miles away. I was to be paired with another student from my PTS named Veronica. Although I had met her during lectures, I didn't know her very well but, seeing as neither Veronica nor I could drive, Bill had volunteered to chauffeur us. We were like a pair of scared rabbits and said very little to each other in the car. The only thing I can remember discussing with Veronica was my fear of being asked questions on diabetes, because I still didn't really understand the difference between hypoglycaemic and hyperglycaemic comas. There was a lump in my throat like a golf ball and it was choking me. Bill drove around until he found the hospital education centre and with a cheery, 'Good Luck,' he abandoned us to our fate.

We couldn't fail to miss the sign in the waiting room instructing us to sit and wait for attention, or the notice on a set of double doors reading: 'Silence, examinations in progress.' We looked at each other apprehensively but, before we could do a runner, the door opened and we were beckoned inside a large hall lined with trestle tables displaying hundreds of different medical instruments and items of equipment. To the left of these tables was a hospital bed with a 'patient' lying there quietly, reading a paperback. The two examiners were ladies and we were introduced to a male nurse tutor whose role was to point out any instrument we couldn't locate, although there was so much equipment about that I doubted we would be able to find anything whatever. We were each handed a card detailing our respective nursing tasks with instructions to read, and were then to discuss our actions and set up whatever equipment the task required. One look at the card made my stomach turn over: 'A known diabetic is admitted to hospital in a coma. Set up anything that you would require for such an admission.'

The one word I had been dreading: diabetic. I felt physically sick. That was it; I was sunk. Panic welled up and then faded; I would just have to make the best of it. Veronica and I had been given ten minutes to discuss the case and set up the equipment, and then we would each be questioned separately by the different examiners. We decided that just because the case was a diabetic in a coma we couldn't assume the coma was due to the diabetes, so we decided to set up everything necessary for an unconscious patient: oxygen, suction, airways, glucose testing equipment, catheter and glucose IV. You name it, we set up for it. We had to place the patient in a coma position (lying on the left side with leg and arm slightly bent to prevent the patient from rolling over) and then, after putting in place everything that we thought we needed, we stood back and waited for the onslaught.

One of the examiners approached and took me to the trolleys that we had assembled. She asked me to explain as fully as possible why we had set them up, the purpose of each item, together with the reason the patient had been placed in the left lateral position. She listened, nodded, scribbled on a clipboard and then asked me about hypoglycaemic comas. I stuttered out a garbled answer, which I am sure was utter drivel. The examiner could see that I was in a panic and told me to calm down and take a few deep breaths. She then very kindly said, 'I am here to find out what you know, not to pick out what you don't.' It was still a relief when the subject of diabetes was dropped, though. I was then asked to go and choose whichever instrument I liked, and give a detailed description of its function and its operation. I searched for an instrument that I thought she couldn't ask me too much about, finally deciding on Rampley sponge-holding forceps. I thought that I was being really clever, as its only function is to hold swabs during operations. She looked at me and smiled, no doubt thinking that I was trying to be a smart-arse, and instead of asking me its name and function, asked me how I would sterilise such an instrument, which took us on to infections and gangrene (serves me right).

Next, I had to set up for two operations, the first an appendicectomy and the other a D&C. I could hardly believe my luck; it was something I had been doing for the last few weeks. Then I had to explain the sequence in which the instruments were used and how they would be sterilised. While I was setting up for the D&C, I stood back to check that I hadn't missed anything, and I felt an instrument being pushed into my hand from behind. The male tutor, bless him, had noticed that I had forgotten to include a silver catheter, an essential piece of kit. He gave me a wink and a smile when I whispered my thanks. With ten minutes to go I began to relax. The examiner sat back, smiled, and chatted about my career and aspirations. It was all over. No more questions. She shook my hand and wished me good luck.

I felt quietly confident that I had done the best I could and successfully answered most of my questions but Veronica, who had been questioned by the second examiner, went out in tears, saying that she had been unable to answer several of her questions and was convinced she had failed. Back in Blackburn we met up with others in our group who had also taken their practical examination that day, dissecting and analysing every question that we had been asked. Now all we could do was wait and hope.

A few weeks later we faced the written exam. One or two students gave the impression of being supremely confident; most of us were just very nervous. When I turned over and scanned my paper I was delighted to recognise several topics which I had studied only recently, although I clearly remember another student, Josie, sitting directly behind me saying, 'Oh God no, oh no, I can't answer anything.' By the end of three hours I was still scribbling furiously and completed the paper with only seconds to spare. Once again it would be several weeks to wait for our results.

Of course the post was late on the day of the results, just as it had been for my O levels. Up in my bedroom I heard the letterbox snap and the post hit the mat. I grabbed my results and ripped open the envelope. The first words I read were, '*I am pleased to inform you*'. It was enough! I screamed and danced around my mum, laughing and crying at the same time. Mum beamed with pride as tears flowed down her face. I ran upstairs to tell my dad, who was still in bed.

'Dad, I've passed my finals! I'm going to be a staff nurse!'

There was surprisingly little reaction from him, although Mum told me that in the working men's club that evening he was bursting with pride and telling the good news to anyone who

198

cared to listen. That was Dad all over, never able to show his emotions in front of us.

My friend and colleague Denise, who was staying with me at the time, telephoned the hospital for her own results and for news about the rest of the group. She was delighted to have passed herself but unfortunately some others hadn't, including Veronica (as she had suspected) and Josie who had been sat behind me during the exam. They would be able to retake the examination some months later if they wished, but at the time they were obviously devastated. Denise and I felt really sorry for them because they were both good nurses who had simply succumbed to nerves, but it certainly didn't stop us going out celebrating that night. We were on cloud nine for days!

6

All newly qualified nurses were obliged to attend an induction course intended to emphasise the much higher level of responsibility and accountability now required at this stage of their career. 'You are now personally responsible for everything you do,' were the sobering opening words from the medico-legal solicitor who addressed us, before going on to detail several actual cases where nurses had been struck off for inappropriate nursing practices, particularly the incorrect administering or misuse of drugs. He cited two particular local cases in our own Health Authority, the first a young male nurse (who tragically at the time was fighting testicular cancer) who had helped himself to sleeping tablets from the medicine cupboard for personal use, and the other a ward sister who had deliberately given an injection into a vein instead of a muscle, thinking that it would take effect more quickly, but which was against a doctor's instructions. Both had been suspended; the sister was eventually struck off and sadly the male nurse died before being allowed to return to work. The solicitor stressed the importance of documenting every incident in a patient's notes, no matter how trivial it may appear at the time. The lectures were both cautionary and thought-provoking. For example, any incident involving the police that resulted in a conviction, even when not on duty, could be reported to the General Nursing Council, with a strong likelihood that the offender would be struck off.

After induction we collected our uniforms and pored over the lists for our first staffing posts. Up until 1969–70, all recently qualified staff had traditionally been offered a choice of wards within their own hospital, wherever possible. However, spending cuts and a reduction in the number of posts altered this, and by 1971 jobs could no longer be guaranteed, certainly not the ones you preferred. Like me, many of my colleagues were simply told where they were being sent; if you didn't like it, you had to apply elsewhere and take your chances. Many of the girls were divided up between the two main general hospitals (BRI and QPH) but I was the only staff nurse to be posted on to the stroke rehabilitation unit, situated within the grounds of the isolation hospital at Park Lee Hospital. It was away from all my friends and not at all the type of nursing I wanted to practise. However, it was a brand-new, purpose-built unit and should, no doubt, prove to be a challenge. I was cheered up immensely when Bill proposed and we became engaged. My life seemed about to change in all directions. My registration was formally declared and on 28 December 1971 I received my letter from the General Nursing Council for England and Wales:

Dear Madam,
    I have much pleasure in informing you that your application for registration has been

approved and your name has now been entered on the part of the register for General Nurses maintained by the General Nursing Council for England and Wales. Your registration number is 444003 and you are now entitled to call yourself a Registered Nurse; your date of registration is 30th November, 1971.

Also enclosed with this letter was a permit entitling me to wear the uniform of a State Registered Nurse.

It was real. It was official. It was ME! I was now an SRN.

* * *

In December 1971 I started my first post as a staff nurse. The function of the specialist unit to which I had been assigned was to rehabilitate both male and female stroke patients to a point where they regained a reasonable degree of independence. On arrival I was greeted with some (not particularly friendly) inquisitive stares from those staff members on duty: the two sisters, one enrolled nurse and two auxiliaries. The older sister, Sister Ashton, a short, grey-haired individual with a permanent scowl, eventually invited me to sit down and have a cup of tea with her before taking me on the compulsory tour. Breakfasts had just been served so the patients were far too busy with the logistics of transferring food from their plates to their mouths to pay any attention to me. There was none of the usual hustle and bustle I was

202

used to at meal times; in fact, it seemed almost too quiet.

I was delighted to find the whole unit clean and sparkling with no unpleasant odours, though. (The absence of incontinence smells on any such unit is always a good indication of high standards of care.) So far so good! Starting on the female ward, the tour began in the large dining room where a number of ladies were at various stages of attempting to feed themselves — some doing really well and others looking quite stressed as they chased the food around their plates. One elderly patient who had been eagerly pursuing the remnants of a fried egg eventually gave up and tossed her spoon skywards in frustration. When one of the auxiliaries went over and put an arm around the patient to comfort her she pushed the auxiliary away. Depressed and angry, no amount of cajoling could persuade her to keep on trying.

At that moment Sarah, a tiny old lady came into view, meandering aimlessly down the corridor mumbling away to herself; knickers over one arm and a soiled incontinence sheet over the other. Seemingly this apparition of loveliness often made her entrance in such a confused condition, but if any of the staff had the temerity to enquire what she was doing, Sarah would look at them in disgust and tell them to 'Mind their own f★★king business!' I was informed that she wasn't actually a stroke victim but was suffering from dementia due to the latent stages of syphilis. In her younger days she had worked as a prostitute but, now in her eighties, was considered to be a 'social problem'. There was really nowhere else to transfer her because every geriatric bed was full and no rest home would take her; so this new 'stroke unit', although still in its infancy, had already been hijacked and used as a dumping ground.

Sarah suffered from a severe mouth deformity due to her illness, which unfortunately meant she was unable to be fitted with NHS dentures, thus leaving her unable to chew properly and severely limited in the type of food she could eat. Not to be beaten, Sarah apparently repeatedly upset the other patients by stealing their false teeth and cramming them into her own mouth, giving herself a comic-book horsey grin. When confronted and questioned as to whose teeth she had borrowed she would fling them angrily across the floor and swear like a trooper. Every day was Groundhog Day — Sarah refused to admit defeat even if it meant trying out every set of teeth she could lay her hands on, the staff permanently retrieving and cleaning the objects of her affection while trying to console the distressed victims of her light-fingered quest.

Sister told me a story about the official opening of the unit. The Mayor and Mayoress of Blackburn were coming to visit the new stroke unit, accompanied by several other dignitaries and members of the press. All was going well, the unit shone like a new pin and the patients were on their best behaviour sitting in the day room either watching television or dozing, when who should make her entrance but Sarah. She shuffled down the ward without a care in the world, knickers draped over her shoulder, dribbling a rivulet of diarrhoea along the shining, newly scrubbed floor. Sister saw her first and frantically gesticulated to the staff to get her out of sight. But have you ever tried shifting an awkward, demented eighty-year-old who doesn't want to be shifted? She wouldn't budge! The sound and distinctive aroma of the continuing discharge increased as the murky puddle on the floor spread ever wider. The harder the girls tried to move Sarah and keep her quiet, the more commotion she made. Then it was too late; they'd been spotted. The dignitaries all came around the corner together as a group, staring in horrified fascination at the delightful scene, as one auxiliary tried in vain to mop up the pool of poo, Sarah screamed 'F★★k off' at everyone, and the staff tried to drag her away into the bathroom. The timing couldn't have been more perfect and everyone had laughed about it for weeks; after all, this was a true picture of life on the unit. Why should everyone be expected to sit up, smiling sweetly at people who basically don't give a monkey's and will all too soon disappear, never to be seen again? Good for Sarah. What a star!

Still laughing at the thought as we moved around the ward, Sister introduced me to Alice, who was ninety years old, her face obscured by the porridge bowl as she licked it clean. She loved her food and was a real sweetie, and did an Oliver Twist impression as we came towards her, asking for more. Sister told me that Alice had spent her life travelling the world as a journalist for a well-known tabloid newspaper but now spent her days reading (without the aid of glasses) and shredding her blankets. She would sit for hours on end unpicking the cellular hospital blanket, piling the cotton threads ever higher on her tabletop. This kept her perfectly happy so no one considered stopping her. It took months for her to destroy one blanket and it was excellent occupational therapy. Mind you, I'm not sure that the Health Authority would have approved of this blatant misuse of valuable resources. The rest of the ladies were eating breakfast and seemed to be very friendly with each other, the more able-bodied helping those who were less capable.

Having been introduced to each of the ladies in turn, it was now time to meet the men. The majority of them were also in their dining room and were equally focused on eating. Some poorly patients, though, were still by their beds, so I was taken to the four-bedded cubicle nearest the nurses' station to meet them. All were in the early stages of recovery after their strokes and still required maximum help and encouragement. The first one, Harry, was about seventy-five years old and reminded me of a little leprechaun. His ginger hair stood straight up and his head looked like a coconut, with the largest dark eyes I have ever seen, and he was slumped lopsidedly in a geriatric chair near his bed. Each of these chairs had a small non-slip table screwed to the front so that patients could attempt to feed themselves without the crockery sliding around or ending up on the floor. Harry was doing a limbo under his table and had slipped so far down that only his head was visible, looking as though someone had put his decapitated head on a platter. I had to giggle when I saw him and asked him where he was going. He gave me a bewildered frown, screwed up his face in anger and screamed at the top of his voice, 'Sling your bloody hook and bugger off!' Sister chuckled and told me that these were the only words he ever uttered; those seven words were the entire range of his vocabulary. At least you were left in no doubt about his feelings! We carefully lifted him up in his chair, gave him a drink in a feeding cup and as we moved away we heard him mutter his catchphrase again under his breath.

The man next to him was Steven, a retired headmaster who, like Harry, was paralysed down his right side and also had limited speech. Roughly the same age as Harry, he had pure white, close-cropped hair and wore dark-framed spectacles held together with sticking plaster. He was sitting in his chair crying pitifully, his head resting on his good hand, and quietly repeating to himself: 'Dear me, dear me, dear me.' It was sad to see this obviously intelligent man so depressed and frustrated, struggling to carry out the simplest of tasks which we all take for granted. Like a schoolboy making a request, he raised his good hand to attract attention and pointed to the floor where he had dropped his spoon. It was hoped that speech therapy would eventually help him to articulate his thoughts, but at the moment it was a constant struggle. I picked up the spoon, washed it and handed it back to him, saying the word 'Spoon' slowly and carefully. He successfully repeated the word and we both gave him a pat on the back and a few words of encouragement, to which he responded with a big grin and a thumbs up.

Then there was Eric, a retired police officer, who was well over six feet tall and around seventeen stone in weight, with such long, bushy eyebrows that it was hard to see his steely grey eyes, even when he could be bothered to open them. He sat bolt upright in his chair, legs crossed and arms folded. A stroke had completely altered his personality; his language had become coarse and he was now often aggressive. Family members said that before his stroke he had been an exemplary officer and a devoted father and grandfather. It was difficult to imagine now and I was warned not to get too close to his feet as he was known to kick out when least expected. When Sister wished him good morning and introduced me, he opened his eyes very slowly and, articulating his words carefully, told her to 'F⋆⋆k off'. Family photographs covered his locker and there was one of him looking smart in his uniform and quite handsome when he smiled.

The fourth man in the cubicle was Richard, a former coal merchant and now ninety-eight years old. He was rather small and plump but he was also the sex maniac of the group. If any female came within reach of his good hand, he would do his utmost to grope her and salivate with enthusiasm at his efforts. The nurses were obviously well acquainted with Richard's antics and would try at all costs to avoid getting too close. Reportedly, during visiting time one day, a lady was bending over her elderly father who happened to be sitting next to Richard when, without warning, he leaned over and pushed his hand up her skirt. When she spun around in surprise he was leaning forward red-faced, slavering liberally and grasping his erect penis, urging her to: 'C'mon, C'mon, C'mon!' Her loud remonstrations brought several staff rushing to the scene. He was hastily covered with a blanket and banished to his cubicle, never again to be allowed in the day room at visiting time. Fortunately, the visitor was very understanding and didn't make too much fuss.

Sister flagged up the antics of a fifth patient who just happened to be wandering past at the time because of his history of going AWOL. Jimmy was an ex-market trader in his mid-sixties; frail and lanky, he was a very unhappy individual who wanted nothing more than to be allowed to go home. He had suffered a number of minor strokes that had not affected his mobility too badly but, unfortunately, his mental state was a constant cause for concern. Weepy and confused, living in the past and feeling imprisoned, it became a game of cat and mouse keeping an eye on him to make sure he didn't disappear from the unit. To date, he had 'escaped' a number of times, usually wearing only pyjamas, a cardigan and some slippers, and was generally brought back within minutes, after getting no further than the hospital grounds.

He would then weep in frustration as he was returned to us. There simply were not enough staff to watch him around the clock and it was an impossible situation. Staff were not allowed to lock doors or restrain him in any way, so it was no surprise when Jimmy disappeared again during one particularly busy day. After an unsuccessful search, the police were informed and a description flashed to all officers in Blackburn. He was eventually found (unbelievably still wearing only pyjamas and slippers) wandering around the outdoor market area some miles away, desperately looking for his old market stall. It was worrying to think how he had managed to board a bus dressed like that, then walk unchallenged through the town centre and across a busy main road. When the police brought him back he was shivering and totally dejected, so we gave him a warm drink and put him to bed. He was examined later by a psychiatrist and put on antidepressants, but it took a week or two before he eventually settled down. Throughout his stay with us he had to be watched constantly in case he tried to escape again.

I could see that I was going to have my work cut out on this unit. It may have seemed amusing at the time, but to see these once respected husbands, fathers and brothers become increasingly unrecognisable must have been agony for their families.

Of course, not all stroke victims end up the same way. One lady even wrote a book about her experiences after having suffered a stroke and her subsequent fight back to near-normality. In her book, she describes how muzzy-headed she had been feeling and then, in what seemed the next moment, found herself in hospital paralysed down one side and unable to speak. Her loss of speech was the most frustrating aspect of all because she felt that everyone was treating her like an imbecile. Her family and friends would visit and have conversations around her as though she was deaf, blind and stupid; even some of the doctors and nurses, who really should have known better, were equally thoughtless. Anger and the sheer resentment at her own helplessness gave her the incentive and determination to pull through. Following months of intensive physiotherapy and speech therapy she recovered well, leaving her with a powerful desire to write an educational book about her experiences from a patient's point of view.

Many stroke victims regain their mobility and speech very quickly, while others never return to their former state and spend the rest of their lives in a personal limbo. This lady had a very positive attitude which probably played an important part in her successful recovery, and her book was an inspirational guide to help all stroke victims and their families to understand about this debilitating illness and the rehabilitation process. Working on the unit helped me to understand the despair she must have felt. It was common for relatives to come and ask if we thought that their mum or dad would like to get some fresh air in the garden or wanted personal items brought in, and yet they had never even considered asking them directly. This greatly frustrated the stroke victim and often sent them into a depression. It was part of the job to try and educate the families as well as the patients about strokes and, in the end, it was very rewarding when patients began to smile at being included in a conversation or simply treated as a normal human being once again.

The process of recovery had to begin slowly and gradually, though. Patients were encouraged at the earliest opportunity to take some responsibility for themselves, starting with their own feeding and dressing. Such everyday actions are so often taken for granted, yet getting food on to a spoon and into your mouth can be surprisingly difficult for a stroke patient because the normal coordination between brain and hand has been impaired. Similarly, trying to fasten buttons or tie shoelaces using only one hand can be unbelievably difficult. It may appear odd to an onlooker, but the patient is struggling to relearn all the basic skills in exactly the same way that a young child does when he attempts them for the very first time. Both the patient and child inevitably experience extreme frustration at times.

I clearly recall one man who had suffered a very dense stroke. He had hemiplegia (paralysis down one side of the body) and his wife insisted on doing everything on his behalf. She was furious with us when we tried to explain that her husband should be encouraged to do more for himself in order to regain some independence and dignity. She was quite indignant and thought we were being cruel, yet when she wasn't there he fed himself perfectly well. The moment she reappeared on the ward, he would instantly down his cutlery, allowing her to feed him like a small child. He made little progress but they both seemed happy with the situation and he eventually went home, presumably to more of the same thing.

It was hard physical work on the unit, although very rewarding, but before too long I got the distinct impression that I wasn't very popular with some of the staff. Because of my enthusiasm to do things correctly, I'd get the odd look or occasional grumble that alerted me to a problem. However, there were one or two incidents which couldn't be ignored. One morning I came on duty early to see a male orderly undressing a gentleman in the open ward. The patient, Michael, was only in his late fifties but had pre-senile dementia and had been doubly incontinent. I watched in disgust as the orderly (unaware I was there) removed Michael's dirty pyjamas, leaving him completely naked in full view of the other patients and, without even washing him first, put clean pyjamas over the top of the filth. I was incensed and confronted the orderly for his lazy and neglectful behaviour. Incredibly, a few days later I was summoned to see the nursing officer and ticked off. The orderly had complained that I had no right to verbally reprimand him as he was night staff and therefore didn't come under my jurisdiction. I had never heard such rubbish in my life and expressed my views clearly, insisting that I would continue to report such conduct whenever or wherever it was encountered. In my opinion the orderly should have been reprimanded and sacked, and I asked the nursing officer how she would like her father or brother to be stripped naked in public and left wet and stinking. Just because the man had dementia and wasn't able to object shouldn't have made the slightest bit of difference to the manner of his treatment. She made no comment in reply to my question and I left the room absolutely seething.

I worked hard and kept my head down for the next twelve months, bathing patients, teaching them basic, everyday skills and helping them to regain some dignity. It was a labour of love, especially when good progress was made and the patients were able to go home. Eric, the retired policeman, was the most difficult. He made very little progress, becoming even more aggressive as time went by and, on one occasion, I made a mistake and forgot for a few seconds just how nasty he could be. When I was bending down to fasten his shoes he lifted his leg and kicked me in the chest, knocking me flat on my back, and then he roared with laughter. Another day I received a punch on the nose which brought tears to my eyes and caused me to react instinctively. I grabbed the collar of his pyjamas and said, 'Do that once more mister and, patient or no patient, I will give you the same back.' Startled, he sat back in his chair and stared at me silently. I could hardly believe my actions, but the pain of a burst nose simply brought about an automatic involuntary reaction. The more thought I gave to my behaviour, the more ashamed I became and I felt I had let my patient down. Surprisingly, however, he never touched me or swore at me again from that day on; it was as though my retaliation had awakened something in his brain. I spent many hours with Eric during my time in the unit and was pleasantly surprised that we got on quite well after that, which did make me question just how innocent his aggression was.

Many of the patients worked hard to get themselves mobile again. It was a daily struggle for most of them and often took many months before they were back to near-normality, but the more determined they were and the harder they worked, the better the outcome.

★ ★ ★

After working on the rehabilitation unit for a year, staff shortages meant that I was to be temporarily transferred to the Isolation Unit at Park Lee Hospital. I wasn't given a choice or even asked if I minded being moved, even though I had previously expressed my real concerns about working with babies and children and the unit was used to nurse anyone with a potentially infective disease. Some patients, for example, were admitted with undiagnosed diarrhoea and vomiting, while others came in with hepatitis A, typhoid or other infections contracted while on holiday abroad. At any one time it was reasonably commonplace to have a number of very sick young babies in the unit, as they easily became dehydrated and were often desperately ill on admission. I detested every second on Isolation, not because I was afraid of contracting a disease, but because I hated seeing babies and young children constantly struggling to survive. I felt inadequate and totally out of my depth. My pleas to move back to the Stroke Unit fell on deaf ears and I began to wonder if they had moved me deliberately in order to get rid of me. I readily admit to having been outspoken on a number of occasions since the orderly incident, but had felt justified in complaining about one or two other incidents that I felt were unacceptable. I had certainly taken issue with one SEN who, unbelievably, was giving out lunches with a cigarette dangling from the corner of her mouth. Ash was actually dropping from the cigarette on to the plate, which she merely removed with a spoon and then carried on. To make matters worse, she was the nurse in charge of her shift that morning. I had literally just come on duty and walked through the doors when I saw it happen. Was I supposed to ignore or allow this? Unfortunately, such poor nursing practices and lack of standards thrive much more easily when the patients are elderly or vulnerable and unable or reluctant to complain. Strong leadership and example is needed to prevent this occurring or to stamp it out, and unfortunately this was sometimes lacking in that unit.

The problem, of course, was my age. I was a newly qualified twenty-one-year-old staff nurse and most of the existing trained staff were much older and just wanted a quiet life. They didn't like being organised by a young kid and perhaps I rocked the boat a little too much. In my defence, I have to say that a number of the auxiliaries confided in me that they were always relieved when I was on duty because they knew that I would roll my sleeves up and do my share of the work. They, at least, appreciated the fact that I didn't spend all my time in the office drinking tea while they struggled with a heavy workload. With hindsight, I may have appeared a little overenthusiastic in my new role, but I was also learning to take charge in Sister's absence and wanted everything to be perfect. It was a new experience for me as well as for them and perhaps indicated to me a need to improve as a supervisor and manager as I got older. In the end, I decided to resign and try my luck elsewhere in a more acute setting, on a ward that would better utilise the nursing skills I had acquired. Considering the existing climate concerning job vacancies, I was extremely lucky that it was only a week later when I applied and was accepted as a staff nurse on general medical ward E3 at Queen's Park Hospital.

★ ★ ★

The ward was situated in the old part of the hospital within the inter-war pre-fabricated section. It wasn't ideal but had served its purpose many times over. Like BRI, there were thirty-two patients in total, split equally between male and female sides, the two being separated by double swing doors. The facilities were even more archaic than in the Infirmary and the day room was merely a small recess on either side where a television was placed along with four comfy chairs. Amazingly no one ever complained.

The two medical consultants on E3 were responsible for the treatment and care of a wide variety of conditions, mainly chest and heart problems. Dr Lyons was one of them and he had been the gentleman who carried out my medical on the cadet induction day. He was a dour Scot who constantly looked preoccupied and didn't suffer fools gladly. His ward rounds could be nerve-wracking at times as he expected nothing less than perfection from his staff. If any patients' records were missing, or if a nurse couldn't immediately produce the appropriate test results for each patient, he was liable to have a mini-tantrum that left everyone on edge for the rest of the day. And yet, he was a superb clinician who cared deeply about his patients and treated each one equally. Irrespective of whether they were a duchess or a dustman, he would often sit himself down on the patient's bed (which would never have been allowed when Matron was in charge) and speak to them openly and with compassion. He genuinely cared about his work and his patients, insisting on the highest standards from everyone on his team. In time I got used to his little idiosyncrasies and learned to admire and respect him for being so thoughtful and considerate.

The second consultant, Dr Ward, was the complete opposite in character. He was tall, elegant and had a rather superior upper-class manner when doing his ward rounds. He could often be blunt to the point of rudeness with the patients, especially if they weren't adhering strictly to his instructions and would never have dreamed of sitting on their bed for a chat. He would regularly tear a strip off any chest patient who persisted in smoking after being advised to stop, then as soon as he left the ward he invariably lit a cigarette. Of course, he thought no one else knew that he smoked but it was common knowledge among the ward staff. He, too, was an excellent clinician and, like Dr Lyons, was very well respected.

Comprehensive reforms to the nursing structure within the NHS, as proposed in the Salmon Report, now made way for nursing officers who were each in charge of their own units. John Fletcher was in overall charge of the medical unit which covered wards E2 and E3. There were two sisters, one senior (Sister Clarke) and a junior (Sister Mills), both of whom had good, solid reputations as excellent nurses, and there were two staff nurses, an enrolled nurse and a number of student nurses. One of the staff nurses, Bernadette Magee (known as Bernie), was a lifelong friend who had qualified six months ahead of me and her brother Michael was married to my own sister Pat. The other staff nurse was newly qualified and was still trying to find her feet on the ward. The enrolled nurse, Jan, was a very capable, friendly, middle-aged lady who greeted me like a member of the family every time we met and had worked on E3 for ages.

Like the majority of wards I had worked on

previously, I knew straight away that I was going to enjoy this one and I settled in immediately. Every day was now busy and challenging, with a much greater variety of patient than on the Rehabilitation Unit. Some of the situations I came across were difficult to deal with, especially one which involved a lady with multiple sclerosis (MS) who had been admitted with pneumonia. Normally she coped quite well at home — a home help visited every day to carry out the household chores and her sister did the shopping. Unfortunately, the pneumonia had exacerbated her MS and rendered her almost totally immobile. She was very poorly but pleaded with us to allow her to go home. The problem in letting her home was twofold; the first was that she lived alone and needed twenty-four-hour care; the second, her chest was so bad that she needed constant access to oxygen along with antibiotic injections every four hours. Community nursing was very different at that time and, although the service was good, it couldn't provide the full twenty-four-hour care that she required. Everyone tried to reason with and reassure her that she would be allowed to return home as soon as she was sufficiently improved but she refused to believe this. One afternoon, after Sister had gone off duty, a student nurse came to me to say that this lady had asked for her things to be packed and transport arranged to take her home. Of course, I immediately went to try and reason with her but she angrily refused to discuss the matter further. She wept and shouted, accusing me of detaining her against her will, insisting that she intended to take her own discharge and would sue the hospital if she was forced to stay. As a junior staff nurse I was completely out of my depth. What should I do? She certainly knew her own mind, but who would look after her? I called the duty doctor, who also came down to try and persuade her to stay, pointing out the practical difficulties and the amount of care she needed. But, alas, all our efforts fell on deaf ears and we had no choice but to let her go. Legally we had no right to prevent her leaving and she knew it.

After getting in touch with her relatives and making them aware of her predicament, I contacted the ambulance service to see if they would agree to take her home — at the time, any patient discharging themselves against medical advice was, strictly speaking, expected to make their own travel arrangements. I also rang her GP and the district nursing team who provided an oxygen cylinder and made arrangements to administer the prescribed antibiotic injections. We were informed some weeks later that she had passed away, despite the district nurses doing their utmost to support her and with relatives staying with her overnight the whole time. I always suspected she must have had a foreboding that her condition was terminal (as do many such patients), so at least she was granted her final wish to die at home in familiar surroundings.

A few months later, Phyllis, an obese, elderly lady who was a chronic bronchitic, was admitted with a severe chest infection and put on oxygen and six-hourly antibiotic injections. After forty-eight hours she had begun to improve to the point where she was allowed to sit in a wheelchair in the day room. At midday I wheeled her back to her bedside to give her an injection. Pulling the curtains around her bed, as was usual, I asked her if she could stand up facing the bed to allow me to give the injection into her bottom. She was rather ungainly and it took some effort to get her on to her feet, but once she stood up she leaned forward to receive the injection. As I lifted her nightdress to administer the antibiotics her legs suddenly began to buckle.

'Stand up straight Phyllis,' I said, 'I will only take a second.'

She tried her best to stand a little more erect but within seconds her legs started to give way again.

'Phyllis you are going to fall!' I shouted, taking the opportunity to push the needle in quickly and complete the injection. But my words went unheard as she slumped forward, stone cold dead. I was frantic and no amount of CPR could resuscitate her. I was totally at a loss, wondering what had happened, even double-checking that I had given her the correct injection. I was reassured by Dr Lyons that it was nothing whatever to do with my actions and a later post-mortem showed that she had suffered a massive brain haemorrhage. Poor Phyllis, there was I urging her to stand up straight when she was on her way to meet her maker! Mind you, several of the other patients weren't too keen on me giving them their injections after that.

Looking back I don't suppose I could blame them, but at the time I felt quite indignant.

In one of the cubicles on the male side of E3, four patients were all recovering from heart attacks. Anthony, a tall, very thin man in his seventies was allowed out of bed to potter around the ward to get some gentle exercise, while the other three were confined to their beds wired up to heart monitors. Since his coronary, Anthony had been confused and a little disorientated at times. One morning he climbed out of bed, put on his dressing gown and spectacles, and then gazed around vacantly as if trying to get his bearings. Appearing to have reached a decision, he headed directly across the cubicle to one of the other patient's lockers. Without any hesitation he pulled down his pyjama trousers, lifted up the lid of the compartment normally used to store the patient's slippers and squatted down. Three buzzers went off simultaneously as the other patients watched in horror and tried to alert the nurses, their heart monitors bleeping like mad and performing a merry dance. The poor bloke whose new slippers Anthony had used as a toilet was in a real state, the tracing on his monitor looked like it had just registered a massive earthquake. Anthony, meanwhile, was at a loss to understand what all the fuss was about and why the other men were shouting at him. I felt sorry for the poor nurse who had to clean it all up.

It was on E3 that I was given the opportunity to see my first post-mortem. I knew the pathologist, who had been one of the junior doctors on Wards 11 and 12 at BRI when I was a student. He came on to the ward quite often and one day I happened to mention to him that I had never seen a post-mortem. His eyes lit up.

'I've got one this afternoon, if Sister will allow you to come and watch,' he said.

Sister nodded in agreement but I distinctly remember wondering what I had let myself in for.

At 2pm, after I had done the medicine round and everything was quiet, I set off to the mortuary, feeling a little jittery. The room was fully tiled with several sinks and metal slabs, one wall comprising large metal doors which opened up to reveal tiers of refrigerated shelves for storing bodies. Jim, the doctor, was already standing there waiting, dressed in white Wellington boots and a floor-length rubber apron, the body of an adult male lay naked on a nearby slab. My eyes were inexorably drawn to a second body, that of a baby girl lying on one of the sinks as though asleep. Initially I thought this was a dummy, until I went closer and saw the tell-tale blue lips. It was an unexpected shock and I looked over at Jim for an explanation. 'Infant sudden death,' he said in a matter-of-fact way. 'You can stay and watch that one, too, if you like.' I declined his kind offer with a shake of my head, wondering how on earth anyone could do this awful job. 'Right, let's get on,' he said. And, with a swift incision of his scalpel, he opened the man's body and began dissecting and examining all the organs.

Jim quickly established the cause of death to

be a coronary thrombosis, taking genuine pleasure in showing me the exposed structure of the heart with its blocked arteries. Very nice! I found the experience utterly fascinating, if a bit gory, yet at the same time I was thankful that I wasn't his wife. The whole procedure seemed so clinical and impersonal, Jim even whistling tunelessly, totally consumed by his work. I wouldn't have liked to work in the mortuary, although it would probably be a good department in which to learn and understand anatomy a little bit better than in the lecture hall, looking at diagrams and illustrations.

⋆ ⋆ ⋆

I absolutely loved working on the medical ward and came to admire both Sister Mills and Bernadette especially during the time I worked on E3 with them. They were hard-working professionals with high standards who rolled up their sleeves and got stuck in alongside the junior staff every day, always using every opportunity to pass on their knowledge and instil a passion for excellence in their work. They were completely approachable for both patients and relatives, never too busy to sit and explain a procedure or treatment and answer questions. Neither of them would tolerate poor timekeeping or laziness but would never hesitate to support their staff or patients whenever the need arose.

All the staff were very friendly and we truly worked as a close team, but during this period I was increasingly occupied by the preparations for our imminent wedding and the modernisations being carried out on our first home. I was just counting off the days and then, on my last working day before the wedding, the staff presented me with a present followed by an unscheduled spin around the ward in a linen skip. The girls grabbed me, threw me into a skip and then pushed me along visiting every patient on the ward, laughing and throwing confetti over my head as we went along. I cried my eyes out as usual.

In September 1972 Bill and I were married, several staff turned up to watch (some still in uniform because they had nipped out from work) and I was blissfully happy. Bill's aunt had sold us her cottage for a song; located on the top of a hill in a tiny village on the moors outside Blackburn, it had magnificent views in all directions and on a clear day we could see Blackpool Tower over thirty miles away. Although the property was originally in need of major renovation and updating, the work was almost completed when we returned from our honeymoon. The place was very quirky; built in 1781, it still retained all the original beams, sloping ceilings, narrow doors and small windows.

Being so high above sea level, the weather could be extreme, though. For half the winter we were enveloped in cloud and at times the snow could be unbelievable. A number of elderly neighbours recalled that in their childhood the snow was much worse, with drifts up to twenty feet high and the village cut off for days. Helicopters had been used in years gone by to drop food when villagers were unable to get out to the shops or go to work. It was bad enough when we lived there, but shovelling snow and having communal breakfasts with the neighbours helped us to meet and make many good friends.

Our new home was only three miles away from the hospital and so I continued to work happily on E3 for another year or so until I became pregnant. It was quite a difficult period in some ways because I was very sick the whole time I was at work and I would be making a patient's bed or carrying out some other routine task when I would have to excuse myself urgently. This went on umpteen times a day and continued for so long that after five months it was deemed advisable for me to go on leave. I had always said that if I was lucky enough to have a baby I would take a break in my career to devote time to my family and in the end this is what I did. It was a very emotional day when I left and everyone was wonderful, wishing me well and buying me yet another gift, this time for the baby.

I was truly content with my lot and loved my little house, all except for the field mice which tended to appear at the most inconvenient times. I remember going downstairs for a drink of water one night when I was heavily pregnant. As I opened the kitchen cupboard door, there were Pixie and Dixie sitting quite contentedly on top of a tin of baked beans. They scurried away frantically, one of them actually running across my bare feet. My screams roused Bill from his slumbers (which believe me was no mean feat), who came flying downstairs ready to ring for the midwife, only to find me sitting on top of the kitchen unit with my dressing gown pulled tightly around my legs. He wasn't amused, poor love; he thought I had gone into labour.

★ ★ ★

In March 1974 I went into labour and was taken into the maternity unit at QPH. At the time the UK was just emerging from two months of miners' strikes and coal shortages, which resulted in the Three-Day Week when electricity was rationed and power cuts were common. At one point I seriously thought my child might be born by candlelight (a romantic notion but not for me, thank you very much!). The midwife who delivered our son Mark was, believe it or not, one of the girls who started as a cadet with me, and trained in my PTS. Kathleen had gone on to do her midwifery exams with every intention of going to work in Africa and here she was tending to me. She had become a highly respected midwife and continued to look after me long after her shift had ended, and she waited with me until Mark was born.

I felt that my life couldn't get any better. The legacy of my children's ward experience gave me the confidence to handle the baby without too much fuss and certainly taught me not to worry about every little spot or sniffle he developed. He must have felt secure straight away, as from day one he slept through from 11pm to 5am. It was heaven. I had clearly picked up so much experience on that ward without realising it at the time, and I was now eternally grateful.

Mark was a doddle because he was such a good baby. When I had resigned from my post on E3, I had intended to stay at home for a year or two and fully expected my time to be taken up with washing nappies and feeding the baby. Instead, six months down the line, I found myself at a loose end and becoming restless. After a long chat with Bill we agreed that I would see if I could return to work part-time. I knew that there were no vacancies back on E3 because I had spoken to Bernie but at BRI there was a newly organised nurse's bank system that allowed qualified staff to work part-time on nights and weekends. When I had left BRI in late 1971, qualified nurses weren't usually stationed on the wards at night and they tended to be staffed solely by students, but by 1974 this was no longer considered best practice. It was now accepted that a level of experience was essential to recognise and deal with the many potential problems that can occur. The new system required at least one trained nurse on each ward, with the night sister still equipped with a bleeper in case of emergency. It was an arrangement that was perfect for me. BRI had even opened a new intensive care unit by this time. Progress indeed.

A bank nurse could choose the number of hours they wished to work but not on which ward; you were sent wherever you were needed within the hospital. I was to meet up with a number of the girls who had started as cadets at the same time as me and who were also now married with children and worked part-time, trying to keep up-to-date with the ever-continuing changes in the NHS. I felt that I had returned home.

The night sisters on duty were virtually unchanged since I was last on nights as a student, although individual nursing officers had now replaced Matron and it was clear, even at this stage, that discipline and standards were not as strict. The wards looked pretty much the same but many new surgical techniques and drug treatments had been introduced in the three years I had been away. The first time I saw the new heart monitors at Blackburn I was flabbergasted. The machines on E3 at QPH had been so big that it took two people to actually move them and they were kept on a trolley so that they could be pushed easily from ward to ward. In BRI a number of state-of-the-art monitors, no bigger than a small portable television, were now taking pride of place on the medical wards as well as in the intensive care unit. Comparatively light as a feather, there was little danger of putting your back out moving one of these in a hurry.

Exciting new procedures and equipment developed in the late sixties and early seventies were now starting to come through into some of the big teaching hospitals and specialist centres, where we were increasingly able to refer some of our patients. Heart bypass surgery, CT scans, increased use of transplant surgery and anti-rejection drugs, ECG machines, and new chemotherapy treatments for cancer patients all promised a bright future. The cost of all this was increasing at a tremendous rate because inflation in the economy was heading towards twenty-five per cent, but with every prospect that funds from the new oil fields in the North Sea would be available to pay for it all.

In 1978–9 there were widespread strikes by many public service trade unions demanding large pay rises to keep pace with inflation. During what became known as the 'Winter of Discontent', NHS ancillary workers formed picket lines to block hospital entrances, which resulted in hospital admissions being restricted to emergency cases only. It was dreadful on the wards, essential cleaning wasn't being carried out and rubbish was piling up outside attracting a small army of rats. I remember Bernie, who was now a sister on Ward E1 (women's medical), telling me that they had to use disposable paper sheets and pillowcases because all their clean linen supplies had been exhausted, and that they had to shake each one vigorously before using them in case they were infested by some of the vastly increased numbers of cockroaches now being seen. The most notorious action at the time was the unofficial strike by gravediggers. As coffins piled up, Liverpool Council had to hire a factory to store them — our own hospital mortuary was full to overflowing. The bereaved families were distraught and I don't think the strikers got much support and solidarity from them.

The very varied experience I gained working over the next five years on the bank was invaluable and certainly increased my confidence. You never knew where you would be sent next but you were expected to deal professionally with any situation. One night I could be working on a busy, acute surgical ward, and the next night on the eye ward. Not that I am saying the eye ward was never busy, because it certainly had its moments, but it was, in general, an endless round of instilling drops into bloodshot eyes. I wasn't too happy the first time a patient asked me to clean his false eye, though! He flicked it out of his eye socket with one finger and dropped it into a kidney bowl, where it peered at me menacingly. I nearly fainted; what the hell was I supposed to do with it? My face must have said it all and the patient laughed and said, 'Oh, it's OK nurse; just give it a clean.' I didn't like to admit to not having a clue what to do, so I took it away and rang a colleague who had worked on the eye ward before. She explained the procedure and laughed when I told her it seemed to be watching me, but went on to reassure me that I only needed to worry if it winked.

★ ★ ★

My son was growing up rapidly and working weekends allowed me to watch his progress while allowing father and son to get better acquainted. It also helped me earn a small income for extras. However, Bill had worked for a large national building society since leaving school, had passed all his professional examinations and for the last two years had been commuting extensively around the UK, so it came as no surprise when in 1979 he was offered promotion to manage a new office. As his was the main income in the family we obviously couldn't afford to turn down the move, even though I wasn't too keen. Mark was five years old and young enough to make new friends easily, so we began house hunting on the Lancashire coast. Just a few weeks later we found a modern bungalow in Lytham St Annes, within walking distance of a good school, and we were soon packing boxes ready for a new beginning.

7

At around the same time as the newly elected
Prime Minister Margaret Thatcher was moving
into No. 10 Downing Street, we were making the
forty-minute drive to our new home. It wasn't
exactly the other side of the world but, for me, a
non-driver, it may as well have been. We arrived
at the same time as the removal men and they
worked hard to get us installed quickly and
efficiently. Being in a modern bungalow felt
strange and unfamiliar after the old cottage and
none of us slept very well that first night. Poor
Mark must have been particularly worried
because he wet his bed for the first time in ages,
which really distressed him. Bill and I made light
of it and tried to reassure him, but he was
obviously apprehensive about changing schools
and worried he wouldn't make any new friends.

On the day he started, Mark and I clung to
each other outside the school gates as if he were
going to the guillotine. I was trying desperately
not to let him see me cry until, just as he was
going into the school and was about to lose sight
of me, he made a last-minute dash for freedom,
sobbing and begging me not to leave him. Tears
poured down my face as I hugged him, feeling
totally pathetic, before a teacher took his hand
and gently led him away. One of the other
mothers came over and introduced herself,
reassuring me that her own son had reacted in

exactly the same way on his first day but now loved being there. Although this was nice to hear, the rest of the day dragged endlessly as I waited for 3pm to come around. I was the first mum at the school gate when he charged out, painting in hand and a huge grin on his face, chatting ten to the dozen with all the other children. There were no more damp beds or tears and he fiercely refused to allow himself to be seen even holding my hand from that day on, declaring that only babies did that. After several weeks, when I was sure that he had settled, I began to scour the local newspapers looking for gainful employment. The job would have to fit in with school hours and ideally be within walking distance. (Bill nagged me to take driving lessons but I kept putting it off because I simply wasn't interested.)

A vacancy was advertised in the local rag for a part-time staff nurse to work in an NHS unit dedicated to the temporary care of young disabled adults. It was situated fairly close to home so I telephoned to see if I could have an informal visit. I had no knowledge or experience of this type of unit so I went along with an open mind.

The unit was housed within the local cottage hospital in St Annes and was much smaller than I had expected. It was quite basic but spotlessly clean and brightly decorated and functioned as a temporary accommodation for disabled adults under the age of sixty-five to enable their home carers to have a well-earned break from the daily grind of providing twenty-four-hour assistance.

It was emphasised from the beginning that these 'clients' were here to give their families a rest and were not coming in for any sort of treatment so should not be referred to as patients. Every month two GPs (who also provided medical cover for the unit on a daily basis), Matron (the post had not yet been phased out at this small hospital) and the unit sister met to consider a waiting list of names requesting respite care. Candidates were assessed for priority in turn and were typically stroke victims, sufferers with MS, amputees and individuals with congenital disabilities. The majority had only limited ability to move around unaided but could usually manage to cope reasonably well with assistance. Accommodation was provided in both single and double rooms, which were adequate without being luxurious, and everyone looked comfortable and reasonably happy. At the far end of the main corridor was a large television room-cum-library and games room that opened on to a beautiful garden where residents could sit out and enjoy the sunshine.

I was offered the job there and then, subject to the usual medical and reference checks, starting more or less immediately. I had been hoping to find a more acute type of post but I felt that I could widen my experience on this unit. From the first day, I was supported and helped by the very friendly staff and I soon settled into the daily routines, which basically consisted of getting residents out of bed and washed or bathed before being taken into a large dining room for breakfast. Help was always given to those needing to be fed and then medicines were distributed. Bedridden individuals received standard general nursing care — bed baths, toileting, feeding, pressure areas, etc. Permanent staffing was mainly provided by auxiliaries but there was one full-time sister, one other part-time staff nurse called Edith and an enrolled nurse, whom everyone knew as Tommi. Rarely were there two trained staff on duty at the same time, although we did get together occasionally for meetings and at shift changes.

The Young Disabled Unit (YDU) filled a valuable role at the time and the girls who worked there were extremely dedicated and genuinely cared for the clients. A prime example of this care comes to mind when recalling a young man, Alec, who was only thirty-two and had been brought in to allow his wife and son to have a break. Alec had MS and was permanently wheelchair-bound, requiring round-the-clock care. His medical records showed a marked deterioration in his condition over the last six months and he was now incontinent of urine and fitted with a catheter. Although still able to feed and partially dress himself, the more intricate tasks, such as fastening buttons or shaving, were becoming increasingly difficult. His fingers were weak and lacked feeling, so gripping small objects was sometimes impossible, yet with the aid of the staff and specialist equipment provided in the unit he was able to cope reasonably well.

Like most other clients Alec had been booked in for two weeks, but one afternoon towards the end of the second week he received some

237

dreadful news that turned his life upside down. His brother arrived on the unit in a state of panic, having discovered that while Alec had been in the YDU, his wife had packed her bags and moved out, taking their young son with her. She had left no forwarding address or contact telephone number, other than that of her solicitor, through whom all future contact would have to be made. She had left without so much as a goodbye, literally abandoning him to his fate. To say that he was totally devastated was to put it mildly and it took several minutes for the news to sink in fully as he desperately tried to make sense of it all. The reality of his situation hit him hard and there was nothing anyone could say or do to ease his pain. He sobbed bitterly, wondering if he would ever see his son again, yet also realising that he simply wasn't able to cope on his own. He worried where he could go and what was going to happen to him. He pleaded with Matron to allow him to stay in the YDU but because it was strictly a short-stay unit this was simply not feasible. His brother wasn't able to take him either, because he didn't have the space or facilities to accommodate a wheelchair. It was a huge dilemma and, in the end he stayed in the unit for nearly six months before a permanent home could be found for him in a hostel for the disabled. He desperately didn't want to go there but two of the auxiliaries, who had become really fond of him, promised to visit regularly and take him out. Poor Alec didn't have much option. It was a very sad day when he left the YDU, many of the staff shedding a tear and wishing him well. He was a picture of abject misery as he was wheeled out to the car taking him to his new life.

It would be easy to condemn his wife for what she did, although I can only imagine that she must have been at her wits' end. At that time there was only very limited domestic support available; she had struggled on for years, holding down a job while looking after both her young son and ailing husband, and eventually it had all proved too much. Whatever her reasons for leaving I could only feel a deep sadness for them both. Alec eventually settled down in his new surroundings and the two auxiliaries did indeed keep in close contact as they had promised, regularly taking him out of the hostel for day trips until his eventual death. They went above and way beyond the level of care normally given to the other clients in the YDU because they had been deeply touched by his predicament and were determined to make sure that the time he had left was as happy as possible.

However, life is never straightforward and I was ticked off more than once for being noisy and making 'clients' laugh too loudly. Apparently the noise could be heard down the length of the corridor. I was lost for words! Surely, if they were laughing they were happy and, for a short time at least, it meant they weren't worrying about their particular situation (I couldn't see how they were disturbing anyone else as there was only one other ward in the cottage hospital and that was at the far end of the building)?

Charles, a stroke victim with marked paralysis

down his right side, had recently come into the unit so that his wife could enjoy a short holiday. He had a permanent indwelling catheter in situ that drained into a bag fixed on his left leg and had a calliper on his right leg to assist him walking. Soon after arrival he mentioned that he was feeling nauseated and had severe pain in his kidney area. He had felt unwell for several days but, not wanting to delay his wife's holiday, had said nothing. Checking his drainage tube, I noticed that his urine was cloudy and offensive so did what any qualified nurse would do: I sent a specimen to the laboratory to check for infection and informed the attending GP about this man's predicament. He readily prescribed an antibiotic for him with instructions to the nurses to push copious amounts of fluids to help flush out the bacteria. Within a couple of days there was a vast improvement, his pain and nausea had gone and he felt much better. The bacteria were isolated by the laboratory and, because the antibiotic he was already prescribed was appropriate for that specific infection, he completed the course of treatment and was soon his normal self.

Imagine my surprise, therefore, when Matron summoned me to her office and lectured me about carrying out inappropriate tests. She implied that I was being too 'nursey', pointing out that I wasn't there to treat clients for their numerous illnesses, and that tests and medications should be sorted out by their own GPs when they returned home. (She made a point of emphasising the word 'client' and not patient.)

240

While what Matron said fitted in with conventional practices at the time, I didn't agree with her. I listened and said nothing, but I knew in my heart that I could never ignore a patient's symptoms, regardless how often she told me off. It came as a surprise to me how much I had matured; having grown up naturally quiet and reluctant to stand up for myself, I was now unwilling to accept such a situation. So, without blatantly defying Matron, I was determined to do this job without compromising my principles.

Several weeks later Pat, a tiny middle-aged lady suffering from MS, was admitted. She lived alone, although friends and relatives visited regularly to ensure she was coping. Unfortunately one evening she tripped and fell to the floor and was unable to get up or call for help. She lay there for two days and, by the time she was found by a neighbour, she was dehydrated, had a hacking cough and a very high temperature. The neighbour called her GP, who just happened to be one of the unit's attending doctors and, after a swift telephone call to Matron, he had Pat admitted to the YDU. This didn't make sense to me; surely she needed to be admitted to Blackpool Victoria, the nearby general hospital. But, as usual, there were no beds. Pat looked very frail and was painfully thin when she was brought in. We washed her and put her to bed before giving her a nutritious drink and within minutes she was fast asleep. I then went off duty for a few days but when I came back I was alarmed to find that she had deteriorated considerably. She was lying flat on her back in bed, struggling desperately for every breath, too weak to move unaided and appeared to be in a critical condition. I immediately sat her upright supported by about half a dozen pillows and put her on oxygen. She squeezed my hand, nodded her thanks and within minutes started breathing easier and was soon sound asleep. As Sister was on annual leave for a week, Edith and I had a long discussion and prepared a care plan to ensure that Pat received appropriate care. It was absolutely essential that she be kept upright, as this helped her lungs to expand more fully and would hopefully prevent her from getting pneumonia. Giving her fluids every hour and ensuring good oral hygiene were paramount, too, along with massaging her pressure area to prevent bedsores developing. There was no doubt in my mind that Pat was dying but we intended that she should pass away as peacefully and as comfortably as possible. Tommi looked quite alarmed when she saw the care plan and said that Matron herself had left specific instructions for this lady to be laid flat, in accordance with usual practice at the time. She clearly didn't want to get into trouble, so I reassured her that I would take the blame if Matron questioned my actions and the care plan was put into action.

A couple of days later, Matron was doing her usual rounds when she stopped abruptly outside Pat's room.

'Who on earth has done this?' she said, pointing at the oxygen and pillows. Feeling a little puzzled at her exasperated tone I explained how I had found the 'client' lying flat on her back, deeply distressed and struggling for every breath, so I had propped her up to relieve her discomfort. Matron replied, 'I laid her flat. The woman is dying and she won't linger unnecessarily in the position I placed her.'

At first I was speechless. To my mind, surely it was more important to allow Pat to not have to fight for every breath? I acknowledged that giving her oxygen and sitting her upright would more than likely lengthen her life minimally, but so what? At least, as I saw it, she would not be suffering! The reaction from Matron was a look that said, 'You're young, you will learn.' She walked away shaking her head in exasperation. After that I tried my best to keep a respectful distance. I didn't want an outright disagreement or confrontation but nothing was going to stop me giving Pat as much care as I thought she needed. The other staff agreed to comply with the care plan so we carried on despite her objections. Pat died two days later; comfortable and warm, but most of all blissfully peaceful and not fighting desperately for every breath.

★ ★ ★

A year went by without further confrontation until one afternoon a thirty-year-old female was admitted for respite care. Heather was a small, painfully thin lady who looked nearer sixty years of age due to her illness. She had MS and was being cared for at home by her husband but had developed massive bedsores on her bottom, hips, heels and knees. Even her elbows were inflamed. The sores were black, painful and offensive, and no matter which way she turned she was unable to find a comfortable position. Once again, I couldn't understand why she hadn't been referred to an acute hospital because of her condition and I voiced my concerns to both the doctor and to Matron, but again was told that she was in the unit to give her husband a rest and nothing more than that. To me her bedsores needed urgent attention and their smell was awful. Decaying flesh is putrid, the smell is dreadful and there was no doubt in my mind that Heather was literally rotting. Three of us gently lifted her into a warm bath, which she hadn't been able to enjoy for quite a long time, so we let her have a good, long soak. When she was clean and at least a little more fragrant we put her back on the bed to dry and examine her sores carefully. They were the worst I had ever seen! I could virtually put my fist inside one sore which was at the base of her spine. This was a terrible situation but it was the smell that worried me most because I recognised the seriousness of her condition. In my opinion she should definitely have been referred to a more appropriate hospital, perhaps even isolation. Sister was unsure how to proceed. She was not used to dealing with acute problems so, even though I knew Matron would disapprove, I suggested we send some swabs off to the laboratory for testing, again masochistically volunteering to put my name on the form. A week or so later, as expected, Matron appeared on the unit.

'You've been at it again, haven't you?' she shouted.

I knew exactly what she was talking about, but said nothing and looked blank. The tests I had sent to the laboratory showed gas gangrene, a highly contagious and very serious infection, so the whole unit would need to be swabbed from top to bottom and Heather would have to be barrier nursed in order to prevent any spread of infection. This meant keeping her completely isolated in one room and anyone entering had to don gown, mask, gloves and overshoes; all of which were discarded into large laundry bags marked 'HAZARD' just before leaving, and then hands had to be thoroughly scrubbed with special antibacterial liquid soap. Matron was absolutely furious. I felt desperately fed up for being in trouble yet again, but carried on and called all the auxiliaries into the office to explain about barrier nursing and then set everything in motion. The laboratory technicians arrived from the general hospital and swabbed every surface in the YDU to check for any further potential sources of infection, which could have been spread by any member of staff who had been in contact with Heather over the previous week. The technicians were pleased to see that all the correct nursing procedures had already been put in place. If gangrene hadn't been diagnosed and isolated, the infection could have spread throughout the hospital, particularly because some of the auxiliaries also worked on the other ward as well as the YDU. The hospital would have had to close. It wasn't my fault that the patient had gas gangrene; she came in with it. Should I have ignored her and done nothing?

After many weeks of treatment and some excellent care, Heather was eventually transferred to an isolation hospital (where she should have gone in the first place) and, eventually, several months later, had extensive surgery to remove all the necrotic tissue on her sores, followed by skin grafts. It was a long, drawn-out process but she survived and did unbelievably well. Her life expectancy improved and she was much happier.

Soon after Heather was discharged Matron sent for me yet again. She wasn't happy and again pointed out that 'clients' came into the unit to allow their families to have a rest, they weren't patients and didn't come in for treatment. By this time I was beginning to get angry. In my opinion every nurse had a professional obligation to look after the people in their care. If clients came in for respite and were taken ill during their stay then I could not and would not close my eyes to any situation where medical intervention was needed. Matron shook her head in despair, and I very rudely told her that she would have my resignation the following day. I was sad to leave behind all those vulnerable people who at times clearly needed more than basic respite care. I felt that I was abandoning them but, in the end, I was clearly rocking the well-established boat, no matter how good my intentions may have been. The one really pleasing thing to come out of this whole episode was that one of the auxiliaries went on to train as a nurse. She had enjoyed being shown how to carry out many of the basic nursing procedures and was very enthusiastic to learn. Over the years I lost track of her, but eventually came across her working as a theatre sister at Blackpool Victoria Hospital.

★   ★   ★

I don't regret 'being difficult', my one aim in life was to look after and care for the sick. If this meant rattling a few cages on the way then so be it. After all, it wasn't a personality competition. It was perhaps another stage in appreciating that, sadly, care may not always be available when and where it is needed. I worked one month's notice and, following a brief interview, started work more or less immediately as a bank nurse in the Casualty Department at Blackpool Victoria Hospital.

On my first day, I was greeted by the nursing officer Mrs Carol Aucott, who seemed genuinely pleased to see me. At interview, she had been perfectly frank and said that although she couldn't give me a permanent post to begin with, working on the bank would provide me with plenty of work (and experience) until such time as a suitable post became available. Another lady named Jean, who was starting her first day as an auxiliary, joined us on a tour of the department. As we were being shown around each of the treatment areas we were introduced to several doctors and nurses, all of them advising us to make a run for it as fast as we could before coming to regret it! I could sense straight away that there was camaraderie and a great team spirit, which immediately made me feel more relaxed and ready to get stuck in.

Blackpool Casualty was a much bigger and busier department than Blackburn. Not only did it have to cater for a much larger catchment area but also for the many thousands of holidaymakers who swelled the population each year. Within the department there was a medical assessment unit, an observation ward, a minor injuries area, a suture room and a major trauma area.

Medical Assessment (which was always staffed by a trained nurse), admitted patients not only from Casualty but also directly from their GPs. Many patients could therefore bypass casualty doctors, thus saving themselves untold hours lying waiting on a hard trolley. Their tests were generally carried out more quickly, too, before being admitted promptly for treatment or sent home. The unit was always extremely busy and saw very poorly patients with many diverse ailments, such as acute asthma, heart attack, pneumonia, overdose, stroke and epilepsy.

The observation ward was used regularly for patients who had sustained head injuries and needed to be kept an eye on for signs of possible concussion. The nurse assigned to the unit would carry out regular standard head injury observations, which consisted of taking their temperature, pulse and blood pressure at least every half hour, as well as checking the patient's eyes to see how they reacted to light (unequal-sized pupils and non-reaction to light can mean a number of things — brain injury being one of them). Although such routine tests often seem trivial, they can literally be lifesavers. The secret lies in correctly interpreting what is observed and reporting on it. Only when these observations are within normal parameters would the patient be reassessed by the doctor before being sent home with written head injury instructions detailing the specific symptoms to watch out for and urging the patient to return if they persisted. The ward also looked after patients who required broken bones to be manipulated into place under anaesthetic. Once the anaesthetic had worn off and the patient was comfortable they could then be discharged. If they were elderly and had no one at home to care for them, then they would be kept in overnight and seen in the fracture clinic the following day.

The minor injuries area backed on to the main waiting room and contained five or six small cubicles, each with an individual door opening directly into the waiting room. Patients brought into this area were mainly walking wounded who didn't require a stretcher, although there were four larger cubicles that contained stretchers, but these were mainly for patients with leg injuries or those who needed to get undressed in order to be examined.

The suture room looked as though it had at some stage been an operating theatre; there was a huge central light fitting and five stretchers permanently in situ, together with five stainless steel instrument trolleys, each of them surrounded by portable screens. In one corner was a shelved cabinet housing everything needed by the doctor and the nurse for suturing wounds, and hand-washing facilities were in an adjoining ante-room. This part of the department saw a seemingly endless stream of lacerations requiring treatment throughout both day and night on just about every shift.

The major trauma area, which was situated opposite the suture room, saw the most serious accidents and injuries, in addition to any other cases deemed to be an emergency requiring urgent attention. Looking back, compared to present-day standards it was extremely basic, but many lives were saved in this room despite the lack of (today's) modern equipment.

Compared to Blackburn the whole Casualty Department was much more extensive and had many more staff. Tour over, Mrs Aucott left me with one of the staff nurses who would be working with me for the first week or so, before going off to place Jean with one of the auxiliaries who had been working there for many years.

Carol Aucott was fantastic and really helped me to become part of the team. As a nursing officer it was quite refreshing to see her with her sleeves rolled up getting stuck in with the other staff. She was the type of senior nurse I had always wanted to be: fair, open-minded, approachable and hard working.

Procedures were very similar to Blackburn, although the doctors sometimes had a slightly different way of treating the patients, but after I had spent the first month or two working all this out, I soon began to feel very much at home. Being a bank nurse meant that once I was settled

I could virtually choose my hours. I preferred nights, for family reasons, so before long I was working two or three nights a week (sometimes more) in and around the department. In some hospitals, trained staff worked in rotation, so that every four weeks or so you did a week of nights, but in Blackpool some worked permanently on nights and therefore had to deal with a totally different clientele.

I settled into my job very quickly and thoroughly enjoyed the challenges, although being 'on the bank' was, in a way, a fairly nomadic experience in that you only occasionally worked with the same staff with any regularity depending who was on shift. Staffing levels on nights usually comprised one sister, two staff nurses, a couple of SENs and an auxiliary. As a staff nurse you were simply left alone and trusted to get on and complete any nursing tasks you were given by the doctor on duty.

I soon found out that the biggest and most frustrating problem at Blackpool Vic was the lack of availability of hospital beds, especially during the main summer holiday period and, at the end of season, during the world famous 'Blackpool Illuminations'. On one (thankfully) rare occasion there were so many patients waiting on trolleys without a single bed available, that the hospital had to close its doors to all admissions other than minor injuries or acute serious emergencies, meaning that all ambulances were diverted to the nearest major hospitals in Preston and Lancaster. Administration staff were contacted in the middle of the night to see if any extra beds could be supplied from storage, while doctors on the wards assessed patients who were near to discharge to see if they could be sent home immediately to free up their bed. Naturally there were complaints from every quarter, but what else could be done? One patient who had been waiting on a trolley for several hours disappeared, leaving a scrawled handwritten note which simply read: 'Gone home to die.' Had it not been so desperate it would have been pretty funny.

Drunks are more often than not the main problem in Casualty at night and could be a damned nuisance at times, but usually there were police officers on hand to help us out. The majority of drunks were easy to handle but during 'Glasgow fortnight' (the traditional two-week annual Glasgow holiday break) some lads could take a little more persuading to leave than others. We often found them snoozing under seats in the waiting room or propped up against the wall in a toilet, too drunk even to stand up. My mop and bucket came in handy on many such occasions. Alcohol was the main factor that contributed to the amount of vomit that was spewed around the waiting areas and toilets.

There was a panic button in the reception area which was rarely needed, although one night we were glad it was there. A dirty, unkempt young man in his twenties, who was complaining that he had sore feet, demanded a bed for the night and, to prove that he was 'suffering', he sat on the floor in the waiting room and threw off his

252

shoes to show everyone his dirty, smelly, blistered feet. Not a pretty sight. His girlfriend had been admitted earlier in the evening with pneumonia so he felt that it was only fair for us to allow him to stay, too. After he had refused a polite request to leave by a member of staff, the doctor was asked to speak to him. The man soon realised that he wasn't going to be allowed to stay and this was the signal for him to lose all control. Trolleys, oxygen cylinders and chairs, even the pictures on the walls, went flying as he punched and kicked his way around the waiting area. He had totally lost the plot and no one could get near him. The panic button was pressed and a number of police officers arrived within minutes. Although it took four burly policemen to subdue him, he did at least get his wish of a bed for the night — in a police cell!

The police were always helpful and quick to respond to problems in Casualty and we had a good rapport with them, so it was heartbreaking when, in 1983, three police officers who we all knew really well were drowned in one tragic incident. A man walking his dog along the promenade in Blackpool threw a ball that bounced over the sea wall and into the water. It was high tide and there were gale-force winds, which created towering waves. The dog jumped in after the ball but immediately got into trouble. The owner followed it in, in a rescue attempt. A passing policeman tried to help but also rapidly found himself in difficulties. Three other officers arrived and attempted to assist both their colleague and the dog owner before the huge waves and strong currents dragged them out to sea. Within seconds they were all fighting for their lives. One of the officers was fortunate when a rope which was thrown to him landed over his head and, despite being almost asphyxiated he was dragged out by the neck. A doctor called to the scene performed an emergency tracheotomy and saved his life. The others were lost without trace and it was several days before all four bodies were recovered. The following evening the local newspaper had a front-page picture of a very distressed policeman carrying the dead dog by its back legs along the beach. Almost inevitably there were numerous complaints about the disrespectful way this officer had treated the 'poor animal', but apparently there was little thought for how he must have been feeling about the loss of his friends and colleagues.

Tourists were regularly being pulled out of the sea: drunks who fancied a midnight swim or wave dodgers (those who, when the sea is at high tide and breaking over the promenade, dare each other to a game of chicken). People could be (and were) dragged into the sea by large waves and sometimes simple heartbreaking accidents happen when least expected. The sea on this stretch of the Lancashire coast can be powerful and deadly, and being a strong swimmer is often not enough. All the officers who had died were excellent swimmers. The emergency services work together so closely that the relationships become personal and these individual officers were popular with both their colleagues and the casualty staff. We were all devastated at their loss.

Because of the close relationship between casualty staff and the police we were all quite protective of each other. But sometimes this was demonstrated with a very strange collective sense of humour. A veteran police constable based at the station closest to the hospital was the self-appointed practical joker, who considered it as his duty to arrange an 'initiation' for each new rookie PC. The favourite trick in his repertoire was to frighten the life out of them by pretending to be a dead body in the hospital mortuary. He arranged for the new PC to be sent to the hospital in the early hours of the morning to check for identification on a body which had been B.I.D. (brought in dead). His plan was for the mortuary assistant to help secrete him in the refrigerated body storage cabinet then suddenly spring to life when least expected. Unknown to him, another officer, no doubt one of his previous victims, intended to turn the tables by getting there first and playing the same trick on him. Thinking that he was just a few minutes ahead of the rookie he lay down on the pull-out stainless steel tray and the mortuary assistant pushed the drawer shut. After about five minutes nothing was happening and the temperature had dropped steeply.

'Bloody hell, it's cold,' he shivered quietly to himself.

'Wait until you've been in here as long as me,' a voice whispered in the inky darkness only inches from his ear.

The older officer sat bolt upright in shock, or

at least he tried to, hitting his head on the heavy steel tray above, splitting his forehead open and giving himself concussion. His injury was sufficiently serious that he was taken to Casualty for treatment. I would have loved to have been a fly on the wall when he eventually got back to the station and was required to explain to the duty inspector why he had been out of radio contact for nearly two hours and had a fresh head injury sporting five stitches.

★ ★ ★

Casualty often had many really busy shifts to contend with, but the time when copycat inner city riots erupted throughout the country and the port of Fleetwood saw fighting on the streets was particularly exciting. Shops and cars were vandalised and police officers were attacked. The department was inundated with minor injuries, ranging from superficial lacerations and contusions to broken noses and limbs. At its height, police were sent into the riot areas to scoop up everyone in the vicinity, seemingly whether they were involved or not, all of whom were bundled into vans and taken to the police station. A neighbour of mine, concerned about the riots, was trying to check his business premises when he was unceremoniously arrested and thrown into a police van. He was furious, especially when his shoes were confiscated before his incarceration in a police cell and, after being released without charge (quite rightly), he found that his expensive leather shoes had been stolen by someone and they had gone home leaving a very tatty-looking pair of trainers behind at the police station.

That same night, one lad arrived in Casualty by car with blood streaming from a head wound and he said that several individuals had attacked him for no reason when he was on his way home from work. His jacket was bloody and torn and he looked genuinely distressed. I had just cleaned him up and prepared the instruments for him to be sutured when several police officers and a dog handler came in, escorting a violent prisoner who also needed stitching. One of the officers glanced at my patient and his face turned purple. He arrested and handcuffed him for assault on a police officer and vandalising a police car. I could hardly believe it and felt sure that there had been a mistake. The officer identified him as one of a group who had attacked and attempted to overturn a police car. The two officers who had been inside were bruised and shaken but not seriously hurt, although the car was damaged beyond repair. He seemed such a decent young man and I had been gullible enough to believe every word he had told me, yet I could see from his expression that he was as guilty as sin. After he had been stitched and taken outside, I found a Stanley knife pushed under his trolley mattress, where he had hidden it in case he was searched. I handed it to the police and he was also subsequently charged with carrying an offensive weapon. I went home exhausted at the end of that shift. It had been non-stop all night but I had really enjoyed the buzz — a bit like Glasgow fortnight all in one go.

One incident on a particular night shift started around 3am. The night had been reasonably quiet until the hospital fire alarm sounded. Casualty staff protocol advised us to stay in the department and await incoming fire casualties, but we were pretty quiet and reasonably well staffed so the sister who was in charge that night asked two of us to go and see what was happening. Adele, an enrolled nurse, and I ran down the main corridor to the assembly point and were directed to one of the wards on the first floor, only to be greeted by smoke and the acrid smell of burning, firemen running around and their hoses snaking across the floor. The officer in charge asked if we were able to carry an old man down the fire escape, so we ran over to his bed where the patient was coughing and looking increasingly concerned.

We initially intended to scoop him up in our arms using a hold known as a 'chair lift' and so we asked him to put his arms around our necks while we tried to lift him. But, as we put our arms under the counterpane to support his legs, we found that he didn't have any! Both legs had been amputated and we had little more than two short stumps to hang on to. I couldn't help myself and began to laugh, and said, 'Bloody hell mate, you don't make it easy for a girl, do you?' Luckily he saw the funny side and also started to laugh. In fact, we laughed so much we nearly dropped him. We were puffing and panting but still laughing when we reached the fire escape.

Then we saw how narrow it was; just about wide enough for one person, and there were three of us. Although it was difficult going down sideways we managed to reach the bottom without mishap, but it was still a big relief to put him into a wheelchair when we reached the ground floor.

The whole ward was evacuated without incident and thankfully no one was hurt, which was the only thing that really mattered, and it is the only time I have been personally involved in such a situation. The fire, which was soon extinguished without major damage, had been started by a male patient sneaking a quick fag in the sluice. He heard someone coming and simply flicked it away without stubbing it out. The burning stub landed inside a large box of papier mâché disposable bedpans, where it smouldered for a while before eventually igniting. The potential catastrophe can only be imagined.

* * *

Blackpool Casualty could be a truly chaotic place, but the doctors and nurses were the hardest-working people I had come across so far in my career. Nothing seemed to faze them and their professionalism was impressive. Working in Casualty taught me a great deal about life, but nothing could prepare me for one incident during my time there. It was around 1980–1, when The Yorkshire Ripper was still at large after having murdered several young women and prostitutes over the previous five years. There was an air of hysteria among women all across the country and when a man rang the hospital switchboard one night saying that he was The Ripper and his next victim would be a nurse, we were all a bit jittery to say the least. I still hadn't learned to drive and after finishing my favourite twilight shift telephoned for a taxi to go home. I always used the same taxi firm and one of the girls who knew that I was nervous said that she would note the registration number, taking particular notice of the driver's face (not really much good to me if I was lying dead in a ditch somewhere). I climbed into the taxi feeling more apprehensive than usual (getting into a vehicle with any stranger in the early hours of the morning always made me a little uneasy), but the driver was elderly and seemed a pleasant sort and we chatted as he drove along. Five minutes into the journey I realised that, even though it was dark, nothing looked familiar and I didn't recognise where we were travelling, yet I had been using these taxis for months and we always went along the same route. We appeared to be going through open countryside and I immediately felt panic welling up inside. My mouth and throat went dry and my heart began pounding.

'Where am I?' I asked. 'I don't usually come this way.'

The driver smiled and told me not to worry as he was taking a short cut to save me some money. His next sentence totally freaked me out, though, as he laughingly announced that he was The Yorkshire Ripper. For several seconds my whole world stopped. I panicked and tried desperately to open the door to get out. It was locked. He laughed out loud until I screamed, 'Let me out!' Tears streamed down my face and I was completely hysterical. He looked at me dumbfounded and immediately began to apologise and tell me that he had only been joking. I was so scared that I wanted to throw up and was literally shaking like a leaf. Yet, once I had calmed down and could see that he had genuinely meant his remark light-heartedly, I cried all the more with relief (while still screaming at him for his stupidity). When we arrived at my home he again apologised unreservedly, but I slammed the taxi door as hard as I could and ran inside. I didn't report him, even though I probably should have done, but he did look genuinely sorry. In fact I think I probably frightened him to death and was sure that he would never dare make such a stupid mistake again. In a way he did me a favour, though, because shortly afterwards I started taking driving lessons.

In the 1970s and 1980s most doctors working in Casualty were senior house officers, a grand title to the uninitiated but most of them had only just completed their first twelve months in the job after qualifying. They relied heavily on the permanent nursing staff, whose experience was often invaluable; although, when it came to making any final decisions, the doctors were totally responsible for their own actions. They had little support and back-up from their own medical body, so it was understandably a difficult and a nerve-wracking time for them.

Every six months all junior doctors changed

wards and departments to obtain experience in other areas of medicine. Nurses dreaded these times, especially in Casualty, and would regularly advise family and friends to avoid the emergency department at all costs in early February and early August if they valued their health. We had to cope with a very diverse range of injuries and illnesses on a day-to-day basis and, in those days, senior doctors rarely based themselves in Casualty, so a new intake of junior doctors provided further complications. To be fair, most young doctors were very capable and enthusiastic and wouldn't hesitate to ask if they were unsure about protocols. However, we occasionally got one who thought it was beneath him/her to ask a nurse for advice, making the inevitable mistakes along the way.

One such young doctor came to work at Blackpool Victoria. This new doctor was swiftly identified as an arrogant upstart and from day one he treated both junior and senior nurses with total and utter contempt. During a lumbar puncture he was handed an incorrect instrument by a young student nurse and he threw it across the room in a petulant rage. He shouted at her in front of the staff and patients, reducing the girl to tears.

Having heard the fracas, I relieved her, winked and told her to take a break, instructing her to leave the instrument on the floor. She fled, still sobbing. Once the procedure had been completed and the patient was comfortable I invited the doctor into the office for a private word, where I advised him calmly but firmly that he should pick up the instrument himself and that if he expected the help and support of the nursing staff he was going about it in totally the wrong way. His response suggested that he felt he was automatically entitled to respect. I maintained eye contact and said quietly, 'Respect is earned and I am afraid you have a long way to go.' I surprised myself; I sounded like Sister White. But I had worked in that very busy emergency department for a number of years by then and had learned how to deal effectively with some really awkward individuals; by comparison he was a pussycat. He did actually pick the instrument up (which amazed me) and tried to curb his tongue, although not very successfully.

He completely alienated many people during his six-month stint, particularly upsetting some of the laboratory staff and even the canteen supervisor. I thought him a spoilt, rude little brat, a snob who considered himself superior both to colleagues and staff. It would have given me great pleasure to administer an extremely large enema to that young man and we all breathed a collective sigh of relief when his six months were completed, although he didn't leave without two pathetically juvenile final gestures.

When the canteen supervisor arrived for work one morning she opened her office door to find a brick wall blocking the entrance. (This part of the hospital was almost deserted at night.) He had 'borrowed' a wheelbarrow plus the materials from a nearby building site and erected the wall, which was his way of showing displeasure with the catering staff. Two workmen were summoned to demolish the bricks and then the cleaners had to clear up the dust and mess, disrupting the kitchens and all the patients' meals, in addition to the cost. Her offence had been to deny him extra (free) sandwiches when he was late for his break.

He had also sent out an official-looking memo to each ward requesting stool specimens from a large number of patients (allegedly because there had been an outbreak of a virulent infection). When the laboratory consultant arrived the following morning, he found dozens of said specimens waiting on his desk, having had the effontery to take the young doctor to task about doing inappropriate tests that were both costly and unnecessary. By this time, the culprit had already departed to pastures new. I heard a rumour later that he had been officially reprimanded for both of these infantile escapades. If the rumour was true, I hope he was reminded of this every time he got above himself.

★   ★   ★

One night, a man was brought in drunk, absolutely filthy and looking very poorly. For reasons which will become obvious, I will never forget Harold. He was persistently wheezing and coughing, totally oblivious to his own body odour and stank of urine. I stood 'downwind' of him when I introduced myself and I could tell that he was really impressed.

'Bugger off!' he said.

I explained that I needed to take his clothes off so that the doctor could examine him and I provisionally promised him a warm drink if he behaved himself. I was rewarded with a wink. He was much more cooperative after that and allowed me to undress his top half, but steadfastly refused to release his grip on the string holding up his trousers. I thought briefly back to the rat episode when I was at Blackburn but persevered, even holding out the promise of new trousers. When he relented I found that they were so crusted with dirt they virtually stood up unaided. His underpants were even worse so, in my wisdom, I left them untouched and moved down to his socks. I began praying quietly as I noticed one sock moving independently! 'Dear God, please help me to cope professionally with whatever I find under this sock.' It was a wriggling mass of fat, juicy maggots that fell out on to the stretcher and I felt myself begin to gag. He had a large ulcer on his leg which was covered in them and I was fascinated to see that the visible part of the ulcer was as clean as a whistle. I covered the area before stepping outside for some fresh air. After two or three deep breaths, I summoned the doctor, an enthusiastic young house officer who was always game for anything.

'Come with me, you have got to see this.'

I introduced him to Harold then pulled back the sheet to reveal his leg ulcer. The doctor's face lit up; he thought that the maggots were heaven-sent, as he was going fishing the following day.

He scurried away for a minute and returned carrying a plastic container with holes in the lid, along with a pair of tweezers. One by one he carefully removed the maggots from the patient's leg and dropped them into the container. When he finished he held it aloft, admiring the contents lovingly. (Apparently he did actually take them and use them the next day). Our 'gentleman of the road' was admitted to hospital with pneumonia and made a full recovery. His chest had improved within a few days, although his legs took time to heal, as they often do. The maggots had done a tremendous job, though, and had cleaned up the dead skin and tissue on the ulcer beautifully, which proved to be a real asset to the healing process. He eventually moved into sheltered housing and was provided with new clothing, meals on wheels and home help. He must have thought that he had died and gone to heaven!

One of my casualty colleagues was Robert (Dr Bob), who was of African origin. He had worked several rotations in Casualty and had been qualified for a number of years but he was unsure which speciality he wanted to work in permanently. We were glad to have him with us as he was highly capable, worked quickly, never panicked and was accustomed to handling drunks and aggressive patients. I enjoyed being on duty with him and felt that the patients were fortunate to have a doctor with so many years of experience to look after them. He was protective of the nurses and inspired confidence in all the staff on duty with him. One night a seventeen-year-old youth, who was much the worse for drink, turned up in

Casualty with blood streaming from a head wound. I took him into the suture room, cleaned him up and, as I was preparing the instruments for suturing, Dr Bob walked in to do the honours. Seeing him, the lad shouted, 'I'm having no n★★★★r near me, so he can f★★k off!'

I went rigid. I had already seen Dr Bob's reaction to racism, as unfortunately such incidents occurred much too often. He went over to the youth on the stretcher and, without saying a word, grasped the lad's collar, lifted him bodily in the air with one hand and 'helped' him through the exit. A police patrol passing the entrance stopped to observe the ejection and gave Dr Bob an approving wave. The lad ran off but returned to reception an hour or so later with his father, himself a large, rough-looking individual, who insisted he wanted to see the doctor who had refused to treat his son. Dr Bob and I were just having a break and heard the conversation, so we both went out to meet them. The lad stood silently as his father aggressively demanded to know why the doctor had refused to stitch his son's head wound. Dr Bob stood straight-backed, arms folded over his chest, looking utterly bored. He took his time to answer, looked directly into the young man's eyes then repeated word for word what the boy had said, adding that there was no way that he would treat anyone who spouted such racist and insulting language.

The father listened in disbelief and with increasing embarrassment. He then turned to his son and asked if it was true. The youth refused to answer but blushed and looked very guilty indeed. Before another word could be spoken the father began punching his son in the face, causing further injuries. I was mortified, begging him to stop before he killed him. After one final slap he shoved the lad forward to apologise. Dr Bob (having now been asked very politely if he would kindly stitch him up) took the son away without a word and sutured all his wounds, both old and new. Afterwards the father shook Dr Bob's hand, apologised once again and was last seen walking down the road shouting and swearing at his son. Dr Bob was absolutely thrilled. Today neither party would be able to get away with such behaviour but it was certainly very, very satisfying at the time.

Dr Bob's considerable experience was invaluable, especially on one occasion when a chap wandered into the minor injuries area sporting a very swollen red eye and obviously in considerable pain. He said that he couldn't remember injuring his eye but that he thought something may have blown into it. Dr Bob came along to see him, using an ophthalmoscope to check the eye thoroughly. I heard him gasp and whisper to himself, 'Bloody hell!' He looked knowingly at the patient and enquired whether he had been abroad recently. Acknowledging that he had, the patient was baffled as to how the doctor could possibly have known. Dr Bob was hopping about in excitement and, without answering the question, called all the other medical staff and nurses together to let them have a look. The poor patient was completely bewildered as his eye was peered at and examined by perhaps ten people. It turned out, the object in his eye was the pupa of an African insect which, at some point, probably while the man was asleep, had laid its eggs in his eye. These eggs had become embedded and, as they developed and grew, had infiltrated his eye, causing him excruciating pain. He was admitted to the eye ward as an emergency. The prompt diagnosis meant his eye was saved, all down to the knowledge of one doctor who spotted a condition rarely encountered in the UK.

★ ★ ★

I thoroughly enjoyed my years at Blackpool beyond all expectation. Casualty was a much bigger and busier department than Blackburn and, although working twilight shifts didn't really help me get to know the staff socially, I found them all to be outstanding professionals. I had been hoping to apply for a sister's post and had already partially completed the application form, but Bill had been promoted again and we had to relocate once more, this time to Sale in Cheshire.

8

Bill could never really understand my reluctance to relocate. For him it was simply a career move and to turn down a promotion when it was offered would have dramatically reduced any future prospects. He worked long hours so it made little difference to him where we lived; he usually came home to a late dinner and relaxed with a newspaper or the television. I enjoy company and missed my friends, who meant the world to me, but with Mark to care for and only working part-time, I accepted that my own career was going to be put on hold. We had already moved for job reasons once before and settled well, so I decided to be positive and look ahead. Only days before Mrs Thatcher had returned to Downing Street with a large majority at the general election, buoyed to a large extent by public reaction to the successful campaign to regain the Falkland Islands only a year earlier, and the country itself seemed in a confident mood with house prices continuing to rise. We were lucky enough to find a really attractive detached house in a much sought-after area and a good school for Mark, who was now ten years old and in his final year at junior school. By this time I had passed my driving test and had my own car so I wouldn't be restricted when job hunting and everything seemed to be going well. Although we soon settled in at home, it took much longer for Mark to settle at school. Most boys of his age had already formed their own groups of friends and he must have felt like an outsider for quite a long time. Eventually, though, he found two or three like-minded fellow pupils and began to relax and smile again. Buying him a Labrador puppy for Christmas also seemed to help a little.

Sisters' posts were relatively few and far between, and part-time vacancies rarely came up. The post I had been considering at Blackpool had been a job share, which would have been ideal for me, but having moved away to a different Health Authority the chances of a similar post coming up were much less likely. So after a couple of months settling in, I began job hunting and applied to Wythenshawe Hospital, Manchester, for a part-time staff nurse post in the Casualty Department. Within a matter of days I had received a letter asking me to go for an interview with the nursing officer, Mr Ian Lee, who asked me a few brief questions about my previous experience before showing me around the very busy unit. I was immediately offered a post and agreed to commence the following week.

On my first shift I was introduced to the unit manager, Sister Julie Barnett, who was tall with meticulously groomed raven black hair. Like in Blackpool, the immediate work would be on the nurses' bank, which at the time was ideal because it meant that I could still take Mark to school each morning and pick him up in the evening. Initially, as in all the other units and wards I had ever worked, Julie scheduled me to work with a permanent member of the unit until I became sufficiently used to the procedures and routines. Valerie, Eileen and Pat were all older senior staff nurses who had worked together on the unit for many years and volunteered to show me the ropes. Each hospital and each individual casualty doctor has their own little idiosyncrasies when it comes to applying special splints and bandages, so I found that I had to constantly remind myself to use the Wythenshawe methods and not the ones I used at Blackpool. As for the casualty doctors, there were just four senior house officers who covered the department twenty-four seven, usually rotating so that there would be only one on duty at night. Unlike the present day, there were no registrars or consultants based within the unit, so literally life-saving decisions had to be made by these young men and women, who usually had little more than a year or two post-graduate experience. It was amazingly difficult for them at times and they did have to rely heavily on the nursing staff.

Wythenshawe Hospital was situated in the middle of a tough, rundown, overspill housing estate, once the largest in western Europe, where patients were often aggressive and demanding. I was soon to become well acquainted with many of the regulars. One particular dysfunctional family was very large and especially difficult. The parents were frequently drunk and abusive, both to each other and to the staff. Their scruffy, unruly children stole anything and everything not screwed down: toys from the waiting room, unattended handbags, bandages, sticking plasters — literally anything — and their language made your hair curl (even the three-year-old had a vocabulary that would make a grown man weep). They were a nightmare of a family. The mother was perpetually in trouble with the police for being drunk and disorderly, stealing or handling stolen property, and she was often brought into Casualty after self-harming (slashing her wrists with a razor blade was a favourite) or taking an overdose. Perhaps best described as belligerent, she was invariably delivered to Casualty by police car or ambulance, usually with bare feet, swearing and fighting fiercely. Her appearance confirmed that soap and water were an alien concept to the daily family routine. One ambulance man commented that they had to wipe their feet when they came out of her house! I often looked at the mother and wondered about her own upbringing. The children were so out of control it didn't take a genius to see how they would almost inevitably turn out. The whole family was a constant concern except, amazingly, for the eldest daughter, who was a reasonably agreeable, normal person, and was often called upon to deal with her younger siblings in preference to their actual mother.

This was one family among many others just like them, usually even more violent and abusive if they couldn't get their own way. The extremely foul language commonly used was quite appalling and at first it was difficult to come to terms with. Sadly, in many instances this was the only language some of these individuals had ever heard spoken or understood, so what chance did the younger ones have? I felt genuinely sorry for the many decent families who had to live in close proximity to these antisocial, feral groups, who thought nothing of picking fights with anyone who simply looked at them the wrong way. Casualty staff were forever having to deal with the aftermath of a good punch-up, drug abuse or the results of drunken domestic violence. Social workers certainly had their job cut out dealing with the children of these out-of-control families.

So with the type of casualty being what it was, one of the first priorities expected of me was to train to suture. Every week the department saw dozens of lacerations requiring stitches. I had never done suturing before as this was always the doctor's territory in the other hospitals where I had worked but, here at Wythenshawe, there were so many to deal with it was deemed sensible to train all the nurses. Of course, it was the doctor's responsibility to examine each wound carefully first to ensure there was no damage to the tendons, ligaments or nerves. Local anaesthetic was then instilled to enable the wound to be thoroughly cleaned before being sutured and dressed. (Nurses were officially only allowed to suture superficial lacerations, as anything deeper was to be left to the doctors.) My training consisted of a senior member of staff, usually Sister or a doctor, working with me and watching my every move. They checked every stitch and then once they felt that I was proficient, I was left to my own devices. I loved every second of it, which is hard to believe since it takes me all my time to sew on a button. But this was different and I took great pride in my work. I would have been perfectly happy working in the suture room full-time.

One day my freshly honed skills were put into dramatic action when four local police officers were brought into Casualty following a road traffic accident involving their patrol car. Although their injuries weren't life threatening, there were several deep lacerations (one officer, in particular, having been almost scalped) and a number of broken bones. The casualty officer quickly prioritised the patients and asked me if I was willing to suture the face of a police officer called Paul, who I knew well. I hesitated at first because, although superficial, the lacerations were on his face and, for cosmetic reasons, it was against protocol for a nurse to suture this area. The doctor saw my reluctance but reassured Paul that I was perfectly capable and would do an excellent job. (I was thrilled to bits that the doctor had such confidence in me, although it was ultimately the patient's own decision.) Paul was perfectly happy to let me have a go, so I took my time and stitched the wound with the utmost care, using the finest-gauge silk available. The doctor checked my work afterwards and said that he genuinely couldn't have done better himself, patted me on the back and carried on to see another patient. Paul returned five days later for me to take his stitches out. The wound looked wonderful, alignment was spot on and I was really happy that there would be hardly any scarring. It made my day when he gave me a hug and a box of chocolates. All the other officers had already been discharged.

One officer we saw regularly in Casualty was Stephen Oake, a tall, gently spoken PC. Always willing to help, he was a genuinely decent human being and family man, who was well respected and liked for his quietly effective way of dealing with the public. In January 2003, during a raid with other officers on a flat in north Manchester, which was believed to be housing Islamic terrorists, he suffered multiple fatal stab wounds while attempting to detain a suspect. There was a national outcry at his death and later his crowded memorial service at Manchester Cathedral was attended by the then Prime Minister, Tony Blair. I felt desperately sorry for his wife and children and have only fond memories of him sorting out aggressive patients for us in Casualty or nipping into the unit in the middle of the night for a quick cup of tea. In January 2009, Stephen was posthumously awarded the Queen's Gallantry Medal for bravery. He was forty years old when he died.

After working on days for several weeks, I was approached by the nursing officer to see if I would be interested in starting on the twilight shift (6pm–2.30am), covering the changeover at the end of the day shift and the busiest part of the night shift. These hours were similar to my shifts at Blackpool Victoria and so I was happy to agree. There were quite a number of very experienced staff working on nights and I was immediately made to feel part of the team. They worked hard, socialised together more than anywhere I had worked previously and many permanent friendships were established that survive to this day. The staff I tended to work with most closely were two of the sisters, Jeanne and Audrey; a couple of the enrolled nurses, Chris and Theresa; and my fellow staff nurse, Wendy. The receptionists Jenny and Edna worked alternate weeks to cover the night shift.

Jeanne and Audrey ran a tight ship and had been in Casualty for many years. Very little came into the department that they hadn't dealt with successfully dozens of times before. Wendy, Chris and Theresa were also very experienced nurses who were trusted and left to get on with the job. Edna was the matriarch of the unit and heaven help any hapless potential patient who messed her about at reception, as they would certainly feel the lash of her tongue. Jenny was more my age but was no slouch when it came to sorting out the drunks and the pests.

Wendy, Jenny and I became close friends over the years and remained in touch long after we all left Wythenshawe. Wendy has a wicked sense of humour, not dissimilar to my own, except when it comes to supporting Manchester United. When she married her fiancé Trevor (another fanatical red supporter), Jenny and I were matrons of honour. I also have Wendy to thank for my nickname within Casualty . . . when I first met the staff on night shift and told her my surname she immediately christened me Timberdick, which stuck with me until the day I left.

The police often brought in drunks who had injured themselves by falling or fighting and one of our regulars, Helen, was a walking disaster area. She was a large, blousy young woman with both a personality disorder and a drink problem, who was commonly overdosing and self-harming by slashing herself. Her arms, chest, breasts and abdomen were a mass of scar tissue, and she had even cut off one of her nipples with a pair of scissors (which certainly makes my eyes water when I think about it). Helen was violent and aggressive at times and could usually be heard bouncing around in the back of the police van halfway up the approach road. Sometimes she would simply wander into reception and announce, 'I've taken an overdose, luv.' And then she would take herself off to the waiting room to catch up on any magazine articles she may have missed since her previous visit. Such cases always had to be treated as an emergency to prevent any tablets she may have taken being absorbed into her system, so Helen always received prompt assessment, which of course was her primary aim.

She loved the attention and didn't care what she had to do to get it. Unfortunately, she wasn't the most attractive girl in Manchester, but would take any opportunity to try and pick up a man, although her chat-up technique needed a little work. I once saw her flashing her ample breasts at some men in the waiting room and shouting, 'Do you want to see my tits?' Whenever she refused to leave Casualty she became aggressive and we had to call the police to throw her out, knowing that she would bite and kick all the way (and she packed a powerful punch). Officers used to groan when they saw who they had come to eject, knowing that she would never go quietly. Helen usually screamed like a banshee when she saw a police uniform and her language was spectacular. Those who knew her well usually asked her politely to leave, despite knowing full well what the inevitable response would be, and then it was all systems go when she kicked off. Two officers grabbed hold of her arms while another removed her shoes, then they ran her backwards to the van (which kept her slightly off balance to prevent her assaulting them) and thrust her inside, the van rocking violently from side to side as she attempted to trash the interior and attack the officers. I can only imagine the scene at the other end of the journey and was glad that I didn't have to go with her and get her out.

On one occasion Helen came in fighting drunk after being arrested for causing an affray in her local pub and her arms had gaping wounds where she had slashed them with a broken bottle.

'Hi Joan,' she said as she was frogmarched in. 'I've cut my f**king arms, luv, will you stitch 'em?' (She had been in so often that she knew all of us by our Christian names.) I went to sort out the instruments while she was busy spitting and attempting to disembowel one of the officers and I eventually stitched her up while kneeling on the floor in the corridor with three policemen holding her down for her own safety. An old lady sitting waiting in a wheelchair declared that she had really enjoyed the whole episode and it was the best night out she'd had in ages! This was despite telling Helen that she was a naughty girl and being unceremoniously told to, 'F★★k off, you old bag.'

We didn't see Helen for several months after that and I wondered if she was in prison or had moved out of the area. It turned out that neither was the case; after becoming pregnant from one of her many liaisons, she was now trying to turn over a new leaf. She eventually had a beautiful baby boy who she brought into Casualty to show to us. The baby was spotlessly clean and we hoped that the child would be her salvation, but sadly this hope was to be in vain. The child didn't thrive as he should have and Helen started making repeated visits to hospital complaining that he was constantly vomiting. Although the baby was admitted several times for tests, doctors could find nothing wrong and began suspecting Munchausen Syndrome by Proxy. This is a condition where an individual, quite often the mother of a pre-school child, deliberately makes the child sick or misleads others into believing that the child is sick by reporting fictitious symptoms. It isn't easy to diagnose because doctors find it difficult to believe that an apparently loving parent can be harming their own child. Such behaviour is meant to attract attention and gives the perpetrator a feeling of importance and power.

In this instance, the child recovered very quickly as soon as he was admitted; until the next time . . . Once the mother's chequered history was taken into account, it became clear what was happening and the baby was taken into care. The child was later adopted by his own grandmother. But Helen was out of control again and some time later she set fire to the block of flats where she lived, was arrested, charged with arson and imprisoned under psychiatric care.

Tony, another regular, was a man in his mid-forties who attended Casualty on a more or less weekly basis. He usually appeared following a blazing argument with his wife, nearly always drunk and complaining of having taken an overdose. He was rarely aggressive but was a true time-waster. We always suspected he was lying but couldn't risk ignoring him. Depending what story he told us, either blood tests were carried out or his stomach was washed out. He must have been masochistic to want these 'wash outs' for fun because they were extremely unpleasant. Eventually even Tony couldn't tolerate them any longer and began to refuse the procedure, opting instead for an emetic medicine called ipecacuanha. The medicine was black and syrupy and was usually given to children in a drink to rid them of whatever unknown substances they may have swallowed. It tastes horrible but empties the stomach by making the patient vomit violently and profusely. Tony opted to have his in a beaker of fruit juice. On one of his frequent visits, Sister and I watched him drink it before we left the room but then continued to observe him through a door which had been left slightly ajar. As he began vomiting he reached into his pocket and took out several pills which he threw into the vomit bowl, but some missed and several multicoloured tablets bounced across the tiled floor. Sister walked in, picked them up and said, 'You missed with these.' Tony looked crestfallen, aware that he had been rumbled and was discharged, yet again, after being given the 'all clear'.

On another occasion he somehow managed to climb on to the hospital roof, threatening to jump off. I was going to my car at the end of my shift, about 2.30am, when I heard a hissing noise. Looking around and seeing no one, I opened my car door pretty sharpish. Just as I was about to get in, I heard a voice from above say, 'Excuse me, luv, will you please tell someone I'm going to jump?' Looking up I saw Tony sitting on the roof with his legs dangling over the edge like Humpty Dumpty. I went straight back inside to inform the casualty staff and several of them dashed outside to talk to him. It was a bitterly cold night and he was shivering violently but he bucked up immediately because he was once again the centre of attention. The police were summoned to 'negotiate' with him and he enjoyed that even more. (There was a very strong rumour going around that some officers who knew Tony well had a little wager among themselves as to whether he would actually jump.) Fortunately, it was a fairly quiet night in Casualty, which allowed the staff time to keep him occupied until, as expected, he eventually came down without any further excitement. After being given a warm drink and a psychiatric assessment he was sent home . . . yet again.

There were so many incidents involving this man, all intensely frustrating because he was wasting time, and taking doctors and nurses away from more pressing matters. Personally, I had a bit of a soft spot for him and didn't mind too much because at least he was never violent and was always grateful for the attention he received. This inadequate human being was just a rather pathetic individual trying to drag himself through life by the seat of his pants. He reminded me of Oliver, the patient in Blackburn, who had finally gone too far and died.

A major problem within the hospital was the local children, who used the public areas as an extended playground. I sometimes found it hard to stay cool when I saw them racing on roller-skates down the main corridors. A favourite trick was to go into the toilet block and put plugs in all the washbasins, turn on the taps and run off leaving the water to overflow. On one such occasion I caught two little blighters disappearing through a window leaving water cascading on to the floor. I grabbed the ankle of one and dragged him back, chastising him for his actions and telling him that I was going to phone his parents. I presented him with a mop and bucket and waited for them to arrive. When they did eventually turn up they thought it was highly amusing and couldn't understand what the problem was, dismissing their child's behaviour as harmless mischief. They even had the nerve to say that they would report me for making their little treasure mop the floor. 'Bring it on!' was my reply. I found their parenting skills exasperating. My own parents would not only have made me clean up but would have disciplined me again when I got home. It was repugnant for me to see such disrespect and apathy.

Wythenshawe Hospital is only a mile or so away from Manchester International Airport and it is one of the designated receiving centres for casualties during any major incident there. To prepare hospitals, especially Casualty and the other emergency services, for any major incident, there are well-rehearsed procedures and scenarios to assess response and critical care timescales. Casualty has a direct emergency telephone to the airport by which any situation involving technical problems or a potential crash situation is relayed directly to the hospital to put all departments on standby to receive casualties. One fairly regular alert was to advise that an aircraft coming in to land didn't have an indicator light confirming the landing gear was down and locked. Needless to say this normally turned out to be a false alarm and was shortly followed by a second call to confirm that all was well. The hospital received many such calls and, while they couldn't be ignored, the staff tended not to get too excited by them. However, early on the morning of 22 August 1985, the emergency telephone rang and this time it was no false alarm.

Sister answered the call and the night shift

nurses, who were about to go home, waited to see if there was a real problem.

'There is a fire on board an aircraft. We are on standby,' said Sister. Night staff groaned and put their bags down, waiting for the expected all clear. The emergency telephone rang again and Sister went pale: 'It's all systems go.'

A major incident had been confirmed and staff moved swiftly to put all rehearsed procedures into practice for the arrival of multiple casualties. Minutes later an airport bus carrying walking wounded arrived, some with burns, others suffering from smoke inhalation and injuries sustained from sliding down the aircraft escape chutes. They were quickly followed by numerous ambulances carrying more serious cases and a second bus, which should have gone to nearby Withington Hospital but had lost its way and also ended up at Wythenshawe. Many of the casualties were in shock and were frantically looking for loved ones. They all arrived so quickly that no one at the hospital had time to contact the off-duty casualty staff, as was protocol. I only heard about it when I walked into my local butcher's shop. He looked surprised to see me and said he thought I would be in Casualty with the aircraft fire victims, having heard a newsflash on his radio reporting the accident. I telephoned the hospital switchboard to confirm the news and twenty minutes later arrived at the hospital to find everything organised, calm and well under control. The staff had done an amazing job. The emergency plans had gone reasonably well, although there were one or two hiccups (not surprising considering the speed of the arrival of the casualties) and so many staff had voluntarily turned in for duty that, quite frankly, by the time I arrived I was surplus to requirements. There were one hundred and thirty seven passengers and crew on board BA flight KT28M. Fifty-five died, forty-eight of them from smoke inhalation.

Bill and I were due to fly on holiday the following day in the same type of aircraft. I hated flying at the best of times but after this incident was even more reluctant to do so and didn't sleep a wink that night. As I climbed the steps on to the flight, two of the flight attendants noticed my panic-stricken face and said, 'How do you think we feel? Some of our friends were on board yesterday.' I felt quite ashamed of myself, but it certainly didn't make me feel any better. It was an enjoyable holiday marred only by the thought of the flight home.

When I got back, my friend Wendy, who had remained on duty that fateful morning, told me about some of the cases she had dealt with and wept at the memories. A man with serious burns had seen his wife and daughter die before his eyes and Wendy couldn't banish from her mind the image that he described. Case-hardened medical staff, ambulance crews and police officers were completely devastated and for several weeks continued to talk about their harrowing experiences. Counselling was rarely offered in those days, not even for the passengers or crew.

Thankfully there were many amusing stories

from Casualty as well as sad ones, like the drunk who was brought in rather the worse for wear. He had a deep laceration to his head after falling over in the road, a fairly regular occurrence for this particular individual. Sister Jeanne Mansfield was in charge that night and went to stitch him up after the doctor had finished his examination. Jeanne knew the man well from his previous appearances and greeted him with her usual smile, asking him what had happened. He gazed at her glassy-eyed and replied, 'Do you know love, you look just like Elizabeth Taylor?' Jeanne preened herself and smiled. 'All tits 'n' arse and over fifty,' he continued. It would be something of an understatement to say that she looked a little disappointed, although she managed to laugh it off and come over to share the moment with us. We chuckled about it for days.

During a well-earned tea break late one night, two uniformed police officers dropped in with a bag containing several boxes of cakes, which were soon polished off by the nurses and porters. We had tidied away the empty boxes and were all relaxing having another cuppa before resuming work when two detectives walked in. They nodded to the other officers and said, 'Sorry to disturb your break, but if you come across anyone trying to sell boxes of cakes will you please let us know. The local Mr Kipling bakery was broken into earlier this evening.'

The two officers virtually choked and, seeing their reaction, we had the sense to say nothing. They had apparently bought the cakes in all innocence from the thieves in the hospital foyer. I don't think they ever made CID!

A pensioner was rushed into Wythenshawe Casualty after suffering a massive coronary and going into cardiac arrest. Despite all efforts by the medical team he was eventually declared dead. As is relatively common in such cases, the patient vomited during the resuscitation process and, boy, did he throw up! What must have originally been a very large portion of baked beans splashed on to the floor and began to spread rapidly underfoot until everyone in the room was slipping and sliding around in a frantic performance worthy of Torvill and Dean. There were beans everywhere!

Sometime later, a police officer turned up with the man's wife to carry out a formal identification of the body. Wendy, who was one of the staff nurses who had tried to resuscitate him, escorted her to the mortuary. A little later, she returned to Casualty alone, doubled up with laughter; not exactly the compassionate, professional reaction one would have expected in the circumstances. On the way to the mortuary, the wife was clearly very upset but volunteered to the PC that her husband had been very fit for his age and was particularly bright and cheerful when he left home earlier that day. The old lady went over to the body, lying on a trolley in a small annexe room located within the mortuary and, as she bent over her husband, gently weeping and stroking his face, looked over to Wendy and said, 'I just can't believe it, he was full of beans when he went out this morning.'

Casualty nurses are a breed apart and it can take years for them to evolve into the unshockable, hard-working and broad-shouldered individuals they invariably become; usually possessing a wicked sense of humour with the ability not to blush easily. The immediacy of often life-saving actions that are necessary in stressful and life-threatening situations requires a highly professional no-nonsense approach to nursing care, which it would be totally incorrect to criticise as hardened or lacking in sympathy. I have regularly seen 'old hands' have a quiet weep after a tragic death, particularly of a child . . . especially me!

Sexual abuse of a child is exceptionally distressing, as well, and I clearly remember one case involving a gorgeous little six-year-old girl who was brought in by a police officer after being missing for several hours. The child's father came into Casualty with her, saying that she had disappeared while playing outside the family home and after a short, fruitless search he and his wife had contacted the police. According to him, before the police arrived he was the one who found her, frightened and hiding under some bushes nearby. The father said that his daughter had told him a man had done naughty things to her, that she was terrified because the man had allegedly threatened her and said she wasn't to tell anyone or he would come back and hurt her. However, we could sense that something didn't quite add up. The father appeared upset and agitated, yet never once went over to his daughter to hug or console her. He didn't even speak to her and the body language between

289

the two was worrying. His eyes bored into hers as if issuing a warning and the child was obviously scared to death of him. Where was her mother? Why was mum not with her daughter instead of dad? It simply didn't make sense and something was very wrong. If the father went anywhere near the child she visibly cringed and turned away. The police sexual offence examiner (SOE) had been requested to attend in order to see if any evidence could be collected from the child and/or her clothing. I spoke to this doctor privately and shared my concerns, asking her to observe the interaction with the father. When we entered the room, dad was speaking threateningly close to the child's face, but went silent the moment he saw us. The SOE asked him politely to leave during the examination, which legally he wasn't obliged to do. Clearly reluctant to go, he left the room warning his daughter to remember what he had told her. The SOE questioned the girl slowly and carefully, so as not to upset her further, but she was clearly too afraid to open up to us while she was in the hospital. Slowly and meticulously the girl was examined from head to toe, with the doctor writing copious notes on specific police reports, also measuring and photographing any scratches or bruises that were found, some of which were swabbed to see if there was any DNA present. Social services were brought in and the girl was taken temporarily into care. The SOE said that normal procedure was to let the girl have a rest that night and she would be seen the next day by a specially trained female officer who would try to get her confidence in order for her to open up. It was awful to see such fear on this innocent little girl's face, and the memory of her dilemma stayed with me for a very long time. At least she was now in safe hands.

Several teenagers had been out drinking heavily one night and four of them were involved in a road traffic accident. One person had volunteered to drive the others home. Some people in the group had sensibly declined his offer because of his drunken condition and decided to walk home but three of them, who were equally drunk, were more than happy to get in the car. I attended to the only survivor, Carl, who was cold, shivering and reeked of alcohol. He had been one of the passengers in the vehicle, which crashed into a river when the driver lost control. The driver and the two other passengers drowned, trapped in the car. The young survivor was still in shock and lay quietly, obviously unsure what had happened. A staff nurse went into his cubicle and asked him for the name of the driver, explaining that she needed to contact his parents. It took some time for him to clear his head but he eventually provided a name and address, still not aware that all his friends had died.

Police officers were urgently trying to identify each body in order to visit the home addresses to inform the next of kin. A policeman attended the house of the young man who had been named as the driver and was actually in the process of telling his parents that their son had died when the young man himself walked in, large as life. Apparently he had sensibly decided not to drive, knowing that he was unfit, but had allowed his equally inebriated friend to borrow the car. The survivor of the crash was so drunk he couldn't remember who was driving and had given the name of the car owner. I can scarcely imagine how the parents felt. The officer was furious at being placed in such an embarrassing situation and stormed back to Casualty to take issue with the nurse who had given him the incorrect details. He quickly calmed down when he realised what had happened, but it was still an extremely stressful situation for everyone concerned.

My own son was a teenager by then and a newly qualified driver, so it really brought it home to me yet again how alcohol can diminish a person's ability to act rationally. My son always felt I was tough on him, which I probably was, but such incidents had a powerful impact on my thinking and my desire to protect him from a similar fate.

I recall one boy who was brought into Casualty one night after being found deeply unconscious, face down in a gutter. We called his parents after a search of his pockets revealed his name and phone number. They were very distressed when they discovered he was completely unconscious and had been doubly incontinent. I advised them that he would need to stay in overnight and asked their permission to leave him in his own filth, hoping that when he woke up it might make him realise just how stupid his behaviour had been. They gave permission willingly but went home in tears. I made sure that I was with him when he came round the following morning and didn't need to say very much to him. His mum arrived with some clean clothes and he literally ran into the bathroom to clean himself up. If I was being too tough then so be it, hopefully the lesson would make him think twice before getting into such a condition again, and it might even possibly save his life.

I also always drummed into my son the dangers of drugs, but I know for a fact that he still tried cannabis because the evidence was in his bedroom after he went back to university! I wrote an extremely forthright letter to him expressing my disgust and didn't hear from him for several weeks (although he did eventually ring to make a grovelling apology). Similarly, a police officer on the drug squad was dismayed to receive a call from the hospital to say that his son had been admitted under the influence of drugs. The man had always emphasised the dangers and tragic results of drug taking to his son, in the hope that it would discourage the young man from experimenting and his intense disappointment brought him to tears. We only hoped that the youngster's embarrassment at being found out, together with his father's obvious distress, would be a turning point in his life.

One teenager high on drugs was brought in by police for the doctor to check him out. He was very aggressive, fighting the police officers, headbutting and punching the wall in temper and frustration. The plaster was literally falling off the wall in lumps yet he didn't appear to feel any pain. After a night in the cells the police brought him back to show him the damage he had caused. He had no recollection whatever of the events and was horrified to see the results of his actions. Shock tactics can sometimes work. He was very apologetic and appeared to be a thoroughly decent person under normal circumstances; again, we could only hope that he would behave more responsibly in the future.

I will never forget the night a young man was rushed in from a club, choking on a burger. After buying the food he had been laughing and joking with his friends and then he went on to the dance floor while still eating. Suddenly he fell to the floor clutching his throat and coughing. His friends thought that he was larking about and laughed at his antics as he gradually turned blue. It was several minutes before one of his friends realised that he was genuinely in trouble. Someone tried desperately to clear his airway until the ambulance arrived and he was rushed into Casualty in cardiac arrest, where we tried in vain to save him. On that occasion several doctors and nurses who had children of a similar age were visibly upset and I still get angry with my family if I see any of them messing about when they have food in their mouths. To see someone choke to death is particularly distressing and the images stay with you for the rest of your life.

A very drunken middle-aged lady was brought in by a police officer who had found her staggering around in the street, wearing only a nightdress and slippers. She was considerably overweight, unsteady on her feet and had somehow injured her arm, which was lacerated and bleeding heavily. She had obviously been heading in the direction of the hospital, although the fact that it was the middle of winter and a freezing cold gale was blowing around her nether regions hadn't made very much impression on her and she remained totally oblivious to her surroundings. The officer had initially stopped to help her, but she had been so aggressive and virtually incapable of standing unaided that he arrested her for being drunk and disorderly. On arrival at Casualty, she was sitting in the police car shouting and swearing at the officer and being totally uncooperative. It took staff several attempts to persuade her to get out of the car and come inside, although eventually she shuffled in reluctantly and gave her details to the receptionist. After being provided with a blanket, the lady was shown into the waiting room, where she very quickly decided that she needed to go to the toilet. The policeman, a rather inexperienced rookie officer who had stayed with his prisoner to make sure she behaved, escorted her down the corridor and steered her into the patients' toilets, stating that he would wait for her outside. He waited patiently for several minutes before beginning to wonder if she was OK.

I had walked past him a number of times, as I wheeled patients backwards and forwards, and wondered why he was hovering outside the ladies loo. It was only when he asked me to check on his 'detainee' that I understood. He was relatively new to the job and had never been to

Wythenshawe Casualty before so wasn't really familiar with the tricks that some drunks got up to. I jokingly said that she had probably climbed out through the window and run off, at which his face turned ashen. I went inside and indeed found the toilets empty and the window wide open, allowing in a blast of arctic air. We looked out to see if we could spot her and there she was, legging it down the road as fast as her uncoordinated inebriated legs would allow, still wearing only her nightdress, egged on by a number of drunks on the passing late-night bus. It was like a scene from a *Carry On* film as the officer and I set off in pursuit. As we caught up with her, she cursed and kicked out at us and the lads on the bus cheered even louder. It took me some time to convince her that we were actually trying to help her before she stopped struggling and agreed to return peacefully. My starched cap had fallen off during the pursuit and by now was probably being blown around some back-street on the Wythenshawe estate, while the policeman was seriously out of breath. We escorted our reluctant drunk back to Casualty and I cleaned up the wounds on her arm, which turned out to be quite superficial, bandaged her up, gave her a warm drink and the last I saw of her she was being 'persuaded' to get back into the police car.

Bert, an elderly man in his seventies, had been knocked off his bicycle and brought into Casualty with leg injuries. I went to help undress him but he clung on to his clothes for dear life and wouldn't let go for love, nor money. No amount of cajoling would see Bert parted from his trousers so we waited for the doctor, hoping that he would be able to persuade him to get undressed so that he could be examined. He still refused to cooperate, but then lowered his head and asked to speak to the doctor in private, looking extremely embarrassed. Eventually he admitted to the doctor that (obviously never expecting to have an accident) underneath his own clothing he was wearing ladies' underwear. His wife wasn't aware of his fetish and he begged us not to tell her. The doctor reassured him that everything would be treated with the utmost confidentiality but insisted that we be allowed to remove his trousers. We were very professional about it and acted as though this was an everyday occurrence, although we had a good laugh about it later (particularly when his wife turned up) and wondered what she would have thought if his little secret was ever uncovered. She certainly didn't find out from us.

Working on reception desk in Wythenshawe Casualty must rank as one of the most difficult jobs on the planet, and it would be unfair not to mention the two brave souls who undertook the task in rotation. They were obliged to endure verbal abuse many times every day (usually patients complaining about the length of time they had been kept waiting) and they had to deal with any number of drunks and drug addicts throughout their shift. A triage system (whereby a trained member of staff initially assesses and prioritises any injuries) wasn't introduced until the early 1990s, so Edna or Jenny, depending which of them was on duty, had to make the nearly impossible decision as to whether a patient needed urgent attention or not by themselves. Hardly the safest practice, but it was the only one we had. Using their considerable experience they got it right most of the time, but it wasn't fair on either the patient or the receptionist. Their job was difficult but they did it with professionalism and patience. Meanwhile, emergency ambulance crews are definitely the unsung heroes of the NHS. Being on the 'front line' often brings them into direct contact with extreme life and death situations on a regular basis. They can be confronted with the most horrendous sights and it beggars belief how they are able to remain sufficiently composed to carry out their duties. Nowadays they have access to counselling as a matter of course but this wasn't available in the 1970s and 1980s, and they were expected just to get on with it.

Two ambulance men arrived outside Casualty with a deceased patient whose death needed to be certified. At that time there were no paramedics crewing the ambulances (who would now be able to confirm a death themselves) and the only person allowed to certify a body was a doctor. Perhaps anticipating something out of the ordinary, the doctor on duty asked me to accompany him, which was a little unusual because they normally just went themselves. As we approached the rear of the ambulance a trickle of blood ran down the step at the rear of the vehicle, forming a small puddle on the surface of the car park. Before opening the doors, the ambulance driver checked around to make sure that no one was about; for good reason, as the scene that faced us has never left me.

Laid out on a thick plastic sheet on the floor were the severed arms and legs of an elderly female. The mutilated torso was alongside and a disembodied head was wedged on one of the stretchers to prevent it rolling around. There was blood everywhere and the two ambulance men were clearly in shock. The doctor looked from one ambulance man to the other and concurred with their diagnosis! The old lady had lost her husband recently and, after leaving a note for her family, had apparently quite deliberately dressed herself from head to toe in black and then, in the early hours of a dark winter's night, stepped out on to an unlit motorway into the path of two large HGVs. She was struck by both vehicles. Despite being completely traumatised, the drivers had been able to summon the emergency services.

The point I want to make is not to shock or horrify but to highlight the awful situations faced by all emergency response personnel, together with many associated services and staff. This one incident unwittingly involved so many different people: the two HGV drivers, obviously both the ambulance and police staff, but also many others including the casualty staff, the pathologist and undertakers, before even considering the lady's family. Working in Casualty, which many would consider to be at the 'sharp end' of patient care, I was always very aware that by the time the patient arrived at our door they had often already been stabilised and no doubt looked much less bloodied and mangled than they had done when the emergency response crews initially arrived on scene.

I got to know several of the ambulance crew fairly well because they were in and out of Casualty all the time. Derek always appeared particularly overexuberant and invariably came bursting through the doors with the patient, looking red-faced and anxious. He cared so much about his patients that each and every individual was of the highest priority for him. On one occasion I was asked to accompany a doctor transferring two young boys by ambulance to another hospital for emergency specialist care, both having suffered serious brain injuries in a road traffic accident. Derek was driving the ambulance and the doctor and I were a little tense knowing how intensely determined he would be to get there as fast as humanly possible.

To speed up the journey we had four police motorcycle outriders, two up front and two bringing up the rear, alternating positions at junctions and traffic lights to ensure our unimpeded progress. Even with their 'blues and twos' they didn't go fast enough for Derek, who was constantly urging them on to ever greater speeds. At one set of traffic lights we were going straight through with two police motorcyclists blocking the intersections at either side, when a little old granny slowly and meticulously overtook the queuing traffic and, in fact, drove around one of the motorcycles, totally oblivious to the emergency vehicles approaching at full tilt with accompanying lights and sirens.

Seconds before the impending impact, Derek saw her and shouted, 'Oh f**k, brace yourselves, she's going to hit us!' I held on to one child while the doctor held the other and only remember being thrown around amid the screeching of brakes, and seeing the shocked expression on the face of the policeman whose bike had been circumnavigated by the elderly car driver. The old lady's face screwed up in terror as she realised her mistake and she slammed on the brakes, only managing to stop inches from the side of the ambulance. There was neither time nor opportunity to remonstrate with her and we completed the rest of the journey relatively uneventfully, listening to a full and varied range of expletives from Derek. The children were admitted immediately and their condition was touch and go for several weeks, although thankfully both survived. Derek always remained hyperactive but sadly died only recently from a massive heart attack, despite his own colleagues trying unsuccessfully to revive him. We all appreciated him because he cared so much and his death was a great loss to the service.

By contrast, Graham was so laid-back he was almost horizontal. He would come in with a patient and introduce me to them as his wife, put his arm around me and kiss my cheek. It was quite funny at first then began to annoy me. I thought he was rather unprofessional and one incident in particular convinced me that I was right. Graham and his partner had to negotiate the steep slope on a riverbank to reach a collapsed patient and decided not to use a stretcher, preferring to take an ambulance chair instead. They checked the patient, secured him to the chair and struggled up the wet slippery slope, laughing hysterically when they dropped him twice and he rolled back down the embankment. On arrival in Casualty they were still chuckling like schoolboys, but the patient was absolutely furious and made an official complaint.

It was some time later when I saw a completely different side to his character, though. There was a big retirement party for Edna our receptionist and Graham and his colleagues were there along with many of the doctors, nurses, police and admin staff. The party was in full swing when one guest collapsed while eating food from the buffet. Within seconds Graham was administering mouth-to-mouth while someone else was carrying out cardiac massage. The patient (as is common with cardiac arrests) vomited, but Graham simply grabbed a napkin, cleared the vomit and carried on, pausing only occasionally to rinse out his own mouth with water. Sadly the man (who was the husband of a staff member) died, but from that day on I considered Graham to be a saint for trying so hard to save him. Few people would have continued their efforts in those circumstances.

★　★　★

Working in a busy casualty unit is not for the faint-hearted, although to be honest I thoroughly enjoyed the buzz. You learn to deal with the blood, the drunks, the abuse and the foul language, but during the six years I had been working there the sheer number of patients and the levels of aggression had increased dramatically. The public started to use the hospital instead of their GP surgery and every evening when the night shift came on duty we were typically confronted by a crowded waiting room full of trivial ailments and minor injuries which the local chemist could have sorted out. There was only ever one casualty officer on duty at night and many genuine injuries often had to wait for long periods before being seen. Needless to say, the time-wasters were the ones who complained longest and loudest. One man waited almost six hours before seeing the doctor, who immediately showed him the door — what was his life-threatening, emergency medical condition? He wanted a tattoo removed from his arm.

What the patients in the waiting room couldn't see were the rear doors where the serious trauma cases and other emergencies were brought in by ambulance, which obviously had to be given immediate priority. When some abusive drunk with toothache started mouthing off about having to wait, I was seriously tempted to drag him through to the trauma area to see the car crash victim oozing blood and guts all over the floor, or the heart attack patient having seven bells knocked out of him by a doctor or nurse jumping up and down on his chest, trying to resuscitate him. I dare say I would have been sacked had I done so, or at least got the hospital sued by the unsuspecting patient for mental cruelty or breaching his human rights in some way but it was still a tempting thought.

It is perfectly possible to get used to drunks being sick down the front of your uniform, or urinating down your leg when you help them up from a chair, but despite the ever-present threat of violence I very rarely feared for my own safety. Wythenshawe was a huge hospital and security officers were thin on the ground, so if the police were busy it followed that we would be busy, too. Every idiot in the area seemed to end up in Casualty some nights and the hospital porters had to step in to save our hides many times. They were a good group of men but it wasn't their job to fight for us physically. After years of working in Casualty I eventually reached the stage when there were some nights I dreaded going on duty, wondering just how aggressive some patients might be.

On one such night, a twenty-three-year-old female who had been beaten up by her partner was brought in by ambulance. The partner followed the ambulance to the hospital and demanded to be allowed in with her. Unfortunately for him a member of staff had recognised the girl as her own sister and waded into the man both verbally and physically. We had great difficulty separating the two but managed to persuade the staff member to go into the suture room with her sister to help patch her up. I was asked to stand outside the room and keep him away. (This is how you get utilised if you are five feet ten in height!) I stood there like a bouncer, denying him access as he ranted and raved inches from my face, demanding that I get out of his way. I held my position, trying to calm him. Sister went to ring for the police and when she came back she nodded silently to tell me that they were on the way, as the man became increasingly agitated. Knowing that he wasn't averse to hitting a woman I felt sick to my stomach.

Two porters who had heard the fracas came into view over his shoulder but, before they could get near him, he took a flying kick at the door behind me and almost took it off its hinges. I was frozen to the spot but thankfully the police arrived at that moment and after a violent struggle the moron was arrested and taken away. My heart was beating ten to the dozen and my legs felt like jelly. I remember thinking, 'What the hell am I doing here?' What no one had bothered to tell me was that his girlfriend was no longer in the building. She had been taken out by a rear door to a place of safety and I could have been splattered against the wall for nothing. I never thought that I would tire of Casualty but I began to consider a future career outside the department. Although, I couldn't imagine what else I would do.

A second incident finally compelled me to make up my mind. Sunday night had been non-stop with strokes, overdoses, coronaries, road traffic accidents — whatever else you care to name, it came in that night! Although it was 2.30am, the time for me to finish my shift, I just couldn't abandon the staff because the place was heaving with dozens of patients still waiting for attention. As usual, I carried on until about 5am when, although it was still fairly busy, Jeanne insisted I went home.

The following night I was on duty again but this time with a different sister. It was just a fairly steady, normal night in contrast to the previous evening and by 2.20am only one patient, who had already been treated, was with a nurse waiting for a porter to take her up to the ward. I checked around the unit, tidied everywhere and went to the staff room. Everyone was sitting down, taking advantage of the break, drinking tea and chatting to two of the regular police officers. It was now 2.25am. I assured Sister that the place was empty and clean and asked if I could go home (bearing in mind that I had worked so much unpaid overtime the previous night). She looked pointedly at her watch and shook her head, reminding me that my shift didn't finish for another five minutes. My face must have spoken volumes because the police officers immediately stood up and made a hasty exit. I couldn't believe what she had just said and at first I thought she must be joking. I said to her, 'Do you know that I didn't get off duty until 5am yesterday? No one told me to leave at 2.30am then because we were all too busy. I stayed willingly, as usual, even though I knew I wouldn't get paid.' She completely ignored me and refused to let me go. I gave her a withering

306

look and, I'm afraid, told her to go to hell! I had had enough and walked out, still a whole two minutes before my shift ended. She followed me down the corridor telling me to calm down but I slammed out through the doors and climbed into my car. Grabbing hold of the car door she tried to stop me, saying that I would have an accident if I drove when I was so upset. I was furious. I had worked really hard in the department for years, routinely and willingly staying beyond normal hours to help; in fact, that was the norm and if this was the thanks I got then so be it. I couldn't sleep when I got to bed, I was fizzing!

At 6am, even though I had only been in bed a short time, this Sister had the nerve to ring and check if I was OK. I told her that she wouldn't be seeing me again because I refused to work with her and the next day tendered my resignation together with a full explanation of what had happened. The nursing officer was very sympathetic and asked me not to leave, but fully understood why I needed to go. While acknowledging that Sister was working by the book, her attitude was totally ridiculous in the circumstances. Over the years I had worked many days, if not weeks, of unpaid overtime. Most of the sisters would try and send me home early if Casualty was quiet (which was rare), but not her. In all other respects she was a decent, hardworking individual, but for some reason she refused to bend the rules an inch. Off duty she was good company, but as soon as she put on that navy blue dress there was a complete metamorphosis. This incident was the straw that broke the camel's back; perhaps I had been subconsciously looking for a reason to leave.

In general everyone was very supportive, even the porters brought a present to my home, saying they really appreciated how I always treated them as part of the team. The girls took me for a night out and bought me a lovely leaving gift which I still treasure today. They were truly a brilliant team and I knew that I would miss them. I kept in touch with Wendy and Jenny for many years and we never failed to raise a laugh when we remembered some incident or other that happened during our time together at Wythenshawe.

Within a matter of days a doctor who worked with me in Casualty (but who was now a general practitioner) offered to interview me for a job in her surgery. So it turned out that I hardly had time to breathe before taking up my first sister's post. I was to be the first practice nurse this GP surgery had ever employed; the post being a relatively new NHS initiative, which was rapidly gaining momentum throughout the UK. I would have my own list of patients for routine treatments and I would be virtually my own boss, thus freeing up time for the GPs. It would be a new and interesting challenge, and certainly less violent.

9

In 1989 practice nursing was still very much in its infancy. For a number of years some GP surgeries had already been employing clinic nurses within health centre settings and they had proved very successful in freeing up doctors to see more patients, saving both time and money. These clinic nurses assisted the doctors during their daily surgeries by changing dressings, giving routine injections or chaperoning female patients; the list varied depending on the requirements of the particular practice. It was a service that was well respected by both patients and GPs alike; after all, nurses were far more used to giving injections and changing dressings than the doctors were, and the patients seemed to like having a nurse around to talk to or seek advice from.

It was proposed that practice nurses should now take on a much wider role than the clinic nurse, and that they would need extra training. In the meantime, talks between the health authorities, GPs and the Secretary of State for Health were very much ongoing, but it would be many months yet before anyone knew just what precise format this additional work was going to take. The onus was intended to be on health promotion for all patients, which included teaching patients how to lead healthier lifestyles (thus avoiding the onset of chronic diseases such as diabetes, asthma and coronary heart disease, saving many thousands of pounds on hospital admissions each year).

The surgery I was to work in was a practice led by Dr Williams. Generally regarded as 'a character', his language was often colourful and, possessing a fiery temper, he definitely liked getting his own way. Notoriously always late for his surgeries, he regularly rushed in at the last minute looking like he had slept in his clothes and was certainly not a person to cross. There were two separate surgeries within half a mile of each other that collectively looked after 12,000 patients and all the doctors divided their time equally between them both.

Initially the doctors were uncertain how to define my job description, never having previously employed a nurse in this capacity, so to begin with I was to hold open surgeries, which simply meant that no appointment was necessary. The doctors were confident that my casualty experience would be an asset, but at interview it had been specified and agreed that I would need to undergo a number of training courses in order to multitask in the various defined medical areas. These included well women issues (which would include smear taking, teaching self-breast examination, pill checks and advising on minor gynaecological problems), as well as coronary heart disease screening, blood pressure screening, obesity and weight reduction advice, child immunisation, family planning services and asthma advice. But for the time being, until these courses were completed, I would be expected to carry out general routine care, plus seeing and treating minor injuries and minor ailments, advising on health issues including obesity, and basically seeing anyone the GPs referred to me — building up to the rest as and when I completed the many required courses.

My first day was obviously going to be quiet as none of the patients even knew that this new service was available, so I felt that the most important thing to do was to introduce myself to the reception staff and explain to them what type of patients I could see. The receptionists were all very welcoming and seemed grateful that there was now someone who could take the pressure off them when they couldn't fit a patient in with a doctor. In the back of reception was the surgery secretary Doreen, who carried out administration duties and typing. A small, dark-haired, pretty lady of about thirty, she offered her services and promised to type anything I needed or answer any queries I may have concerning the practice. She was so friendly that I felt like I had known her for years.

She stood up and offered to show me the treatment room, which was a large, light and airy room that I had been told was mine to do with as I chose. A large wooden desk and chair were in the centre of the far wall, with a second chair for the patient. An examination couch with a curtain surrounding it was on the left of the room with a dressing trolley next to it, and a whole range of wall and floor units for dressings and medical equipment were on the right, next

311

to a white sink unit. I thought the facilities were good, although untidy and not particularly clean (which was unacceptable), but once I put my stamp on it I hoped it would be perfect.

I spent that first day cleaning out cupboards in the treatment room and discarding any out-of-date materials. I even unearthed a bundle of rusty acupuncture needles, which went straight into the sharps bin for disposal. Only moments later (Sod's Law?), in walked Dr Williams. He was certainly not impressed by the fact that I had thrown precious needles away and advised me in no uncertain terms that I could collect my P45 on Friday. When I pointed out that they were rusty and tentatively mentioned the word 'tetanus' to him (tetanus can commonly be contracted from rusty objects), he simply wagged a finger at me and walked out.

A few minutes later, in the same cupboard, I found a specimen jar that had furry black spores creeping up the inside of the container. Its contents were unrecognisable until I spotted a patient's name on the label along with the word 'urine'. The date on the jar was at least six months earlier and I have to say that I wasn't particularly impressed with my discovery. Rather than risk being unreasonably chastised a second time for throwing out 'valuable' items, I donned a pair of surgical gloves and took it along to the senior partner.

'Yours, I believe,' I said, smiling sweetly as I presented it to him. His answer was unrepeatable and, remembering some real characters I had encountered among the casualty doctors, I knew

312

this one was going to be a big challenge.

Unbelievably, in the middle of my cleaning frenzy I actually got my first patient of the week. A stooped elderly gentleman with a walking stick came to reception asking if there was a district nurse available to have a look at his leg. The district nurses came into the surgery once or twice a week to carry out minor treatments such as post-operative suture removal and things like ear syringing. The practice had never had a clinic nurse, so the district nurses provided this service on top of their already very busy schedules. I could hear the receptionist ask him if he would like to see the new practice nurse and seconds later he was knocking on my door (after she had helpfully brought me his records). I welcomed him and introduced myself but, before I could ask him to sit down, he was rolling his trouser leg up to reveal a rather grubby-looking dressing on the side of his leg. He had missed his appointment with the district nurse the previous week and needed to have his dressing changed.

'Reyt lass,' he said. 'Let's see if tha can sort this aht. Ah've bin comin' to see t' nurses 'ere for o'er twelve month. I 'ad summat removed from mi leg and it just won't 'eal. I've tried everythin' but it still won't 'eal. Let's see 'ow good tha are.'

I asked him to sit on my couch so that I could get a better view and, after removing his dirty dressing, I switched on a small inspection lamp so that I could see what I was doing. The wound was only tiny but still gaping open. Cleaning it gently I prised the opening even wider to see if I could see deeper inside and, lo and behold, I

313

could just barely see a tiny blue speck deep down in the fatty tissues. After asking him to keep very still, I went into the cupboards and searched for a magnifying glass and a sterile needle. I told the patient (who said to call him George) that I thought he had a piece of stitch left inside his wound and that if he could tolerate the discomfort I would try and remove it.

He was absolutely elated and said, 'Ah've bin tellin' yon male nurse for months that I thowt there was summat in it. Go on lass; see if tha can get it aht.'

Holding my breath, I took the needle, eased the tip under the 'foreign body' and seconds later a sliver of blue silk stitch emerged, which was surprisingly nearly half an inch long. The feeling was quite rewarding as I brandished the offending item in the air for him to see. He beamed from ear to ear as he grabbed my hand and shook it enthusiastically. A small dressing was needed and I asked him to see me in two days to check how it was doing. He was virtually dancing as he left the room and I documented my actions in his records. I have to admit to feeling rather pleased with myself, although it would be interesting to see what the outcome would be when he came back. He returned as requested two days later and I held my breath as I took the old dressing off. It looked wonderful and the wound had already healed over. He was thrilled to bits and made a point of shaking my hand once again before leaving. I had made a friend for life.

★ ★ ★

My clientele gradually increased and before long I began to see my own list of regulars. There was one lady whose predicament I will simply never be able to forget. This particular lady was almost eighty years old; she shuffled slowly into the treatment room and sat down wearily on the chair. She looked worn out and in considerable discomfort. When I asked how she was, she put her head down and began to weep. She had not been registered with the practice very long, as she had just moved house to be nearer to her daughter, but was feeling very run down and exhausted. Worse still, she said that she was in pain 'down below'. After persuading her to let me see what the problem was, I pulled the curtain around the bed, donned some surgical gloves and helped her on to the couch. As she reluctantly parted her thighs I could see a massive protrusion dangling between her legs and I can honestly say I have never seen anything like it in my career, either before or since. At first I hadn't a clue what it was (I had seen a prolapse before but this was the size of a large grapefruit) and it was inflamed and ulcerated where her inner thighs had rubbed against it. She was extremely embarrassed and kept covering it with her hand until she eventually allowed me a closer look.

I asked how long she had had the lump and why she had never seen a doctor? Her reply sickened and annoyed me. She had been to see her GP on innumerable occasions over nearly

315

twenty years because it often became ulcerated and infected, yet the only thing he said to her was that many ladies suffer from this as they get older and not to worry about it. He said that if it didn't cause her pain then it was better left alone. I was absolutely horrified and asked her if she minded if I brought a doctor in to have a look. I squeezed and held her hand a minute to reassure her before leaving. I asked Dr Williams to look at her because, unfortunately, there was no lady doctor on duty that day and, although he was in the middle of his own surgery, once I described the mess this lady was in he followed me back to the treatment room.

When he first saw the huge bulge he was almost speechless; he swore in disgust under his breath and went on to reassure the old lady that something could be done to sort it out, although it would mean an operation. He said that her problem was a prolapsed womb which had dropped down completely and, because it had been hanging there for so long, not receiving a sufficient blood supply, it was now wasting away. He was very kind and told her that he would refer her urgently to a gynaecologist who would more than likely have to carry out a hysterectomy. He patted her arm as he left the room shaking his head, while I tried to explain to her what the operation would involve. She left soon afterwards, but not before I gave her a big hug and told her not to worry.

Unlike Casualty, the good thing about general practice is that you usually get to follow a patient's progress and see the outcome of any treatment. This sweet old lady was admitted to hospital shortly afterwards and went through her surgery without a hitch. I saw her some months later shopping in town and she looked marvellous. She said she had never felt so well in years and thanked me for helping her.

The district nurses eventually all came in to see me and introduce themselves and, in general, were friendly and glad to be able to get on with their own patients. They instructed me how to carry out ear syringing (which I had never done previously) and advised me on the correct treatment for leg ulcers and other common wounds, which I would probably not have come across in Casualty. There was a lot to learn but I was ready for anything.

As soon as possible I enrolled on the practice nurse course and I met several other nurses there who, like me, were also new to the role. It was interesting to hear how doctors in other practices treated their staff, along with the completely different expectations of the various surgeries. Some of the nurses complained that they were not allowed breaks, others had few holidays. One or two didn't like the poor facilities they had been provided with and I soon began to consider myself extremely lucky to be working where I was. The course itself lasted some three months and, although worthwhile, was pretty basic. We were given the usual compulsory discourse by general practitioners and nurses who were already doing the job, plus lectures covering everything from leg ulcers to taking smears and administering child vaccinations. There were many new areas of nursing that I needed to learn and I realised that these could not be done overnight. However, the course flew by and I had made new friends who vowed to keep in touch. I had not realised that at the end of the course there was an examination to provide a valid nursing certificate to all the candidates who passed but, at this stage in my career, examinations were synonymous with the job and no longer scared the wits out of me. I was pleased and relieved to pass the course exam with flying colours.

Within a matter of weeks I started my family planning course, which also took three months to complete. The theory was studied at the Nurse Training School in Manchester, while the practical sessions were held at Palatine Road Clinic, Manchester, which was classified a family planning clinic school of excellence. I was also able to work a few hours at the surgery at the same time, where I put what I was being taught to good practice, albeit under supervision of the doctors until I had been assessed as competent. I thoroughly enjoyed the course, which I found well organised with excellent tutors. I learned so much about family planning, sexually transmitted diseases, breast checks and smears that I was buzzing with enthusiasm to put even more of my new-found knowledge into practice on my own patients.

Again the course culminated in an examination, but this time there was also a project to complete. I thought the theory paper was hell but I managed to pass without any problem. The fairly unusual subject of my chosen project was 'sexual problems and the handicapped', for which my paper was awarded 93% (I couldn't quite believe it) and was assessed second in the group. As a result of this, I was asked to give a lecture about my project subject to a number of subsequent groups attending the course. What amazed me even further was that I was actually paid for doing this! Some of the equipment I used to illustrate my lectures created a certain amount of interest among the course members.

This further training allowed me to see a much more varied clientele within the practice, as I was now able to do smears and breast checks, give family planning advice and carry out contraceptive pill and HRT checks. My confidence and abilities continued to grow, helped by brilliant support from the doctors and staff at the surgery, and I was soon seeing patients for all types of diverse problems and loving every minute of it.

★ ★ ★

After I had been working at the practice for over a year, patients began complaining that they could never get in to see me because my appointments were always fully booked. I was asked if I would work full time but, even though Mark would soon be going off to university and I would have more spare time, it wasn't really what I wanted to do. I offered to increase my hours temporarily to see if this eased the pressure.

In late 1991 the doctors had also decided that

they would opt to become a fundholding practice, essentially meaning that they were allocated a budget from which they could purchase selected healthcare services within the NHS for their patients. To receive this funding they would have to introduce a number of specialist clinics that were intended to educate patients about healthcare issues and promote healthier lifestyles, thus reducing hospitalisation. It meant a lot of hard work and added pressure to put the systems into place. Computer terminals were introduced for all the staff throughout both surgeries and all patient records had to be checked manually before the information was put on to the system. Everybody was on edge and cranky, especially the senior partner Dr Williams, who was becoming a nightmare to work for. He was not known for his patience at the best of times but this added work made him very difficult to approach. He was moody and permanently short-tempered with everyone, including his fellow doctors. He would often shout at staff (and sometimes even the patients) and this made them scared of approaching him for advice. Some of the receptionists were extremely wary of him and tried to give him a wide berth. They didn't know how to handle his ever-changing moods, and this sometimes caused problems that could have easily been avoided. There was only one receptionist, Cheryl, who really knew how to handle him. She had known him socially for several years and possessed a similar sense of humour, but she was no pushover and refused to accept his moods without putting up a fight.

Few people really understood the senior partner. He was a very clever but complex man and he was not only a general practitioner but also taught post-graduate students, practised hypnotherapy and acupuncture, and had a deep interest in alternative medicine. I always felt that he was simply bored by his job. Once, when I asked him why he had become a doctor, his typically sarcastic reply was that he stood in the wrong queue at school and had really wanted to be a vet. The majority of the patients he saw presented with trivial ailments that could have been dealt with by any pharmacist and this frustrated him to the point where he was often flippant and/or rude. Patients were increasingly beginning to complain about his attitude; indeed, this caused some of them positively to refuse to see him. The receptionists were at the end of their tether and felt unable to consult or confront him on even routine matters. They tried to avoid him by going to one of the other partners with their many queries, until eventually even the other doctors became totally alienated by his attitude and refused to deal with his problems. Something had to be done.

The commencement of fundholding gave rise to an opportunity which I hoped would help to solve the problems without causing too much unpleasantness. The fashionable word in GP practice at the time was 'audit', which to my mind was a fancy name for a survey. The basic objective was to improve standards by highlighting potential problems, collecting accurate data pertaining to that problem, then offering constructive criticism and viable alternatives. Knowing how unsettled everyone had become I decided to do an audit of all the staff and patient complaints that I received personally and then I planned to present my findings to management. Little did I know what I was letting myself in for.

During the following four weeks I had received over twenty unsolicited complaints regarding the senior partner, a number of which were serious. I remember sitting at home wondering what on earth I was going to do. As a professional I knew that I couldn't ignore my audit results but I decided to contact my union, The Royal College of Nursing, first for advice. They recommended that I speak with the other partners because they felt that it should really be handled by them (at the time we didn't have a practice manager). I was asked to contact them again if I needed support.

I consulted two of the partners the following day, showed them my audit figures and asked for advice. Amazingly, rather than agreeing to approach Dr Williams themselves, they offered me more bullets to fire (which I declined to accept) and wished me luck. They couldn't have made it any clearer: I was on my own. What a bunch of wimps! I set about detailing each complaint, naming the patients and, with their permission, giving dates and times of the alleged incidents. I couldn't back down now. The strange thing was that I felt somewhat protective towards Dr Williams and certainly didn't want to get him into trouble. So, heart in mouth, after morning surgery one day I tentatively knocked on his door and walked in. I could actually hear my own heartbeat pounding in my ears and I felt as though I was choking. He smiled and seemed to be in one of his better moods, not that I expected it would last.

'Now, what can I do for you Joany?'

I took a deep breath and asked if I could make an appointment with him to discuss the results of a recent audit that I had carried out. His eyes lit up because he was pleased that I had undertaken the exercise on my own initiative.

'What's the audit about?' he asked. I advised him that it was about patient and staff complaints. He at first found this highly amusing, until I told him that most of the complaints were about him. His expression changed and he looked quite perturbed. He quietly asked me to go through it with him straight away. After a brief hesitation I asked to be allowed to have another representative with me to witness the conversation as I didn't want to create any conflict or risk any misunderstandings. I could see that I had worried him even further and he almost pleaded with me to give him the audit feedback. I agreed, as I knew that if the situation was reversed I, too, wouldn't be able to relax until I knew the worst.

It was one of the most difficult tasks I have ever had to carry out. We went into a quieter room so that we wouldn't be disturbed and I went through each individual complaint in detail. Throughout the meeting he didn't speak a word and, for once, he listened intently. After what felt like a lifetime, although it was in fact only an hour, I finished what I had to say and sat back waiting for the flak. He looked completely stunned and it took a couple of minutes before he responded. He stood up, shook my hand and said, 'Thanks for that. You may just have saved my career.' He left the surgery shortly afterwards to do his home visits, looking totally preoccupied, sitting in his car for several minutes before moving off. Surprisingly I felt truly sorry for him, but it had to be done, otherwise he could have ended up in big trouble and I certainly didn't want that.

The other doctors, who had been waiting in the wings to see if I survived, came rushing in to see how things had gone. I felt numb, yet relieved by his response. Everyone expected a difficult afternoon but it never happened. Although Dr Williams was subdued and deep in thought when he returned to the surgery, he made no further comment and the matter was never mentioned again. I know that he tried hard to modify his behaviour with both staff and patients and I genuinely admired his efforts, apparently accepting the audit findings in full and without question. One problem that he did admit had shocked him was that people misunderstood his sense of humour, which was often seen by others as flippant and inappropriate. They couldn't see that, underneath it all, he really cared. I am certainly not saying that this episode turned him into a saint, because believe me it didn't, but it had at least given him food for thought.

★   ★   ★

Knowing the pressures that doctors and staff were under during the transition into fundholding, the Primary Care Trust offered practical assistance by sending a member of their team to help with the transition. Before being allowed to become fundholding, a practice had to put in place monitoring and budgetary control systems, with achievement of specific government and NHS targets being one of the main criteria, but it was a laborious and boring task. Before too long a new post of practice manager was created to help with the day-to-day administration. New IT systems were brought in and the massive task of transferring all 12,000 patient records on to the computer was commenced. In anticipation of the increased workload, and because I had declined their offer to work full time, an advert was placed in the local newspapers for a second practice nurse. Several of the proposed new clinics were also instituted, including: new patient medicals; diabetic clinics; asthma clinics; baby vaccination clinics; holiday travel vaccination clinics; hypertension and coronary heart-screening clinics; minor operations clinics; and well woman clinics, which were more comprehensive than my previous clinics.

Rita, who was working as an occupational health nurse and already knew Dr Williams, applied for and was employed in the full-time post. We were expected to carry on with our general nursing duties as well as setting up and running the new clinics. There still weren't enough hours in the day and soon after Rita's arrival a third nurse, Denise, was subsequently employed. The job rapidly became unrecognisable from that which I first started only two years earlier.

The actual transition to fundholding status was extremely time-consuming and stressful for all concerned. Computer templates needed to be set up to ensure that all the various clinics followed their own specific protocols — standardising the gathering and recording of information and treatments, etc. — all of which basically boiled down to performance measurement. My previous computer experience was non-existent and initially I found it difficult to come to terms with these new systems but after a few weeks of trial and error I eventually managed to see a glimmer of light at the end of the tunnel, and before long I was tapping out the keys like a (two-fingered) professional. Doreen's assistance was invaluable to me during this period and without her help I would have been lost. I like to believe that we became quite good friends during my time there. Her husband was a patient at the practice who I saw fairly frequently. He was a real comedian. Everything was funny to him and he usually spent his appointment time telling jokes while I was trying to teach him about low-saturated-fat diets and he didn't take a bit of notice.

I will never forget turning forty. Doreen had obviously told him about my birthday and he had purposely arranged an appointment with me about a week later. As he came into the surgery he couldn't stop grinning. I checked his blood pressure and started to ask how he was coping with his new diet. He laughed out loud and said, 'Low-fat diet? Do *you* practise what you preach?'

'Of course I do.' I said, 'Why?' Reaching down to the floor he picked up a plastic bag from under his seat and handed me the parcel inside.

'Happy fortieth birthday Joan,' he grinned.

When I cast my eyes over the contents I roared with laughter. There was an oversized T-shirt printed with MY photograph, showing me lovingly trying to cram the biggest cream cake you have ever seen into my mouth. Several staff members had attended my birthday party where Doreen had been the official photographer. I hate being photographed, so when it was my turn, I had grabbed my neighbour's huge portion of chocolate gateau and posed with it in front of my mouth. This was the photo which her husband had had printed on the shirt. I kept that shirt for many years and regularly wore it for a laugh until it fell to bits. Strangely enough, I have continued to see the pair of them nearly every week during the intervening twenty years; they are both extras on ITV's *Coronation Street* and are usually propping up the bar in the Rovers Return.

★　★　★

My friend Wendy had by now left Wythenshawe and was in charge of occupational health for a large local authority. One day she was asked by a colleague who worked in the occupational health unit at the BBC studios in Manchester whether she knew anyone who could tell a funny medical story. BBC2 were planning a medical theme night called 'Docs on the Box' and were going to be rerunning selected episodes of classic old soap programmes such as *M*A*S*H, Dr Finlay, Dr Kildare* and *Emergency-Ward 10.* Not having commercial breaks on the Beeb, they were looking for a link between the programmes and someone had come up with the bright idea of using real doctors and nurses to tell amusing true stories. My name came up in conversation and, after a telephone interview with the producer, arrangements were made for Wendy and me to travel to London. Train tickets arrived courtesy of the BBC and we were picked up at the station by car and whisked off to Battersea Studios. The place itself was a dump but everyone was friendly and supportive and we really enjoyed ourselves. There were six doctors/nurses and we each took our turn in the recording studio, seated in front of the camera and microphones surrounded by medical paraphernalia. I recorded three stories from which two were selected for the programme. The tramp and the maggots won hands down and Wendy's number one was her story about the deceased cardiac arrest patient covered in baked beans.

It was a hoot and, after a late lunch (which was nothing more than a few curly butties, crisps and biscuits), we were put in a car and driven back to the station. When the recordings were shown on television two months later the telephone never stopped ringing with friends and relatives laughingly asking for my autograph. Fame at last! I even had a write-up in the *Mail on Sunday.* A big headline by the TV critic announced 'Docs on the Box' followed by (and I quote):

If only I hadn't been eating mushroom risotto. But then, how could we have known? It was 8.35pm, not an unreasonable time for a TV supper, when a chirpy nurse from Manchester started telling the story of a tramp who had been brought into Casualty. She approached the tramp gingerly, not least because his sock appeared to be moving by itself. Underneath, and please feel free to skip the rest of the paragraph, was a spectacular leg ulcer on which several maggots were dancing the hokey cokey. Apparently, a resourceful doctor removed them with tweezers and put them aside for his fishing trip the following day. That was the bit that put me right off the BBC2's medical theme night 'Docs on the Box', not to mention my mushroom risotto.

The story of the tramp and the maggots — say it quickly enough and it sounds almost wholesome, like an Aesop's fable — was the ikkiest of the real-life medical adventures recounted during 'Docs on the Box'.

I thus experienced my few minutes in the spotlight. Pity I didn't get a fee, but what a fantastic experience. Many of my patients and the staff at the practice had seen me and I was famous for weeks. A patient commented to one

329

of the doctors how much younger I looked on the television. Damn cheek.

★   ★   ★

Before working at a GP surgery I had never experienced dealing with a person who was a transsexual. Generally considering themselves to have been born into a body of the wrong sex, many of these individuals seek gender reassignment surgery in order to enjoy a lifestyle they feel has been denied to them by nature. Before they can be considered for surgery they must receive intensive psychological counselling and live and dress as a member of the opposite sex for two years. Michael was a small, rather shapeless man in his forties. Usually dressed in a skirt and blouse he looked like Dick Emery's comic drag character, but not quite as attractive. Denis, his friend, was seventeen stone and six-feet-three. Plastered with thick makeup, false eyelashes and lipstick, he normally wore a dress.

Both attended the practice regularly for hormone treatment and health checks in advance of their scheduled surgery. I was on duty one morning and wandered through the waiting room where they were both sitting patiently, trying to ignore the stares of the other patients, when in came a young mother with a little boy of about four. The child's eyes immediately fixed on Denis and, fascinated, his mouth started to form the words of what mum knew would be an awkward question. Clamping her hand over his mouth she tried to distract his attention, but to no avail.

'Mam, why's that fella got a frock on?' All other conversations stilled instantly, as mum dragged the protesting child away to sit with her at the other side of the room, apologising to Denis as she went.

Although Michael and Denis were no doubt used to such embarrassing incidents by then, and it was after all their own choice, I felt that it took an awful lot of guts for them to be there. I suppose that to be able to deal with it success- fully demonstrated how badly they wanted to have the procedure.

★ ★ ★

The most significant lesson I learned as a practice nurse was the importance of document- ing all treatments and information arising during a patient consultation. Some two years after I had left the GP practice, I received a letter from a firm of solicitors acting on behalf of the partners. A patient was alleging negligence at the practice, complaining that she had been suffering from chronic urinary problems that had been inappropriately treated, resulting in the loss of a kidney. She had only ever been seen by me and one of the partners so I was asked to submit an account of my consultations with her after, of course, refreshing my memory from her notes. I had seen her twice, first for a new registration medical and second some months later for a general health check. On both occasions I had checked her urine and it was normal. She had been asked the standard questions: have you had any hospitalisation or treatments for any serious medical problems? Have you any ongoing problems at present? She had replied no to each question.

The doctor had also fully documented each consultation and there was definitely nothing to indicate the patient had complained of kidney problems. The legal case was thrown out. Although we were confident of the outcome it was a wake-up call to all the other practice nurses and doctors.

★ ★ ★

In August 1995 everything was put on hold when my mum became seriously ill. The doctors were very kind and insisted I take time off to care for her. They were terrifically supportive throughout that period for which I will always be very grateful. Mum had often been ill and spent a lot of time in and out of hospital. She rarely complained, shrugging off her illnesses, but sometimes confided that her greatest fear would be to lose her mental faculties. Sadly, she became more and more forgetful and one day broke her own heart after she had unexpectedly found herself incapable of signing her name for a postal delivery. She said that she had felt so utterly foolish, although thankfully the postman had been very understanding. I tried to reassure her that everyone had memory lapses from time to time and she wasn't to worry, but we became increasingly aware that she wasn't herself. Mum had always been meticulously clean and tidy but it was now difficult to watch her eat, as an increasing loss of coordination caused her to spill her food and drink and her clothes were permanently food-stained. Then, to make matters even worse, a muscle-wasting illness affected her legs, necessitating callipers to walk, and a stairlift had to be fitted in the house to enable her to get to the bathroom.

Mum's memory deteriorated before she lost her speech. She was unable to recognise me or my sister Pat and she referred to Dad as 'that young man'. Poor Dad wasn't too healthy himself and had great difficulty accepting that Mum was suffering from a form of dementia. Totally illogically he said that he thought Mum was pretending, although of course we knew this wasn't the case. Pat and I were sitting chatting to her one afternoon in the dining room when Dad walked through to the kitchen. Mum smiled at him and nodded her head. After he had gone she leaned forward conspiratorially and whispered, 'That young man got into bed with me last night.'

Pat and I choked with laughter and asked her what she had done. She smiled and said proudly, 'I put two pillows under the duvet and kept them between us. I'm having no hanky-panky in this house.'

We chatted on about our children, with Pat talking about her grandchildren and the mischief they got up to. Mum looked sad then and, out of the blue, sighed and said, 'I wish I'd had children.'

Pat and I looked at each other and tried to tell her that we were her daughters. She looked absolutely flabbergasted and in a loud exasperated voice shouted, 'Well, nobody told me.' We laughed again and hugged her, but it was quietly killing us to see her like this.

A very worrying incident occurred one day when Dad and Mum were together in the house and Mum decided to go for a walk. Dad was watching television (he was as deaf as a post anyway so couldn't hear her) when she went out of the back door and crossed a busy main road. She managed to walk up a very steep hill towards where her sister lived a few hundred yards away. Surprisingly she found the correct house and knocked on the door. Her sister Norah was startled when she opened the door to find Mum standing there looking lost and anxious.

'How have you managed to get here on your own Agnes?' she said.

Although there was a flicker of recognition when Mum saw Norah, she simply looked at her vacantly and smiled. Norah took her inside the house and telephoned my sister, angry that Dad had allowed her to come out unaccompanied. He hadn't even noticed that she had gone, so an unfortunate argument ensued, ending with Norah and Dad not speaking to each other. That incident was really the beginning of the end as Mum became increasingly disorientated.

A few days later, when Dad was out of earshot, Mum needed the toilet and somehow managed to use the stairlift to get upstairs to the bathroom. Coming down again was a major problem because she couldn't remember what this contraption was that blocked the stairs. She couldn't get past it or shout for Dad (who wouldn't have heard her anyway) so she tried to climb over it wearing her callipers and fell all the way down the stairs. It was obvious from her screams that the fall had caused serious injuries; Dad was panic-stricken and rang my sister for help. She called an ambulance and Mum was taken to hospital. The casualty doctor wanted to admit her; not least because she was taking anticoagulants following heart surgery and would, therefore, need observing for internal bleeding. But Mum and Dad had other ideas; they had both had enough of hospitals over the years. Mum spent half of her life going in and out of one hospital or another for a variety of serious operations and, although she was always grateful and appreciative for the care she received, now she had simply had enough. She was tired and weary and just wanted to go home. In Casualty she had apparently been hysterical and the slightest movement had caused her to scream and push the doctors away, so they hadn't been able to assess her properly. They suspected internal bleeding but, amazingly, because of her aggression, had missed a very obvious fractured femur.

Although they wanted to admit her, Dad told them that I was a nursing sister and would look after Mum. The doctors had tried desperately to persuade him to leave her in the hospital; at least overnight so that they could assess her properly once they had her pain controlled, but he refused and signed a form for Discharge Against Advice. At first I was livid that I hadn't even been informed of her discharge and, by the time I had received a telephone call from Pat and rushed to Mum's house in Blackburn, the ambulance crew had just arrived and were trying their best to carry her inside. She was screaming for England and hitting out at everyone who came within smacking distance. The crew couldn't believe that she had been sent home in such a dreadful condition and, even though Dad (as her guardian) had signed her discharge, I felt angry that she had been allowed home without any of the medical staff even checking with me whether I could cope with her care. They didn't have a clue who I was or what experience I may or may not have had. However, Dad was officially her next of kin and legally there was little else the hospital could do because this was what Mum and Dad wanted.

Pat and her husband Michael had managed to bring a bed downstairs, so while the ambulance crew were putting her to bed I called the family GP to see if he would come and assess her for pain relief. She was grey and clammy and looked gravely ill. I realised that Mum was dying and, after discussing it with Bill, I decided to stay with her and Dad for as long as I was needed. Unfortunately her own GP was on sick leave, so an on-call locum (who had never even met Mum and had no idea about her medical history) turned up a couple of hours later. He prescribed mild analgesics but seemed oblivious to the seriousness of her overall condition. He even suggested that I get her up and sit her in a chair as soon as possible to prevent chest problems. That would have been fair enough normally, but with the leg injury and her mental state it was impossible. I pointed out the injury to her leg, which was shortened and rotated (all the signs of a fractured femur) and told him about her being on anticoagulant medication — extensive bruising was already visible and rapidly spreading across her buttocks, legs and back. He looked unimpressed and left after promising to call back the next day.

When he arrived the following morning he immediately asked why she wasn't up in a chair as he had suggested, ignoring the fact that she was, by this time, only semi-conscious, sweaty and had navy blue bruises covering much of her body. I couldn't believe his lack of understanding and his inability to see the plight that she was in. I told him that there was no way that she would be able to sit in a chair as she was in too much pain from her leg, but I did suggest that he was welcome to try to get her out of bed himself. He roughly took hold of her arm and tried to sit her up, yet even though she was barely conscious she groaned in pain and hit out at him. The poor soul was totally unaware of what she was doing but was obviously in considerable discomfort. He soon gave up and promised to send the district nurses to help with her care, but again suggested that I get her up. I could have slapped him.

Mum deteriorated rapidly over the next few days as the bruising spread inch by inch over her entire body. In all my years of nursing I had never seen anything like it, nor had the district nurses. Around the sixth day her own GP, Dr Joshi, came to see her. He was still officially on sick leave following an eye operation but had called into the surgery for whatever reason and had been told about Mum, of whom he was quite fond. He was dumbfounded when he saw her and looked at her leg in dismay, even suggesting that I consider legal action against the hospital for allowing her to come home in such a condition, regardless of what Dad had instructed. My only wish at the time was that she shouldn't suffer, so Dr Joshi (realising, too, that she had little time left) arranged for her to have a cocktail of drugs to alleviate the intense pain. I knew that Mum would have wanted to remain at home surrounded by her family and I was reasonably confident that I could cope, provided I had some back-up from the district nurses, although it is very different nursing someone you love to nursing a stranger. There is so much more emotion involved that it is difficult, if not impossible, to stay impartial.

I hadn't slept a wink for eight days and was completely exhausted. There was a knock at the door and when I went to answer it, I couldn't believe my eyes. Bernadette, my friend from QPH who had been battling serious illness herself for the last couple of years, was standing on Mum's doorstep offering help. Wheezing, emaciated and fighting for breath in the terminal stages of breast cancer, I was humbled to see her and will never forget her turning up like that.

After she had a cup of tea and a chat, I urged her to go home. I remember going out for some fresh air while Dad watched over Mum a bit later and tears flowed down my cheeks as I prayed with all my heart that both Bernie and Mum would soon be at peace.

One of the district nurses offered to arrange a night sitter so that I could at least get one night in bed. I was really grateful for this help because I hadn't been able to relax for a minute with Mum being so restless, particularly during the night, when I was also worried that she might fall out of bed (not having cot sides in situ). A Marie Curie nurse attended that night and I can't begin to describe what a difference it made. Her presence relieved me of so much pressure, allowing me to have several hours' rest, if not actual sleep. Although these nurses normally attend terminal cancer patients, they also occasionally help with the dying, regardless of cause.

Even though I hadn't slept, I felt revitalised the next day because the rest gave me the strength to carry on. By this time bruising now covered Mum's entire body except for her face. Even her neck and ears were dark blue, yet her face showed no sign of bruising whatsoever. It was uncanny. I gave her a bed bath and encountered no resistance; the drugs had relieved her pain to the point of euphoria (for which I thanked God). I cleaned and moistened her mouth and massaged her elbows, knees and heels to prevent bedsores. She hadn't recognised me for several months but now stirred gently, opened her eyes, smiled and whispered, 'Hello Joan, what are you doing here?' Before I could reply she closed her eyes and fell deeply asleep. Those were the last words she ever spoke to me and I felt so privileged to have been there for her. She died peacefully some hours later surrounded by our family in the comfort of her own bed.

★ ★ ★

Returning to work after that was difficult. Patients and staff were all very kind and sympathetic but during that first week, with everyone giving me their sympathy, I seemed to spend a great deal of time crying in the toilet. Eventually one of the doctors, Dr Regan, talked to me privately. He had just lost his young niece to bacterial meningitis and was distraught. We both found it easier to talk about our loss because we were each experiencing many of the same feelings. After a while, I felt able to begin to talk openly about my loss to the other members of staff who were really supportive, and they helped me start to readjust. I deliberately kept busy and threw myself back into the daily routine.

It was only eight months later and Dad, who hadn't really got over Mum's death and, during her illness, had been constantly rubbing his left ear and was obviously in pain, stubbornly refused to listen to advice or see a doctor. He was irrationally afraid of doctors, even though he denied this emphatically. After Mum died, I asked Dr Joshi if he would call in on him on the pretext of checking whether he was coping on his own. I had mentioned Dad's ear problem and stressed to the doctor that I was concerned because there was a particularly unpleasant smell coming from the ear and I suspected that something serious was going on. Having been alerted, Dr Joshi took his auroscope when he visited and checked him out thoroughly. He was very concerned by what he saw. Dad's ear was badly infected and he was urgently referred to a specialist. Within two weeks he had seen the specialist and was booked in for surgery. The consultant was horrified to find that even part of Dad's jaw was diseased and said that he hadn't seen anything like it in his entire career. With a history of three previous coronaries, Dad was a massive risk for anaesthesia, but he could well have died without the operation; therefore, he had no real choice. He survived the surgery and after just three days went home.

I went to see him the following morning, after a telephone call from my sister telling me that she was worried about him. She said that he was constantly rubbing his chest and complaining that he was aching and felt unwell. As usual he said he had flu but he always said everything was flu. He looked drawn and grey and I knew from experience that something was seriously wrong, but he wouldn't let me call a doctor. I had taken a blood pressure monitor with me to check him out, but his blood pressure was fine, as was his pulse. The problem was you couldn't argue with Dad. I told him that if he was no better by the following morning then, regardless of his wishes, I would call the GP. I offered to stay the night but he said he wanted to have some peace and quiet and be on his own, so I left reluctantly, certain that he needed to go back to hospital. First thing the next morning I rang early to ask how he was.

'Awful,' he said. 'I've been up all night aching and sweating. I've got really bad flu.' For Dad to use the word 'awful' I knew he must be feeling pretty rough. With his permission I rang the surgery and requested a home visit, and then I rang my sister to see if she could go and stay with him to see what the doctor had to say. Later that morning the locum arrived (the same one who had been less than useless with Mum). He examined Dad and stated that he had a virus (parroting my Dad's words). Pat tentatively told the locum that I had seen Dad the previous day, spoken with him this morning and was worried that there was something more serious going on. He looked angry and asked if I was the same lady who had looked after Mum? When she nodded her head, he grudgingly asked if someone could take Dad to the health centre for an ECG (heart tracing). Thirty minutes later my brother-in-law Michael took Dad for the test and waited with him for the result. When the locum saw the result of the tracing he looked shocked, instructing Michael to get Dad home immediately and pack a bag ready to take him into Blackburn Royal. In the meantime he said he would try to find him a hospital bed as a matter of urgency. Pat telephoned to tell me what was happening and I set off hoping to accompany Dad to the hospital if he hadn't already left.

It took me half an hour to get to the house and when I got there I saw an ambulance parked outside. I thought, 'Thank goodness, I'm in time.' But I wasn't. Dad was already dead. He had gone upstairs to put a few things into a bag to take to the hospital, brought the bag downstairs and sat on the sofa. He took one last deep breath and died. For months afterwards I blamed myself for not insisting on summoning a doctor the previous day, or at least insisting on staying with him that night. But he didn't want me there; he was a proud man who didn't wish to appear weak. He died at home, just like Mum, as he would have wished. The post-mortem showed that he had suffered multiple emboli (clots) and hadn't really stood a chance of surviving. I will never understand why the doctor didn't send him straight to hospital. Dad would have been taken to Casualty and, even if no bed was available, he would at least have been in close proximity to equipment and expertise that could have given him a fighting chance.

When the funeral was being discussed the undertaker asked if we wanted any special message written on the family wreath. I grinned and said that we did. 'Please write,' I said to him, 'Joan told you it wasn't flu.'' He looked at me as though I were mad and said that he couldn't possibly include such a remark, but when I insisted he agreed, especially when I said that Dad would have seen the funny side. On the day of the funeral I purposely checked the wreath on top of the coffin, found the card hidden among the flowers and, sure enough, the undertaker had obliged. Everyone who read the card laughed, knowing Dad's obsession with flu.

Some months later I was thinking about Mum and Dad and how they had always said that they wanted to die at home. The nurse who cared for Mum on her final night had been very kind and her presence had allowed me to have several hours of much needed rest. I decided to investigate this service further because I knew there were so many families out there in a similar predicament and I felt that providing this type of care would potentially give me a great deal of job satisfaction.

After a bit of research, I applied to join the Marie Curie nurses and was invited for an interview. All seemed to go well until the question was asked, 'Have you had any personal bereavement within your family during the last two years?' I wasn't sure how to answer; I had not only experienced the deaths of my parents but eight others in that period, including my husband's father and stepmother. At first I remained silent thinking of what to say, but then decided that I had to be truthful. The nursing officer's jaw dropped in surprise and she shook her head; they didn't accept applicants who had suffered any family bereavement within that period, let alone ten. I was dismayed and pleaded with her at least to give me a chance, explaining about Mum and the nurse who had inspired my application and doing my best to convince her that I felt perfectly ready and able to undertake this nature of work. She pondered for a few moments and then rather reluctantly agreed to grant me a trial period. I was so pleased I almost kissed her.

As always, the doctors at the practice were supportive but they, too, were concerned that it was too soon after my parents' deaths to be carrying out this type of work. However, they wished me well and after working a period of notice I left to become a Marie Curie nurse.

10

Marie Curie nurses care for the terminally ill, whether in a hospice or in the patient's own home, and are funded mainly from charitable donations and public fundraising activities, with some additional financial support from the NHS. The service basically enables the patient's family or carer to get a good night's rest, knowing that an experienced nurse is looking after their loved one. Palliative care nursing doesn't suit everyone and many nurses find it depressing. It is sad yet also deeply rewarding to help a dying patient do so peacefully and with dignity in familiar surroundings. After the traumas of nursing my own mum and with all my previous nursing experience I felt confident that I could face any situation. In the community, the hours were worked on a night duty bank system, which allowed me to choose the number of shifts I wanted to cover and still left plenty of time available for my family, although Mark had now completed his studies at university and was living in Nottingham.

All nurses who work in any capacity in a patient's home are required to have a Criminal Records Bureau (CRB) check carried out, to ensure they have no convictions or other detrimental information recorded on the Police National Computer database. (Indeed, these checks are now commonly made on many professions and occupations, especially those dealing with children and vulnerable people.) While waiting for my own checks to be carried out, I attended an induction day at the local health centre that covered the expected standards of care for terminally ill patients, along with providing meticulous, step-by-step instructions on established protocols pertaining to the health and safety of a lone worker in a patient's home. Once the CRB check was completed (which took about four weeks), I collected my badge and uniform from the community nurses' building and was ready for my first call.

Normal procedure was for a doctor or district nurse to assess a patient's condition and establish whether the existing carers were struggling to cope or needed some additional support. If such was the case, a Marie Curie nurse could be called in; the district nurses usually telephoned first to give the patient's details, reporting on their condition and individual requirements.

I expected my new job to be a challenge and couldn't wait to get started. Some of the other bank nurses, who I had already met at the health centre, had warned me to take an extra cardigan or jacket on my first shift as it was often cold and not every household kept their heating turned on during the night. They had also suggested I take a flask or bottled drink plus my own mug on a first visit because not all homes provided them (or weren't too fussy about hygiene!).

A few days later my first call came in. The district nurse asked if I was available that night and gave me full details of a patient named Marian. The shift normally ran from 10.30pm to 7am, unless the patient died first, in which case the doctor would attend and all the formalities had to be completed before I could go home. (The patient's carer would always be given the name of the nurse who would be attending and that nurse was then expected to ring them about thirty minutes in advance of their arrival, a procedure intended to prevent bogus callers.)

On my arrival I was met at the door by the patient's live-in companion/housekeeper, who told me that Marian's condition was critical and that her son, who was with her, was not coping at all well. She took my coat and showed me into the bedroom. The son was a stout balding man in his sixties who sprang to his feet as I introduced myself. He had clearly been crying and was very agitated. He immediately put on his coat and started to leave before anything else could be said, although one quick glance at his mother convinced me that she couldn't hang on much longer. I sat him back down as gently as possible and encouraged him to stay.

'Please don't leave on my account,' I said. 'Your mum looks very poorly and perhaps you ought to stay a little longer.' At this he began to cry hysterically and rocked manically backwards and forwards in the chair, unable to accept that she was about to die. I put my arm around his shoulders to try and comfort him as he sobbed, and suggested that he hold her hand and talk to her. As he took his mother's hand, Marian took her final breaths. He hadn't realised that she had died until I broke it to him as gently as I could, whereupon he became totally inconsolable. It took quite a while for him to regain control of himself and then, looking puzzled, asked me how I had known that she was about to die. I could hardly say that I had seen hundreds of people die over the years, so I just said, 'Experience.' Unsure what he was supposed to do next, I explained that the first thing was to ring the doctor who would come to certify her death. And then he would need to call an undertaker of his choosing who would come and remove the body after establishing his requirements. He looked panic-stricken, declaring that he just couldn't face talking to anyone and he asked if it would be all right if the housekeeper could deal with everything because she had all the details. He passed me a slip of paper with the name of the undertaker he wanted to use then made a rapid exit, sobbing again as he went. I called the GP who arrived within twenty minutes, certified the death and said the certificate would be available from his surgery the following day. The undertaker arrived soon afterwards to remove Marian's body. It was then eerily quiet. The housekeeper looked completely worn out but, knowing that she wouldn't be able to sleep, asked me if I would keep her company for a while and stay for a cup of tea. She was obviously very distressed and told me that Marian had been more of a companion than an employer. This lady had been a resident in the house for many years and was starting to worry about where she would now live. We ended up chatting until daybreak, when she eventually decided to go to bed and I made my way home.

It had been a strange start in one way because I had been able to do so very little for Marian herself, but I had at least been able to give some support to both the son and the housekeeper. The following afternoon my manager rang to see how I had coped. I was relieved but not really surprised to report that my own recent personal losses hadn't affected my work in any way. The family very kindly sent a letter of appreciation to the Marie Curie service together with a substantial donation towards the fund.

Only two days later I was called out to a young man called Neil, who was twenty-nine years old and had been married for less than a year when he was diagnosed with a malignant brain tumour. Within a matter of only a few months he was terminally ill and the district nurses reported to me that he was now semiconscious and no longer eating or drinking. On my arrival, his pretty young wife, Pauline, answered the door looking frail and exhausted, her hair uncombed and her face devoid of any makeup. The sight of her stooped shoulders and incredibly sad expression spoke volumes of her inner turmoil. She smiled weakly as I introduced myself and then took me upstairs to see Neil, who was resting quietly, his huge frame seeming to fill the king-sized bed. Pauline bent down and lovingly stroked his forehead; gently telling him who I was and at the same time kissing his face and squeezing his hand. I felt myself beginning to choke with emotion (wondering how I would feel had it been Bill lying there) as I watched the tragic scene unfold. There was no response from Neil, who lay motionless, only now and again taking a noisy breath as though sighing. His head was hugely distorted due to the rapidly growing tumour, making his appearance somewhat grotesque. For several minutes Pauline and I stood quietly watching him until she snapped out of her reverie and told me that she intended sleeping alongside him during the night, and would shout for me as and when I was needed.

No matter how hard I tried I couldn't persuade her to sleep in another bedroom where I felt that she would get more rest. She was insistent and who could blame her? She took me downstairs to show me the toilet and the kitchen facilities and then went back to her husband, after telling me to help myself to drinks. She knew that Neil had little time left and she wanted to spend every last second with him.

It felt strange being away from my patient; the idea of the service was to allow the family or carer to rest, but it was their home and I was only a visitor. I spent the first hour reading a book and having a look around the room at the many wedding photographs proudly adorning every surface, all showing the bride and groom smiling happily without a care in the world: Neil in his morning suit, tall and handsome with short blond hair and athletic build, both sets of parents looking so proud. Life can be so unfair.

I decided to creep upstairs to check that all was well but immediately regretted it because every stair and floorboard creaked as I moved, and I had so badly wanted not to disturb them. Thankfully they were both fast asleep; he in a foetal position and she cuddled into his back with her left arm reassuringly around him, like a pair of spoons. I left them in peace and didn't venture upstairs again until Pauline called me. She had woken up at around 2am to find herself soaked with urine. Neil had been incontinent and she was wet through, as was the bed, but at such a time that was the least of her worries. So while I stripped the bed and started to give Neil a wash and change his pyjamas she had a quick shower before returning to help me change the bottom sheet. He clearly objected to being moved from side to side and moaned his disapproval, but once he was clean and dry he appeared much more settled. I moistened his dry mouth and massaged his pressure areas with cream, before whispering in his ear that Pauline was there with him. He sighed as if he had heard me and I left the room to let them rest. My services were only required again once more during the night and I said my goodbyes at 7am, giving Pauline a hug as I left. The district nurses rang me later that afternoon to say that Neil had died not long after I left, still wrapped in Pauline's arms and surrounded by his family.

The young and terminally ill were the most memorable. They clung to life so much harder, lingering in a kind of limbo, often drugged-up to the eyeballs with painkillers. The district nurses asked me to sit for Jill, a lady aged thirty who was terminally ill due to breast cancer, advising me that she was quite likely to die that same night and that Jill's husband and her best friend would both be there. Apparently she had seen her GP two years earlier after discovering a hard lump in her breast. He had loftily dismissed her obvious concerns saying that women of her age didn't get breast cancer. He told her to forget about it, but some months later she found the lump had become much bigger and returned to see him again, only to be told exactly the same thing. A year or so later when the lump was even bigger, she really didn't know what to do but eventually plucked up her courage and went to see a different GP who referred her urgently to a breast clinic, where she was diagnosed with cancer which, by that time, had spread to her lungs.

If this had happened to me then anger and bitterness would be the very least of my feelings. How could anyone possibly accept or come to terms with such a situation? I felt ashamed on behalf of the medical profession, quite illogically because I had never even met her before, and felt rather awkward when entering her home. Jill's husband Duncan let me in. Lost in his own thoughts, he showed me to her bedroom, where the best friend was sitting, holding Jill's hand and talking to her quietly. But Jill was deeply unconscious and beyond hearing, unaware of the affection around her, looking skeletal and ravaged by the disease. I felt numb looking at this sheer waste of a young life; I looked across and saw their wedding photograph, the beautiful young bride bearing no resemblance to the emaciated scrap of indignity lying on the bed. It was heart wrenching. I bathed Jill and moistened her mouth; she was no longer taking fluids and it was just a matter of making her remaining hours as comfortable as possible.

The family's dog had been Jill's constant companion since he was a puppy and had slept at the end of her bed throughout the long months of her illness, stubbornly refusing to leave her side. That morning the dog had slunk out of the bedroom and no amount of coaxing could bring it back. Jill died peacefully about an hour later, thankfully free from pain. Her husband and friend were with her to the end and asked me to ring the GP (her new one), who had insisted that she would attend if anything occurred, no matter what time of day or night. I telephoned the number umpteen times, letting it ring for long periods, but got no response. Eventually, after trying several more times we called the locum service.

I knew the locum doctor who turned up shortly afterwards and, aware that he could unintentionally appear flippant at times, warned him before he came in to be careful how he handled the situation. I explained the difficult circumstances of Jill's misdiagnosis and naturally he carried out his duties with the utmost care and sympathy. When he left, I contacted the undertakers and stayed with the family until Jill's body was removed, making my own exit soon afterwards. After I returned home, I left word on the district nurse answerphone, letting them know the situation.

The following morning the GP telephoned

me, angrily demanding to know why I hadn't called her. When I told her that both Jill's husband and I had tried numerous times without response she was immediately apologetic. There was no accounting for the doctor not hearing her telephone ring, especially when she was such a light sleeper and had checked her telephone which was working normally. Fate sometimes deals a rotten hand and this family certainly got one of them.

★ ★ ★

The inner-city area of Moss Side in Manchester is infamous for gun crime and gang culture, a place where you think twice before stopping at a red traffic light after dark. So I was more than a little apprehensive when I was asked to care for an elderly West Indian gentleman who lived in this area and was dying of prostate cancer. One of the Marie Curie nurses had been mugged and robbed there only the previous evening, having got lost and been obliged to make a call from a public telephone box to ask the district nurses for directions. Leaving the telephone box she was pushed to the ground and had her bag stolen. It was assumed that, because she was in uniform and carrying a small black bag, the perpetrator thought she was carrying drugs. She wasn't. I found the house easily (thank God) and on arrival was shown into the front room by his son. My patient, Winston, who was almost ninety, was in bed trying to get to sleep but looked very uncomfortable. He was so tall (at least six feet nine inches) that his legs stuck out way beyond the end of the bed and were resting on pillows on top of a coffee table. His eyes were dull and vacant, and he seemed to be totally beyond caring.

While I was looking after my patient in the front room his son had invited a few friends around for a get-together in the kitchen. Several large young men, smoking what smelled suspiciously like cannabis and drinking copious amounts of white rum, were playing loud reggae music into the small hours, causing Winston to toss and turn restlessly, unable to sleep. Personally I loved the music and could have happily listened to it all night, but it was completely inappropriate and this was definitely neither the time nor the place, so I felt that I had to have a word with them about their thoughtlessness.

With my heart in my mouth I asked the son and his friends very politely if they would mind turning the music down because it was disturbing my patient. Without hesitation they apologised unreservedly, the music was immediately turned down and the party soon broke up, finally allowing the old man to sleep. I was very impressed with their good manners but the following morning felt duty-bound to report to the district nurse about the alcohol and suspected pot smoking. The son was caring and attentive to his father but alcohol and weed are not a good combination in such circumstances. These lads were basically decent young men, in their own way only supporting a friend in his hour of need, but there was a clear potential risk for any lone female going into that house. Very diplomatically the district nurse asked Winston's son if he would like his father to go into the hospice to give him a break. He wasn't too keen at first but, after discussing it with the family, arrangements were made for Winston to be admitted. He died there peacefully and in much greater comfort several weeks later.

A few days later, I was asked to care for a frail elderly man named Vincent in a house on the edge of the Wythenshawe estate, not too far from the hospital. As soon as I arrived, Vincent's daughter and son-in-law decided to go to the pub for last orders, leaving me locked in the house with my patient, while their nineteen-year-old son Ronnie and his friend were downstairs in the living room drinking beer and eating pizza. At one point, Ronnie came staggering into the bedroom clutching a slice of pizza which he offered clumsily to his grandfather. I thanked him for the kind thought but told him that his granddad was unable to eat solid food, so he turned around and disappeared back downstairs.

The daughter and son-in-law returned a couple of hours later much the worse for alcohol; in fact, they were stinking drunk. I had just managed to get Vincent to sleep when they both staggered noisily up the stairs and into the old man's bedroom. His daughter was shouting incoherently and climbed on to the bed, cuddling and hugging the old man, even though he visibly winced in pain. I had to insist very firmly that she stop. Out of the blue she suddenly turned to me, trying to focus through the haze of alcohol, and asked me how I felt having been left alone in the house with two armed robbers; Ronnie and his friend had apparently just been released from prison! I tried not to react to this statement because at the time I was more worried about Vincent's condition and his general situation. When I first arrived his bed had been saturated with urine and there were at least six full mugs of cold tea littering his bedside cabinet, although there was no possibility he could reach any of them. More worrying was the electric fire that was inches from the bed and showing exposed wires.

When the drunken bunch eventually staggered to bed, I moved the electric fire and the cups, cleaned and tidied the room and spent the rest of the night making sure my patient (who was clearly partially dehydrated) drank copious amounts of tea and fruit juice. Poor Vincent was really grateful for everything I did and repeatedly squeezed my hand in thanks. After all those drinks, not surprisingly, he was incontinent all night long, necessitating three complete changes of bed linen and I spent most of the night washing and changing my patient. I felt very strongly that in view of the incontinence, the lack of fluid intake (when he was left with the family in charge) and a very dangerous fire so close to the bed, that his case needed reviewing urgently and my concerns needed to be highlighted to the district nurses. When I was due to go off duty at 7am I found that I couldn't waken anyone to say I was leaving and, in any event, wasn't able to get out because the doors were locked. I was beginning to wonder what to do when the 'armed robber' appeared on the landing to let me out, wearing only some skimpy little underpants and reeking of stale alcohol. I couldn't get away fast enough.

The following morning I put in my report to the district nurses and when they went round to do their daily checks they couldn't get in because everyone was still asleep. The doctor tried some hours later, also without success. After lunch the district nurses tried again and were met at the door by the old man's daughter, bleary-eyed and stinking of booze. They found Vincent in pain, wet, dirty and desperate for a drink. As they washed and changed him he told them about an 'angel' who had looked after him the previous night and they rang me to pass on his thanks. Alarmed at how the old man was being neglected, that same day they organised for him to go into a hospice where he died peacefully a week later. It was my privilege to look after this vulnerable gentleman and to have helped ensure his life ended with some degree of dignity. I honestly believe that his family tried their best; it certainly wasn't enough but at least they tried, so what more could anyone ask?

Walter was eighty years old and dying of prostate cancer. As I went into his room he gave me a wonderful beaming smile. His family were very supportive and had worked out a rota system to ensure that at least one person was with him at all times during the day. Night-time was Marie Curie time. He looked very frail, yet for some unknown reason wasn't in a bed. A little alarmingly, but entirely by his own choice, he lay on a sofa and didn't look at all comfortable; although, my main concern was that he could fall off if he turned over in his sleep.

My first shift passed without incident but the following night his son came to the door and took me aside; he felt that his father was deteriorating and asked me to ring him straightaway at home if his condition got worse. After being reassured that I would do so, he said good night to his father and went home. As I walked in Walter waved weakly and gave me a smile. He seemed puzzled, though, and was looking directly over my shoulder. I clearly remember turning around and asking him what he was looking at. He whispered, 'Why have you brought your mum and dad?' I smiled but wasn't really sure what to say; how could I tell him that they had both recently died? I felt the hairs on the back of my neck stand on end and had goose pimples all night. No matter what I did, I couldn't get warm. Walter died that morning soon after his son turned up.

Sandra was a woman in her thirties who was in the terminal stages of ovarian cancer and the district nurses had warned me that she was unlikely to survive the night. Going in to care for younger patients is always distressing and somehow seems much more tragic, so I was a little apprehensive as her anxious husband ushered me into the bedroom. The wasted skeletal figure lying in the huge bed looked, quite frankly, horrific, little more than skin and bone, and in all my years as a nurse I had never before seen anyone look so emaciated. Sandra was drifting in and out of consciousness, unable to speak or move. A device called a syringe driver was attached to her chest, dishing out regular metered amounts of morphine. Looking at her, I was convinced that she would die that night.

Soon after my arrival, her husband Phillip brought in their two children to say goodnight to their mum. The little boy and girl each carefully climbed on to the bed in turn and kissed her goodnight. I choked back my tears, remembering my own mum and feeling fortunate to have had her in my life for much longer than these two unfortunate children would. The little boy said, 'Good night Mummy and God bless.' The girl said nothing but was very distressed. It was an emotional scene and I needed all my strength to control myself when Phillip went out to settle the children into bed.

Amazingly Sandra survived the night and, in fact, survived a further eight days. No one could believe the fight she put up. The family asked if I would personally look after her until the end, which I was pleased to do, but I never really expected to see her alive again after the end of each shift. The family were very close and there was always one of them by her side at all times. Those shifts allowed me to get to know them very well. They were clearly a loving, caring family and we built up a close bond of friendship and trust in that time. We spent many hours together during these long nights, sometimes in silence, sometimes listening to stories of their happy childhood.

My last visit will remain with me forever. By this stage Sandra was deeply unconscious, unresponsive and even thinner than I could believe possible. The children went through the usual routine of kissing her goodnight and then being put to bed, and I remember watching and praying in silence that God would take her soon; the family all looked worn out. I begged them to go to bed and rest, assuring them that I would call if she deteriorated further. I sat for several hours holding her hand and watching her closely. Her breathing altered dramatically at around 3am and I knew instinctively that it was time to rouse the family (although we let the children sleep on). The family filed in around her bed, each in turn saying their last goodbyes, and she passed away peacefully soon afterwards.

Eventually, the children were allowed to say goodbye. It was when I saw their distress that I couldn't hold back any longer, no matter how hard I tried, and I sat on the top stair with tears streaming down my face. A few minutes later, one of Sandra's brothers came out of the bedroom. Through his tears he said that she looked beautiful. Although I had done my best to make her look as presentable as possible before the children saw the body, I was far from sure that this comment was particularly accurate.

I went back into the room to make her ready for the doctor. Everyone in the room was weeping and obviously deeply upset, yet I could only stare at Sandra in astonishment. Her lips were parted very slightly in a serene smile and even her cheeks appeared to have filled out. She looked peaceful and at rest, and I was completely speechless.

★ ★ ★

Sandra was my final patient before Bill and I moved back to the Fylde coast in what was hopefully our last relocation. I would have loved to continue with Marie Curie but it wasn't to be. Because each individual Primary Care Trust provided some of the funding towards nurses' wages, I had to re-apply in my new administrative area and was told that there were no current vacancies. Once again, I was on the lookout for a new job.

Almost a year had gone by since I had begun working for the Marie Curie Service, sometimes up to three nights per week, and I can truthfully say that the work was the most rewarding I had ever done in my life. From the minute I had been blessed with a Marie Curie nurse caring for my mum on the last night of her life, I knew that the work was for me. In my experience, everyone needs special care and comfort at the end of their lives and they don't want to die in unfamiliar surroundings being looked after by strangers, and I believe that this is what the Marie Curie Service provides.

After working for Marie Curie I became very unsettled. I enjoyed my independence and really missed the reward of being able to give such personal care to each individual patient. It was hard to imagine doing anything else that would offer me the same job satisfaction.

11

Moving back to the Fylde Coast was like coming home. I had never truly settled in Cheshire and we had always intended to move back to the area at some stage. Mark had completed his studies by this time and was now settled in Nottingham with his girlfriend Emma; so settled, in fact, that they had even adopted a rescue dog, so we didn't expect him home any time soon. We bought the show house on a new housing estate, fully decorated and furnished, which suited Bill down to the ground because he didn't have to lift a finger before we moved in.

One of my new neighbours, a registered nurse also called Joan, pointed me in the direction of the local cottage hospital in Lytham where she worked and I started as a part-time staff nurse in Out-patients. The patients at this small local hospital were basically looked after by their own local GPs but a number of out-patient clinics were held there by consultants based at Blackpool Victoria Hospital. After my first week I realised that I had made a big mistake; nice friendly people, monotonous routine and out-of-date equipment sum up the experience, which lasted about a year. During that time, Joan, who was by now also a good friend, had been headhunted by a local GP surgery as one of their practice nurses and when she alerted me to a vacancy I applied. Soon I found myself once again working as a part-time practice nurse, this time at Holland House Surgery, Lytham.

Although the doctors were great to work for and had a glowing reputation among their patients, the work was very much the same in this practice as it had been in Cheshire and I no longer found it particularly challenging or rewarding. I had kept in touch with Edith, the nurse I worked with in the Young Disabled Unit nearly fourteen years earlier, and one day she told me that her husband Alan had been diagnosed with a brain tumour and was terminally ill. He had refused chemotherapy and his one wish was to be allowed to die at home. The next few months found me working my shifts at the practice and then calling round to check on Alan's situation. It was difficult to see a friend in so much distress but, between us, Edith and I managed to cope with his gradual deterioration and were both with him at home at the end. Doing this reminded me just how much I missed working for the Marie Curie Service so, when a friend from Cheshire was herself diagnosed with terminal cancer, I had a chat to Bill who agreed I should resign and devote myself to helping her during the time she had remaining.

I had been at the surgery for about three years and it was suggested that they would leave my post open for me. However, I had no idea how long this situation might go on for, so decided against it. The doctors were all very understanding, with one of the partners, Dr Steven, trying to alert me to how difficult it would be nursing a friend who was so very poorly. (This doctor was particularly thoughtful and well respected by his staff and patients. He would often make unsolicited visits to his own terminally ill patients; even popping in to see them when he was officially on annual leave.) But I had made up my mind and, after working a short notice period, left to help my friend in any way that I could.

Catherine's situation was particularly sad because her husband Barry had died suddenly not long before from an undiagnosed congenital heart defect. Now their three teenagers, who were all away at university, were facing another dreadful situation. Bill was still travelling to work every day in Cheshire and initially he dropped me off at Cath's a couple of mornings each week and picked me up in the evening. At the time, I was simply needed to do some housework or help to make a meal. Cath spent most of the time in her bedroom upstairs so that she could be nearer to the bathroom when necessary or lie on the bed when she became tired. She looked exhausted and washed out; it was heartbreaking to watch her struggle through her discomfort, although two of her closest friends visited regularly to try and keep her spirits up and also volunteered their help. Between the three of us, we tried our very best to take as much pressure off the family as we could.

Gradually the general deterioration became increasingly evident. She began to experience more pain and became so weak that she was unable to get around without support, yet never once did she ever complain or grumble. She was an amazing lady. As her cancer progressed she began to need more nursing care and I visited more regularly, and the district nurses started to come in every day to help to control her pain. The children had by now returned home from university and I showed them how to change her bed without having to get her up and how to prevent bedsores from developing. When a patient (for whatever reason) isn't eating or drinking enough, they quickly become dehydrated, manifesting itself with an unquenchable thirst, dry, cracked lips and an ulcerated mouth. These are added, unnecessary discomforts that can easily be avoided with a little extra care. Cath was always so grateful for any help we three friends could give and the children did their best to follow the basic hygiene steps I had shown them. They did a wonderful job looking after her, which I am sure gave them all great satisfaction, and I had nothing but admiration for the way they applied themselves to the unwanted task in hand. Louise, the eldest daughter, became the chief cook and often made large pans of delicious homemade soups to keep us all going, while Andrew and Clare did the shopping and cleaned around the house without a grumble. They were a total credit to Cath.

I had been going there for three months and it was coming up to Christmas. When I arrived one morning, Cath looked at me with resignation and whispered that she had two final hopes and desires; she wanted to remain at home with her children for as long as humanly possible and she wanted to live through Christmas, for their sake. She had already spoken to her GP, who had agreed to try to do as much as he could. He thought that she was slowly haemorrhaging internally and, although he didn't share his thoughts with her at the time, he felt that a 'top up' from a blood transfusion might just give her a boost. She was admitted to hospital overnight a number of times for a quick transfusion, and this did seem to give her more energy, albeit for a short time. It was soon noticeable, however, that the time in between each one was getting appreciably shorter. She was a very intelligent lady and she knew herself that time was running out. Without fuss or complaint she sorted out her will and began to get her affairs in order.

Day in, day out, I kept her company and sometimes we did relaxation exercises together and played gentle music to bring a calming atmosphere to the room. It really did seem to help; in fact, one day the two girls joined us and afterwards we were all yawning to the point of nodding off. Sometimes the children would all come in to keep her company and would lie on her bed cuddling her and trying to keep her spirits up; it broke my heart to see the pain etched on their young faces. One particular day, Clare crept on to her mum's bed and, with tears streaming down her face, told her mum that she didn't want her to die. Catherine quietly and calmly put her arms around her and held her tight, reassuring her that she would cope and not to worry. I left the room to give them some privacy, crying my eyes out as usual.

Two days before Christmas I could see that she was rapidly going downhill, so I decided that it was time to give her an early Christmas present. I had wrapped a big basket of toiletries up in seasonal wrapping paper, plus one very special item that I hoped would make her smile. I told her that I probably wouldn't be able to come over on Christmas Day so had brought her present round early. Her eyes lit up and she begged to open it, beaming at the special gift smuggled in the centre of the toiletries — a black furry gorilla that played a tune and whose shoulders went up in time to the music. She laughed out loud and jiggled her own shoulders up and down in enjoyment. The children were thrilled that it had brought her so much pleasure.

The following day was Christmas Eve and, when I arrived that morning, Cath looked like she was having a hallucination. Her eyes were open but glazed and unseeing, and her hands were clutching at thin air as if she was trying to grasp an invisible object. The children were alarmed and I called the district nurses to see if they could help. They arrived shortly afterwards and rang the GP who prescribed extra medication through a syringe driver, which they set up as soon as they had collected the drugs from the chemist. The drugs helped relieve her pain and allowed her to relax and sleep. When I was due to leave for home that evening she was barely conscious and unable to communicate. Her father and brother arrived and sat by her bed, holding her hands and talking to her gently.

I knew that I couldn't help her any further and, though reluctant to leave, felt that it was time to go. I squeezed her hand tightly and made my exit. Catherine died on Christmas morning. I was devastated when I got the telephone call; this was exactly what she had fought to avoid and it took a lot of coming to terms with, but it had been my privilege to help her stay at home with her family. Looking after someone you know is, indeed, very different to caring for a complete stranger. My emotions were in shreds and I can honestly say that I felt completely numb for a very long time afterwards.

★   ★   ★

It was a while before I could even consider working. I needed a rest, emotionally and physically. But I couldn't stay idle forever, however much I missed my friend. One morning, I was idly scanning the situations vacant when I saw a small advert looking for bank nursing staff to work in the Healthcare Department of a prison. Crikey! I had never even thought about nurses working in prison, but I made my application and received an invitation to go for interview. Bill thought the idea was hilarious and made a number of daft remarks about *Prisoner Cellblock H*, but I was really excited and could feel another challenge coming on.

The inmates of this prison were mainly those convicted of minor offences such as car crime, fraud or theft. The infrastructure and many buildings were substantially unchanged since the war and accommodated approximately six hundred inmates. The majority were serving short-term sentences, although increasingly others have been transferred from high-security establishments to serve out the remainder of their long-term and life sentences. These offenders work in the community following a programme that helps them to integrate back into society and I found that these men were usually far less troublesome than the minor offenders simply because they risked losing parole if they misbehaved.

Always an early bird, I arrived half an hour before my interview time and drove up to a barrier controlled from a small gatehouse. Having been forewarned to have my interview letter ready as a means of entry, I nervously flashed my credentials and was duly admitted. A prison officer showed me where to park my car and, in no time at all, a young inmate appeared to escort me to the Healthcare Department. As we walked the several hundred yards to the department, he pointed out the various work-shops and extensive fields where most of the inmates were obliged to work during the week. He explained that he currently worked as an orderly in Healthcare but was due for release the following day and it was obvious that he couldn't wait to go home. He complained that the food in prison was awful and the accommodation was even worse, although at the time I paid little attention to this and thought that he must be exaggerating.

We passed the inmates' accommodation buildings. Each block housed about twenty inmates and had single room facilities that contained the most basic amenities: bed, chair, cupboard, small chest of drawers and a sink. Each block had showers, toilets and a washing area, plus a kettle and tea-making facilities, but were generally tiny, damp, cold and overdue for replacement. The beds were very narrow, hard as a plank and the pillows had the appearance and texture of breezeblocks. A pillow fight could have resulted in serious injury but at least it would have been almost impossible for one inmate to use a pillow to suffocate another (which presumably was the point).

As we walked along I didn't feel at all intimidated by the inmates, they were just as curious about me as I was about them. A few nodded and said, 'Good morning,' and everything seemed perfectly civilised. There was an abundance of wildlife, particularly baby ducklings. There were literally hundreds of them wandering around following their mums in long, trailing processions, one behind the other, and inmates were feeding them crumbs and taking care not to tread on them. The orderly said that occasionally it was known for an inmate to stamp cruelly and deliberately on one but the main danger to them were the seagulls, which often would swoop down and carry them off. Fortunately, most inmates seemed to care for and protect these babies, but if anyone was seen to deliberately harm them they were formally 'punished' by the prison authorities and lost their privileges.

The Healthcare Centre seemed to be miles away. Luckily the day was warm and sunny but I dreaded to think what it would be like when it was raining hard. As we went along, Chris, the orderly, warned me not to accept anything to drink from an inmate as they sometimes, shall we say, 'contaminated' the cups. I was beginning to wonder what I was letting myself in for but on arrival at the centre I was immediately made welcome and offered a cup of tea. I wasn't too sure about accepting it and watched the orderly who was making it very closely until I had the cup in my hand. Chris stood to one side smirking as he observed my reaction. I did then wonder whether he had been telling a big fib so that the orderlies wouldn't be given the job of brewing up.

I had just settled into a chair with a cup in one hand and a biscuit in the other when I was called for interview. Several orderlies wished me good luck as I went in. The interview was conducted by the Nurse Manager, Tracy, and the Healthcare Governor, a short, bespectacled individual who was in charge of the day-to-day running of the department. With several other applicants also waiting their turn for interview, it was good to know that if I was accepted I wouldn't be the only starter on what would be a new 'bank' system. It was a very strange, short interview. Tracy asked me about my nursing experience but said little else, and the governor warned me at great length about the inmates presenting themselves with fictitious illnesses in order to avoid work, adding that they would steal the fillings from your teeth given half a chance. That turned out to be the entire interview and I left to go home after being advised that I would hear from them in due course.

On my way out of the department, the Healthcare Officer (the prison officer assigned full-time to the department) introduced himself and volunteered to escort me back to the main gate. It was a beautiful summer's day and he readily admitted that he was looking for an excuse to get some fresh air. As we walked along he chatted on at length about himself and his long years of service at the prison and how, before the Healthcare Department was established, he had been in charge of the inmates' health and well-being. He began to grumble about the poor nurse management and left me in little doubt that he resented having nurses in charge, remarking that he could run the department better with his eyes closed. I had no doubt that he'd probably completed a first-aid course at some time, but suspected that this man didn't see himself as part of the team.

A couple of weeks later I received a job offer and then, along with several other staff, I began this new phase in my career; although, I have to say my first day was very different from anything I had ever experienced previously. Tracy welcomed me and took me on a tour of the prison, explaining that it was a working prison in which all inmates were obliged to carry out some form of manual labour. There were many acres of land devoted to market gardening, which produced vegetables and plants for both internal and external customers, together with workshops that manufactured wooden products such as garden furniture, bird tables and dog kennels. There was a bakery, a meat packaging plant and many inmates worked in the kitchens preparing food for the staff and inmates.

Orderlies (who were the most trusted inmates) worked in Healthcare, the gymnasium, the prison offices, the library and the education centre. Every day saw a hive of activity in each different area of the prison. Tracy made the point quite strongly that some inmates tried their best to avoid any form of work, while others were willing to work but didn't like the particular job they had been allocated. While an inmate could appeal for a move to a different job after a certain period of time, they still had to wait for a suitable vacancy. In the meantime, they would try every scam in the book to get out of work and Tracy warned me that Healthcare was their first port of call. I couldn't wait.

After the tour I was taken along to the security offices where I was given a short talk about personal security. I was warned that inmates would test me to the limit to see if they could persuade me to bend or break the rules, put them on sick report in order to avoid work, post letters for them or bring articles into the prison, all of which were strictly against regulations. I was told never to leave an inmate unsupervised when in the Health Centre as anything not screwed down would be stolen and quickly sold on.

Two very important rules were: never get too

familiar with inmates and never enter an accommodation block alone without first informing the
security office, who would send an officer as
escort. Occasionally I would be obliged to carry a
two-way radio, which was briefly demonstrated,
and we were advised that all female staff had to
be addressed as 'Miss' and male staff addressed
as 'Boss'. (I had the urge to laugh every time I
heard these terms at first, feeling like a school-
teacher, but this form of address eventually became
commonplace and, after a while, I never gave it a
second thought.) With all the rules and regulations to learn my head was spinning. After the
tour and security talk it was back to Healthcare
to familiarise myself with the daily routines of
prison life. I was expected to observe the routine
on my first day, although I was encouraged to
join in where appropriate.

The day began with all inmates who took daily
medications rushing into Healthcare to collect
them, which initially looked quite intimidating
because they were in a hurry and could miss
breakfast if they were delayed. Meal times were
on a first-come, first-served basis, so it was not
surprising if their prescriptions couldn't be
found immediately, that inmates became rude,
impatient and sarcastic. It was a stressful time
for everyone, and a time when mistakes could
easily be made. Identification always had to be
produced and checked to make sure that the
correct medication was given to the correct
individual, and no inmate was ever allowed to
collect medication on behalf of someone else. It
was quite surprising, even on that first morning,

how many inmates suddenly couldn't find their I.D. badges (which itself was an offence) then became obnoxious when they were refused their medicines. This was the time when the Healthcare Officer came into his own, because his imposing frame and confident attitude quelled any aggressive behaviour before it could get out of hand. He took no nonsense from any inmate and sent them packing until they could produce their correct identification. I felt rather apprehensive about these morning routines and hoped that it was just because it was new to me.

Sick parade came immediately after breakfast. Appointments to see a doctor were usually booked by the nursing staff the previous evening, although there were apparently always the 'chancers' wanting a day off work by feigning sickness who would come in and say that they had been ill all night and needed to see the doctor. A panel of doctors, who were in fact my own GPs, had a contract with the prison service to provide healthcare. They came into the prison every morning for surgery and had done so for many years. They stood no nonsense from the inmates and soon gave them short shrift if they were perceived to be trying it on; although, this wasn't always easy to spot as some of them would have done well at RADA. A nurse was always in the room with the doctor during sick parade and if treatments or medications were required it was her/his job to sort them out.

After sick parade came treatments and this is where I knew I would be happiest. Having done years of casualty work and practice nursing this was my forte. I watched as a queue of inmates arrived, wanting attention. Most had regular appointments and were typically lads in for dressings to be changed or wounds from various injuries through their job or assaults by other inmates to be seen to. Some needed stitches removing and others needed their ears syringing or blood tests ordered by the doctors. There were a whole variety of ailments and injuries that required blood pressure checks and temperatures taking. As I gave a helping hand with dressings, one of the other nurses repeated the message never to leave an inmate in the room alone, as you could guarantee that 'medical equipment', especially syringes, would go walkabout. It was apparent chaos up until almost lunchtime, although one of the orderlies did comment that the numbers had risen that morning because they wanted to see who I was and if I would be a pushover. At midday there was a further distribution of medicines which again was a frantic scramble, this time because of the inmates wanting to get to lunch, followed by health checks on any new arrivals.

A prison van arrived early that first afternoon and ten new inmates tumbled out of the van, hot and sweaty and obviously glad to be out in the fresh air. Being naturally curious, I asked if I could have a look in the van and was horrified to see that each inmate had been enclosed in a small claustrophobic cubicle inside it. There was virtually no room to move and I am sure that I would have passed out if I had been cooped up as they were. The Healthcare Officer showed me the list of medical questions that needed to be answered, which included asking about daily medications. Any regular medications had to be brought with them from their previous prison or from court and no medicines, apart from asthma inhalers, were given back to the patients; everything was logged and locked away until medicine rounds the next morning for the doctor to see. Once everybody had been clerked in, I was informed that they were then seen by the board of officers who allocated jobs to them all, depending on their medical health.

After the paperwork on the newcomers was dealt with, the next job of the day was to speak to all the inmates who were going home. Happy to be leaving, for many it was the first time since their admission that they were cooperative and helpful. Anyone who had been ill during their time with us had to be given a letter for their GP outlining any current problem with appropriate information in terms of medications (which, if they were on regular treatment, were collected as they left). Each inmate also had to be weighed and the reason for this staggered me; it was not unknown for individuals to try and claim compensation for new clothes because they had either lost or gained weight during their incarceration. Finally we came to the last medicine round of the day before going home. Phew!

After locking up, all the staff trudged back to the car park together, handing over any department keys to officers on the gate. My first day was completed and I felt shattered.

Constantly busy and very challenging, I felt sure that I would enjoy working at the prison; my head was in a whirl but I couldn't wait to get cracking.

Each day followed a similar pattern and my favourite work was carrying out treatments and first aid but, even in prison, nursing wasn't for the faint-hearted. My casualty experience was to prove invaluable, not only for the illnesses and injuries but also in dealing with the bad language and aggressive behaviour.

The most common ailments were back pain, diarrhoea and sore feet. Back pain was a favourite complaint, as it was difficult to diagnose without x-rays or scans, which made it convenient for getting out of work and for obtaining pain-relief tablets (which inmates could then sell on within the prison). The most effective miracle cure at our disposal was to tell the inmate that they wouldn't be allowed to go into the gym for at least two weeks if they had back pain because they wouldn't want to aggravate their condition and make it worse. They rarely tried that scam more than once.

Diarrhoea was also a useful ploy, particularly for anyone who didn't like working in the kitchens or in the meatpacking unit because health and safety regulations dictated that their job had to be changed (albeit temporarily) until tests established that they weren't infectious. Inmates claiming to have diarrhoea were meant to be kept in Healthcare until they could provide a specimen. The imaginative ways they came up with to provide this specimen for analysis were genuinely noteworthy. It was astounding how many inmates suddenly couldn't 'go' once they had been given a specimen pot, in spite of swearing blind that up until then they had been running to the toilet every few minutes. One 'gentleman' conned an inexperienced nurse into allowing him to go back to his room in order to produce his specimen. Only minutes earlier I had told him to stay in the department but I had been distracted while attending to someone else and my colleague, unaware of the rule, allowed him to leave. He returned a few minutes later producing a container with the strangest-looking faeces specimen I have ever seen. He was told that he would be allocated a different job while awaiting the results but he was not impressed with this news and argued that he felt far too ill to work and needed to go back to bed. However, he had no temperature, his pulse and blood pressure were normal; he had no abdominal pain and looked far too healthy. Although sympathising with his predicament, he was referred to a panel of senior officers who allocated him a job cleaning the prison officers' administration block, which allowed him immediate access to a toilet, if necessary. He was not pleased. Working with this type of prisoner really made me become cynical and eventually I tended to disbelieve everything I was told until it could be proved otherwise.

Ten days later this man's results came back from the laboratory saying that the stool specimen comprised of nothing more than 'Weetabix, curry powder and gravy browning'. I immediately sent for the inmate and presented him with the report. He read it and exclaimed, 'Yeah. So what? I eat a lot of curry.' He looked at me as if I was totally stupid. I informed him that food goes through many changes during the process of digestion and doesn't magically 'reappear' in precisely the same format as it has been eaten. I warned him that I was no fool and that if he didn't get his act together I would put him on report. He slammed out of the room with the 'F' word ringing in my ears, so I reported him anyway. Any staff member can put an inmate on report if they break the rules or misbehave and a written complaint has to be filled out with a short résumé of the allegation. If it is deemed sufficiently serious, the inmate has to go in front of a disciplinary panel, usually made up of senior prison officers and including the duty governor. Each inmate is questioned to establish their side of the story and a fine or loss of privileges can result if found guilty. The ultimate punishment is for the inmate to be transferred to a higher security prison where they will have greatly restricted freedoms. On this occasion the inmate was given a warning about his behaviour and had his privileges reduced, although it wasn't long before he was shipped out anyway after being caught trying yet another scam.

Like bad backs and diarrhoea, feet were an equally persistent problem. Under health and safety legislation, many inmates were obliged to wear work boots with steel toecaps because of the type of job they were assigned. These were provided by the prison but were often ill-fitting and caused blisters. They also made feet sweat, resulting in fungal infections and, unfortunately, fungal powders (which were the best medicine to help prevent these annoying infections recurring) were banned from prison because of potential misuse by drug addicts. All aerosol sprays (whether deodorant or medicinal) were also banned because they could be used as weapons, so treatment was generally limited to antifungal creams and hygiene education. Scissors were also strictly banned (for obvious reasons) and nails had to be trimmed using clippers. It is surprising how such basic everyday procedures are taken for granted.

Most of the other problems and treatments tended to be the same ones that every practice nurse and casualty nurse has seen and dealt with a thousand times before. Inmates often arrived bleeding from deep cuts and abrasions, which is when it was indeed like being back in Casualty. There was also the occasional coronary, asthma attack and diabetic problem, along with some rather serious injuries due to assaults or accidents.

One such incident involved a middle-aged inmate who had only just arrived that day. On this first night he couldn't get to sleep because of someone's snoring. After tossing and turning for what no doubt seemed like several hours, he climbed out of bed and boiled a kettle of water. He then proceeded to pour this over the head of the snorer. The victim was rushed to hospital with first-degree burns and the perpetrator was arrested and charged with assault. He was shipped out immediately to a secure prison and was subsequently prosecuted. In due course the victim was returned to prison, his face, neck, chest and shoulders covered in dressings which all had to be changed daily. Although I say it myself, we did a fantastic job and his burns healed beautifully. When he was eventually discharged after completing his sentence, the inmate came to see us to say thanks, which was a rare event in prison, and gratefully accepted. Despite his snoring he seemed a decent young lad, yet he was a prolific serial burglar and had already served a number of prison sentences.

The prison didn't have twenty-four-hour medical cover and the doctors only went in for one hour each day, Monday to Friday. Healthcare was open 7.30am — 5pm during the week and on Saturday and Sunday mornings it was open from 7.30am — 12pm. At all other times, competent prison officers with first-aid qualifications were meant to deal with any emergencies as best as they could. Anything beyond their capabilities was sent to the nearest general hospital.

There was normally only one member of Healthcare staff on duty at weekends and it was usually fairly quiet. In general this was because most inmates weren't obliged to work at weekends and, rather amazingly, rarely became ill on Saturday or Sunday.

On this particular weekend an inmate called Kevin, who was a known thug, attended Healthcare asking for 'strong painkillers', saying that he had hurt his face slipping in the shower. The nurse on duty was at that moment in the middle of dishing out medicines and offered him mild painkillers, which were the standard analgesic used for any ache or pain. He refused the tablets, demanding something stronger, but when he was advised that no alternative was available without a doctor's prescription, he became abusive and started shouting obscenities, before storming out of the building. The nurse didn't feel it was necessary to document the incident in his notes because he had refused the treatment offered, and she thought nothing more about it.

However, when I arrived for duty on Monday morning the same inmate was waiting anxiously to see whoever was on duty and didn't even give me time to take my coat off before badgering to see me. By this time his face was grossly swollen and he was clearly in agony, could barely speak and straight away started to complain through clenched teeth about the nurse who had 'ignored him' at the weekend. Not being aware of the circumstances, I knew to tread carefully. Without preamble I warned him: 'If you tell me that you have slipped in the shower I will throw you out. [This story was routinely used as the explanation when there had been a fight or if there was an opportunity to try to make a claim for compensation.] It's obvious to me that you've been beaten up, so don't insult my intelligence by telling me some cock and bull story; simply tell me the truth please.' He admitted fighting but refused to give any details other than to say that, according to his mates, he had been knocked unconscious for several minutes. His facial injuries were so painful that he wept like a baby and looked desperately uncomfortable.

As the doctor wasn't due in for another two hours I examined his injuries carefully and checked his observations before organising for him to go to Casualty. While waiting for the prison transport to be arranged, I checked his records to see who had been on duty over the weekend and what had been documented. To my dismay there wasn't a single word in the notes about the incident and, although it wasn't strictly my place to do so, in the absence of anyone more senior I felt obliged to have a word with the nurse who had been on duty to warn her about the complaint and to ask her (in view of the patient telling her that he had fallen in the shower) if she had filled in an accident form as per protocol. She said she didn't think it was necessary because he had been offered tablets which he then refused. She was therefore convinced that he had not fallen, and that he had obviously told her a pack of lies.

Kevin was taken to Casualty and from there he was admitted to the ENT Ward, where he underwent urgent surgery after x-rays revealed a fractured jaw. The hospital consultant was very concerned when he saw him and, after the operation, rang the prison governor to complain about the delay in sending him to hospital. The weekend nurse was beginning to realise just how vulnerable her position was. The inmates all had an acute awareness of their legal rights and would think nothing of trying to sue for negligence in their treatment. It was now too late to draw up a statement. However sceptical we were, caution needed to be the key word every time; as trained nurses we were all responsible for our actions and could personally be sued, which could lead to being struck off.

★　★　★

One particular individual was the bane of my life at the prison and, no matter how professional I tried to be, I found myself bristling with annoyance every time this inmate came into the department. A career criminal who had spent most of his life in prison, he was a known troublemaker and invariably ignored the rule that written permission was needed from his boss to visit Healthcare (a sensible rule which ensured that staff knew where every inmate was at any given time). Presuming that the rules didn't apply to him, he would simply slip out of work without permission and present himself to us demanding attention. He was so aggressive that some nurses were intimidated by him and gave in to his demands. This is where my casualty experience came in; dealing with rude, irate and demanding people was part of the job. I had the ability to assess patients fairly quickly and could usually tell if someone needed urgent attention, and this man didn't. Usually he came in shouting and swearing at the orderlies to book him in straight away, threatening them and generally being a damn nuisance. Calmly reminding him of the prison rules for the umpteenth time, I always flatly refused to see him without a letter. The problem was he never ever had a letter.

The very first time I met him I asked for the usual letter and when he couldn't produce it I told him to leave. 'I only want a f**king paracetamol for a f**king headache,' he yelled. I stood my ground and asked him to leave. 'You f**king bitch!' he screamed, and then banged out. This happened a number of times and he even started bringing new inmates with him to see how I reacted to them when they also had no letters. Of course, if they didn't need urgent attention they were also turned away. It became a battle of wills and I was determined to win.

On the final occasion this same man turned up, yet again he demanded to be seen and, clearly feeling masochistic, I volunteered to find out what he wanted. As I walked into the waiting room he groaned audibly and swore. At this point I am pleased to say the Healthcare Officer, sensing a problem, came into the room and made his presence very apparent. I smiled at the inmate, kept my voice quietly calm (although my heart was pounding) and asked him for the letter from his boss. He totally lost the plot and went berserk, swearing, kicking the orderly's desk and finally punching a window before storming away. The inmates in the waiting room had all scattered and were looking at me to see how I reacted. My stomach was churning but I managed to keep my self-control, smiled and remarked, 'He's madly in love with me really,' at which they all burst out laughing and sat down.

After I had stopped shaking and calmed myself down, the officer advised me to put in a report to security about him. (This individual had been put on report several times previously by other members of staff without any action being taken, so I decided not to hold my breath.) The following morning, however, one of the Healthcare orderlies took me to one side and reassured me that I wouldn't be bothered by this man again because one or two inmates had been disgusted by the way he had spoken to me and had had a quiet word with him. Wondering what had happened, yet at the same time not really wanting to know, I was alarmed to hear that he had been given a heavy beating. I didn't know whether to laugh or cry. Bill thought it was brilliant and said I was a gangster's moll, although I have to admit that the whole incident worried me. I saw the inmate in the compound the following day, badly cut and bruised, but he never came back to Healthcare nor did he report the men who had assaulted him. When questioned by officers on how he had sustained his injuries, he told them he fell in the shower. He was, in fact, shipped out soon afterwards for threatening a female civilian employee. He didn't seem to learn from his mistakes and would very probably spend the rest of his life incarcerated in one or other of Her Majesty's establishments.

Although prison rules and regulations were necessary, they did sometimes cause problems, such as the one about producing a letter from a 'boss' authorising the inmate to come to

Healthcare. It wasn't always possible to get such a note, especially from the officers out in the fields as they had acres of land to cover and weren't always close by. Sometimes they didn't carry the necessary paperwork (although they usually had two-way radios) and they didn't always have access to standard telephones, so the nurses had to use a modicum of common sense.

On one occasion there was an urgent knock at the door and when an enrolled nurse went to answer it, I heard her ask the inmate quite abruptly what he wanted. A worried voice said that his mate had got chest pains and needed urgent help. Without so much as glancing at the patient she asked for the letter from his boss, only to be told that he hadn't got one as he worked in the fields and the officer in charge had driven off in the van. They didn't know where he was and felt that it was better to come to Healthcare quickly than mess about trying to find him. The nurse refused to let the man in saying that unless he had a letter he wouldn't be seen. She was about to close the door when I intervened and decided to at least see if the inmate genuinely looked poorly. He looked awful. He was hot and sweaty and his breathing was laboured. He said that he had pain in both sides of his chest, especially when he breathed in and he felt like he was burning up.

I sent his fellow inmate away to find their boss and to tell him where the patient was, while I took him into the treatment room to check him out. The enrolled nurse was annoyed that I had countermanded her instruction and stormed off complaining loudly to anyone who cared to listen. I don't think it occurred to her that the inmate's symptoms were potentially serious, so after finding that his temperature was sky high, I contacted the doctors at the surgery who advised me to send him to hospital. The Healthcare Officer sorted out the appropriate paperwork and organised a prison car to take the patient to Casualty where he was found to be suffering from double pneumonia and pleurisy. He wasn't admitted to hospital but was prescribed anti-biotics and pain relief and given a letter suggesting he have complete rest. He was, in fact, really quite ill and unable to work for a month, so I felt fully justified in my actions. My priorities were always firmly with my patients, but of course my past nursing experience helped me to make quick, firm decisions and if that meant breaking an occasional rule and ruffling a few feathers then so be it. The inmate came to see me when he felt better to say thanks. That meant everything to me knowing that I had done my job.

The majority of prisoners gave me very little trouble and, provided they didn't abuse my trust, I treated them as I would any other patient in my care. During my time at the prison I did catch several lads attempting to 'lift' things from the cupboards when my back was turned and I always reported them, not wanting them to think me a soft touch. They soon learned I was no pushover. If they reported sick and wanted to rest in bed, I checked them out thoroughly and put them in front of the doctor if I thought the illness was genuine. If I believed they were pulling a fast one, I kept them in the department and refused to let them go back to their accommodation. They soon became bored and in a very short time usually said that they felt much better. I would let them go, but not before the Healthcare Officer stepped in to tell them that he was ringing their boss to let him know that they were miraculously cured.

Despite the aggravation caused by some inmates, nothing could spoil my mood when in May 2003 my darling grandson Ryan was born. Taking some time off to help look after mother and baby down in Nottingham when they came home from hospital was a welcome break from the routine, although Bill wasn't too pleased to pick up yet another speeding ticket rushing up and down the M6 to be with us.

★ ★ ★

Throughout the prison working day, injuries and ailments were dealt with as and when they presented. The other nurses who also started working on the bank in Healthcare when I did were all good, experienced nurses and we quickly formed a very capable team. It was quite amusing to see how often inmates failed to realise that these new faces didn't come down with the last shower. They tried every trick in the book to fool us, usually to no effect.

One man in his early twenties came in supposedly doubled up in pain, saying he was unable to work and thought he had appendicitis.

I checked his temperature, blood pressure and pulse, which were all normal. He wasn't tender anywhere on his abdomen but, just to be on the safe side, I decided to keep him in Healthcare for an hour or two to keep an eye on him. When I enquired about his bowels and waterworks he looked disgusted and told me to mind my own business (or words to that effect). After checking on him every half hour, I said that I would like to take a blood test from him and needed to check his urine. He stood up and refused to have any investigations, saying that all he needed was a couple of days in bed. I tried to explain that this was not possible without some basic tests being done, at which point he swore, gave me a V sign and walked out. I made sure that his boss was informed that he had left our department and I found out later that he had failed to return and was discovered shirking elsewhere. He was reported and lost privileges. What a complete waste of time.

Robert was carried in by his mates, one bright spark saying, 'He's broken his ankle, miss.' They put him down in a chair and left, giggling and laughing like a couple of schoolgirls. Julie, one of the other new nurses who had been a sister on an orthopaedic ward, helped me to remove both his shoes and socks to compare his ankles for swelling. There was nothing to see apart from a layer of dirt. He had full range of movements and, when asked how he had done it, he couldn't give an answer. Julie and I stood him up to see if he was able to bear his own weight, which he could do without a problem. She winked and smiled at me as she told him that he needed a rather painful injection directly into the joint and reached for a large syringe. I agreed and went on to say that I would have to leave her to it as I couldn't bear to watch! Without further ado, he was up and out of the door in a flash, shouting that it felt much better. We watched as he ran like a whippet down the main thoroughfare, needless to say he was never to darken our doorstep again.

★　★　★

The old blocks were being demolished to make way for more modern accommodation; responsibility for the inmate's healthcare was transferred from the Home Office to the NHS and, because of severe overcrowding in the prison system, increasing numbers of more serious offenders were sent earlier in their sentences to the prison where I worked. There were a number of changes in the air and there was strong speculation that the Healthcare Officer was being moved out of the department to be redeployed elsewhere in the prison, which was rather worrying to say the least. Despite his claims to the contrary, this individual's nursing skills were little more than that of a qualified first-aider but a prison officer's presence in the department was both necessary and reassuring if there was any trouble. Any reduction in staffing would leave the remaining (mainly female) staff in a potentially vulnerable position. The Number One (Main) Prison Governor's attitude was that if we couldn't cope with the inmates then we shouldn't be there. He had a point but I wasn't getting any younger and had been thinking about taking early retirement for a while. It was challenging work at the prison with all these men and I didn't want to have to be constantly worrying about my personal security as well. As luck would have it, a colleague told me about a totally different type of job being advertised, based at Royal Preston Hospital, so I was off again.

12

The Lancashire Sexual Assault Forensic Examination (SAFE) Centre was opened within the grounds of the Royal Preston Hospital in 2002 by HRH Princess Anne. The concept of the SAFE Centre was that the police should have available a specialised resource to examine medically all complainants of sexual assault and rape, record the findings and gather physical evidence, including DNA, to support any subsequent court proceedings. It was the first purpose-built unit funded by Lancashire Constabulary specifically for this purpose and quickly became recognised as a centre of excellence.

The Clinical Director of the unit was a highly experienced senior doctor, recognised nationally as a clinician and expert witness in court matters involving sexual assault and forensic medical evidence. She had planned the design and operation of the unit in conjunction with the police authority, training fellow doctors to carry out specific detailed forensic examination and giving support and training in presenting evidence during subsequent court prosecutions.

The centre manager, Carolyn, supervised the day-to-day running of the unit and was in charge of support training, organising protocols and procedures, and setting the standards of care. She was a registered nurse with many years of experience at a senior level and was one of only a very limited number of qualified Forensic Nurse Examiners in the UK. She was ideal for the position, with good traditional values and a passion to do things correctly.

The third permanent member of the team, Pip, was a counsellor trained in general counselling but specialising in sexual assault and rape victims. Her duties included some general administration and she was also trained as a crisis worker.

In addition to the permanent staff, there were a number of experienced doctors trained as Sexual Offence Examiners (SOE), as well as several supporting crisis workers who were usually, but not necessarily, experienced female nurses whose function was to support the complainant (as the victims of any alleged assault were generally referred to) and the SOE during each examination. All non-permanent staff were employed on a bank system, working from home on an on-call rota covering a twenty-four-hour period, seven days a week.

I had seen the job description for a crisis worker when a co-worker at the prison had applied a while back. At the time I had thought it seemed interesting and different and, as the post was organised on a bank basis, it sounded ideal for me. I decided to take pot luck and sent a letter and CV to the centre manager enquiring if there were any vacancies. Although all the positions were filled at the time, I received an application form with the promise of an interview as and when one became available.

Within a matter of weeks I was in the centre

being interviewed and I felt from the moment that I stepped inside that this was a job I really wanted. I had routinely dealt with numerous rape cases previously in Casualty and knew that I was perfectly capable of dealing with the particular nature of these distressing cases, but was confident that this unit had far more to offer than the NHS ever possibly could in such difficult circumstances. The manager showed me around, clearly bursting with pride in the facility she had helped to create. Every room was spotlessly clean and highly organised; it was an absolute pleasure to see such high standards. After a fairly lengthy interview, I was offered a post and, in the meantime, Carolyn furnished me with a thick file to study, containing extremely comprehensive step-by-step protocols for virtually every eventuality likely to be encountered by the crisis worker (this was to become my Bible and I never left home without it). The time and effort it must have taken to compile the file was a credit to the management team and demonstrated the high standards expected within the team. After my references and CRB check were cleared, and following a general induction day in the Hospital Education Centre, I was put on rota and given a starting date.

Every month the SOEs and the crisis workers submitted their availability for duty to the manager and a rota was issued and circulated, including full contact details, with each shift being covered by both a doctor and a crisis worker. Although crisis workers tended to be on call mainly at night, they also covered day shifts at weekends and Bank Holidays. Initially I was to shadow two experienced crisis workers until I was deemed competent to support the SOE unaccompanied, and my first shifts were obviously correlated to those of my mentors.

The centre was open Monday to Friday, 9am to 5pm. Carolyn and Pip liaised with the police and made appointments for complainants to attend for examination and counselling, in addition to dealing with 'historical' cases and those involving children. It was unusual to see a child at night on a call-out as they tended to be far too tired or upset and therefore uncooperative. Historical cases were usually people who had plucked up the courage to come forward some time after the assault, perhaps months or even years later. Forensic testing in such cases would be pointless but the complainant could at least be offered support and information about counselling, which was often the start to recovery.

The night shift started with a handover from the day staff and the usual procedure was that between 5pm and 9am the police would first make contact with the duty doctor directly via their Force Incident Manager, who held all the appropriate telephone numbers centrally on an updated SAFE Centre rota. The officer would briefly outline the allegation to the doctor and a decision would be made to either examine immediately or by appointment during normal daytime hours. If it was deemed to be urgent then an appropriate time was agreed for all parties to meet at the centre. The doctor would then telephone the crisis worker to arrange for her to open the centre and set up all the necessary equipment.

The first case to which I was called out involved a young woman in her early thirties who was the victim of domestic violence; her partner of several years had allegedly beaten and raped her. The crisis worker on call rang to give me the time of examination and we arranged to meet half an hour earlier in order to show me the preparation procedures. SAFE Centre staff didn't wear a uniform (the reasoning behind this being that a uniform would appear too formal and authoritative) so, provided we were clean and presentable, we could wear whatever we liked. As it turned out the doctor came in wearing pedal pushers, a T-shirt and trainers, looking as if she had come straight from a run. I felt distinctly overdressed in my cotton blouse and tailored trousers.

The complainant, Eileen, and the accompanying police officer turned up as scheduled and rang the doorbell. The entrance door was kept locked at all times and the area was scanned by a CCTV security system. The woman was very distressed, sported several facial injuries, including a black eye, and her left arm was in a sling. After briefly introducing herself, the doctor took the police officer into another room to discuss the nature of the allegation while Kate (the attending crisis worker) and I took Eileen into the pre-examination room where she was made comfortable. As we waited for the doctor, Kate began her well-rehearsed explanation of the proposed examination by the SOE and the procedures to be followed. It was legally important that Eileen fully understood the reason why she had been brought to the centre, in order to ensure that she could make an informed decision about agreeing to the proposed examination. It was made abundantly clear that every procedure was to be undertaken entirely voluntarily and that, even though there was police involvement, she could stop the examination at any time.

Soon afterwards the doctor came back in, having been brought up to date with details of the alleged assault. The doctor introduced herself for a second time, although this time more informally as Christine, and reiterated everything that Kate had already explained, making doubly sure that the woman fully understood what was proposed. Intensive questioning then followed pertaining to past and present medical problems, social background, general lifestyle (including drinking, smoking and drug taking) and a brief résumé of any obvious injuries. It was a tedious session which took at least an hour; each answer being carefully documented, as the information might eventually be used in a witness statement for the courts.

During the subsequent physical examination various forensic materials were collected for DNA analysis, particularly intimate swabs from the genital and rectal area, as well as swabs from any area where the complainant had been bitten, licked or kissed. Bruises, cuts and injuries were measured, recorded and photographed, captured on video or catalogued on to body charts; even Eileen's clothing was seized and bagged for forensic testing. The doctor handed each individual item or specimen to the crisis worker as they were collected so they could be labelled and placed in order, including the time of collection. The whole procedure was completed with a polished professional efficiency. Eileen was at this point allowed to take a break, which gave her time to have a shower and get some refreshments, and then it was back into the examination room to complete the process.

The centre has the facility to offer post-coital contraception, advice on sexually transmitted infection, prophylactic antibiotics if there was a possibility of exposure to HIV, Hepatitis B vaccination if there had been exposure to likely infection, pregnancy testing and details of access to counselling and multi-agencies, such as women's refuges. By this time Kate had already explained the assistance available and issued a centre leaflet to Eileen that confirmed the information provided and contained all the relevant contact telephone numbers, so once the evidence bags had been handed over to the police officer the complainant was at last allowed to go home. The forensic specimens would be taken directly by the police officer to the force laboratory, while the photographic and video evidence would be stored in a vault within the centre until such time as they may be required. Regrettably, very much like in Casualty, we rarely found out the result or whether a case ever went to court because it could well be several months before the Crown

Prosecution Service even decided whether to proceed on an allegation.

Kate and I then had to clean the pre-examination and main examination rooms to remove any residual DNA traces and make all surfaces forensically clean. The centre had to be left tidy and equipment restocked to prepare for any subsequent cases, as we could well be called out a number of times during any one shift. This was a typical standardised procedure for virtually all cases, although it took several shifts before I felt totally confident. Usually there were up to twelve doctors on rota, each following the established protocols but with their own little individual idiosyncrasies, which took me quite some time to get used to.

The evening that I was rostered for my first solo night shift found me at home waiting by the phone. At 5pm the manager rang to say that all was quiet and no cases were booked in or pending. I carried my mobile phone everywhere, even to the bathroom. My bag, shoes, car keys and centre keys were placed near the front door, ready to go. I was like a cat on hot bricks, unable to sit still for two minutes, rehearsing the dialogue that I was meant to go through with each complainant; determined to appear confident and relaxed if called into action.

My telephone remained silent, so around midnight I decided to go to bed. I laid my clothes out in the bathroom ready to throw on quickly, although I was still half-dressed under the duvet. My head had scarcely touched the pillow when the voice of Peter Kay rang out:

'Everybody in. It's spitting!' I made a mental note to change the ring tone on my mobile, as Peter wouldn't sound very professional while I was at work (we had to keep our mobiles switched on at all times when on call) and I hadn't yet mastered how to put it on vibrate, technology not being my strongest point. I leapt out of bed to answer the call and almost fell over the dog. It was the doctor saying that we had a case on the way. She gave me a few details and agreed to meet me in the centre about an hour later.

My heart was pounding as I rushed into the bathroom to dress, dropping everything I touched and trying to focus myself sufficiently to insert my leg into the correct trouser leg. 'More haste, less speed' went through my mind as I overbalanced and almost fell into the bath. My head was spinning, having jumped up too quickly and Gino the dog was getting excited, thinking he was going walkies. A few minutes later I found myself outside in the car, even having remembered to pick up the centre keys. I headed off towards the M55 and covered the fifteen miles in about twenty minutes, not bad for someone who hates speed and motorways. Arriving in the car park and remembering my personal security routine, I searched for my keys first before opening the car door and scanning around to see if anyone was lurking in the shadows. It was a fairly well-lit area and I parked my car facing the exit, ready for a quick getaway should it be necessary. All was quiet so I entered the building, switched off the alarm and rushed around preparing the examination room. Minutes later a police car pulled up, followed closely by the doctor. A female police officer came in with a teenage girl and the girl's mother, both looking extremely distressed. The doctor introduced herself and went off with the police officer, while I took mother and daughter into the pre-examination room.

Hannah, the young girl, was nervous and uncooperative, initially refusing even to listen to what I was trying to tell her about the procedures likely to take place within the department. She had been drinking heavily at a house party earlier that evening and had woken up alone in a nearby alley. Her underwear had been removed and she was convinced that someone had had sex with her, but could remember nothing whatever of the incident and was still more than a little inebriated. The body language between mother and daughter was strained and it was obvious that the two had been arguing. However, after a few minutes once hostilities had eased a little, I was able to explain the objectives of the examination and to answer their questions. From then on the case ran reasonably smoothly, although Hannah insisted that her mother wasn't to be present during the doctor's examination. This didn't go down very well with Mum, but when I pointed out that we might be able to collect possibly vital physical evidence she understood and went outside. There were no further delays or problems and within two hours I was on my way home.

By the time I arrived home I was wide awake. I crept upstairs quietly and slipped into bed, ignoring the dog's wagging tail beating against the bed, and tried to get to sleep. My adrenaline was still surging and details of the case continued to run through my mind. Before too long Peter Kay again interrupted my husband's snoring and I hit the road for a second time.

★ ★ ★

Although the actual routine of each case over the next three years followed a broadly similar pattern, the complainants themselves came from every strata of society. Ages ranged from babes in arms to eighty-year-old grandmothers; from gang-raped teenage boys to drug-raped married ladies; from brutally beaten and assaulted total strangers to domestic and sexual abuse of several children within the same family; from mentally and physically disabled pensioners to drunken schoolchildren. Regrettably, the largest and by far the most common category were young females, more often than not totally incapable through drink and/or drugs, barely able to remember even the most basic details of the incident.

When I opened the SAFE Centre door one evening, Lisa was standing with her friend, accompanied by a female police officer. Clearly in shock, she just stared at the floor and didn't speak a word as I went through our procedures and explained what would happen next. When I asked her to confirm that she was happy to continue or had any questions, the only response was a shrug and a shake of the head. Observing the expression on her face I was worried and would have been far happier if she had been screaming and crying. Although I wouldn't get to know the full story until later, the police officer told the doctor that Lisa worked in a hotel bar and, the previous evening, had suddenly felt sick and developed a bad headache. As it was almost the end of her shift the other staff urged her to go home, so she put on her coat and left, but this was the last thing she remembered before waking up naked the next morning in a strange bed next to a snoring man she had never set eyes on previously. Grabbing her clothes, which were scattered around the floor, and dressing quickly, she fled downstairs and out of the front door. She had no idea where she was. After walking for a few minutes she recognised the area and made her way home. In what is a fairly classic reaction to such a traumatic situation, although she had no idea what had happened to her, she had a long, hot shower and flung all her clothes in the washing machine. Unfortunately, from our point of view, this potentially destroyed the DNA evidence on herself and her clothing.

Resolving to say nothing to anyone about this episode and to put it behind her, she decided to go to work as usual. However, her colleague immediately recognised that something was wrong. When Lisa eventually told her what had happened, her friend persuaded her to contact the police who brought her to the SAFE Centre because there was still an outside possibility that intimate swabs could produce DNA evidence if sexual intercourse had taken place. The doctor also took blood and urine specimens to check for drugs and alcohol, as it seemed a possibility that someone had spiked her drink with a 'date rape' drug.

Only after the examination did Lisa break down. She was distraught, especially when I had to advise her to get checked out for sexually transmitted diseases. My heart went out to her as she was offered the morning-after contraceptive pill and advised of the counselling services available to her.

The SAFE Centre treated each case consistently and impartially, simply gathering evidence and providing medical reports for the police, and offering support and advice to the complainant (and their families). These nights became routine and I loved the unit and the work, feeling privileged to be part of a well-respected professional team. I worked with all the SOEs at some stage and was impressed with the care and dedication with which they fulfilled their shifts, often in addition to a full-time position as a GP or hospital doctor. The other crisis workers were all very experienced nurses who I met during regular meetings at the SAFE Centre. We all got on really well and had a similar pride in doing the job well, although we never got the opportunity to work together.

★ ★ ★

After I had been at the centre for a year, Carolyn handed in her resignation; she was emigrating to America. Shortly afterwards, the Clinical Director also resigned; she was moving to Cumbria to work with the police authority there. We had lost the two most important members of the management team and the staff found it very unsettling, wondering how soon replacements would be appointed and what quality of applicant would be available to fill such specialised roles. We were determined to pull together, though, and work hard to keep the centre operating efficiently. The experienced senior staff pulled out all the stops during this transition period, working extra shifts and also supporting the administration of the centre. A new post of administration clerk was created to answer telephones, book appointments and update computer data; the new member of staff being trained by the counsellor and one or two of the crisis workers in the continued absence of any formal induction programme by the NHS or the police.

The centre continued to operate efficiently despite the lack of leadership. The post of Clinical Director was advertised and one of our senior SOEs was appointed, thankfully avoiding the need to familiarise the centre and staff to a new face. Inexplicably, it was almost a year before the centre manager vacancy was advertised and the post filled, although standards had thankfully remained high due to the outstanding efforts and contribution of all the team.

I had become an old hand at the job and, by this time, was also acting as mentor to new recruits. One particular case remains fixed firmly in my memory because it involved an eighty-year-old lady who suffered from Alzheimer's disease. She had inadvertently allowed a male stranger into her home thinking that he was her carer. The district nurse's daily visit found Maud distressed and confused, although she was able to tell the nurse some of what had happened, saying that this man had stolen her money and 'touched her'. The nurse contacted the lady's daughter, who in turn called the police. After spending a considerable amount of time trying unsuccessfully to coax information from Maud, it was decided to bring her to the centre to see if any forensic evidence could be found to support her claim.

I remember opening the door to a frail old lady who was weeping quietly and clasping her daughter's hand tightly. Maud was introduced to the doctor, who then went off to speak to the police officer while I took the old lady and her daughter into the pre-examination room. Within a couple of minutes I realised that it would be pointless going through the usual dialogue with her because she was tired, confused and continually asking if she could go home. She begged her daughter not to leave her alone and I felt a huge lump in my throat as she stared at me fearfully, like a rabbit caught in a car's headlights, and I couldn't help thinking of my own mum. I held Maud's hand and spoke gently, reassuring her that I would look after her. She gripped my hand and smiled, saying, 'Can I go home now? I'm very tired.' I gave her a hug and said she would be able to go home as soon as the doctor had checked her out. I explained to her daughter how the examination would be carried out and a few minutes later the doctor came in and took Maud straight into the main examination room. I helped her to get undressed and put on a gown and soon had her laughing. The gown was much too small for her and I made several silly comments about eating too many chips and sticky buns and, in no time at all, she started chattering away incessantly. Her favourite TV programme was *Strictly Come Dancing*, which she said she watched every week without fail. We shuffled around doing a slow waltz as the doctor checked her back and legs, and when she laid her head on my chest, I whispered, 'Hey, missus, who said you could lean on my bosom?' She laughed out loud at this and hugged me all the more, and we carried on our banter until the examination was completed. Maud had hardly even noticed the doctor's swift examination or the numerous swabs being taken, and when the time came to leave she gave me a big smile, said that she had had a lovely time and hoped she would be allowed to come again.

Waving her off, after doing a foxtrot to the police car, I couldn't hold my emotions back any longer and sobbed my heart out, wondering what sort of swine would do that to an old lady. Thankfully, whatever may have happened that day would soon be forgotten, her short-term memory loss would be a blessing in disguise. The swabs proved inconclusive and sadly this outcome was extremely unsatisfactory. Her case never did get to court; she couldn't even remember what day it was let alone stand up and give evidence.

I dealt with many such distressing cases

during my three years at the centre, which made me really appreciate how the unit impacted so directly on the lives of the public at such a difficult time, but the time had come to hang up my apron for good. It had been a privilege to work in such a professional unit with many dedicated and experienced colleagues, some of whom I am still in regular contact with today; so it was with a deep sadness that I finally made the decision to end my nursing career, but this would allow me to now spend much more time with my family and walk my beloved dog along the beach in the sunshine.

Afterword

If every nurse and doctor had to experience being an in-patient for at least a week as a compulsory part of their training, I am utterly convinced this would guarantee a more attentive and sympathetic medical and nursing profession. Going into hospital as a patient can be an extremely traumatic experience; people are often afraid and vulnerable, needing care and compassion from every member of staff they meet, regardless of stature.

When I began my nursing career in 1966 my one and only aim in life was to nurse the sick and the dying. I wasn't academic in any way and, fortunately for me, I didn't need to have a diploma or a degree to be able to achieve my ambition. It was a particularly strict regime under the old-fashioned matron system but one that I became increasingly proud of, although I can't truthfully say I enjoyed the enforced discipline, which sometimes put me on edge in case I made a mistake. With hindsight, though, I realise how lucky I was to have been trained in the era when a nurse's main concern was for their patients.

When I worked on the wards, excellent nursing standards were the accepted norm but, sadly, in more recent years I have witnessed some dreadful situations, one of which concerned my elderly next-door neighbour Lillian.

Aged in her eighties, she had been a skilled seamstress for nearly seventy years and was still very spritely for her age, being extremely particular about her dress and appearance. She was very much a lady and lived with her daughter Margaret. One morning Margaret came round to tell me that her mother had been taken ill and had been admitted to hospital for tests and was very poorly. Just after lunch, when I had finished my shift at the GP surgery where I was working at the time, I went to visit her in the geriatric ward. The sister in charge and several nurses were sitting around their station drinking tea and sharing a joke. One or two were writing reports, the others were just chatting. I asked where Lillian was and Sister pointed to a four-bedded bay directly opposite the nurses' station. The only occupant was an old lady who was sitting slumped over her table, face down in her congealing meal, both slippered feet surrounded by a puddle of urine. As I approached her, the stench of faeces was nauseating and I had great difficulty believing what I was seeing. I was disgusted that my elderly neighbour and friend could be treated in such a manner. Tears welled in my eyes and I had to hang back for a moment until I regained control. I went over, bent down and held Lillian's hand. She didn't even have the strength to raise her head so I helped her sit up, her face and hair covered in gravy.

She whispered, 'Is that you, Joan?'

I assured her that it was and asked whether she would mind if I cleaned her up.

She smiled, nodded and said, 'Yes please. I've

told that lot over there you would look after me.'

I was seething with rage. None of the staff knew me and I wasn't in uniform, yet they all just sat and watched me take a trolley from the sluice and pull the curtains around the bed. She had been doubly incontinent and her nightdress, dressing gown and slippers were stinking so I bagged them all up, washed her from head to toe and changed her clothes. She whispered her thanks over and over again but was so weak that she could barely move. Without a second thought I lifted her into bed and could immediately see the relief spread through her weary body. She just lay there, all her energy gone, and it seemed to me quite clear that she was dying. I pulled back the curtains and saw that the staff were still sitting there, not one of them having offered to help. I gave Lillian a drink and told her I would ask her daughter to visit. She held my hand, nodded and then fell into a peaceful sleep.

I dumped the dirty trolley in front of the nurses with a bang and presented myself to Sister, angrily pointing out that it now needed cleaning. Trying to remain calm, I asked, 'Have you let Lillian's daughter know how poorly she is?'

She looked at me like I had two heads and dismissed my concerns, saying that Lillian was just tired and sulking because she didn't want to get up. I looked at this 'angel' with distaste. There was a total absence of empathy, care or professionalism.

'She is dying,' I said, but this statement simply brought looks of derision from the assembled nurses and was completely ignored. My parting statement was, 'She is dying and if you don't inform her daughter, I will!'

As I left the hospital Margaret was just coming in. I made her aware of all that had taken place since my arrival, then went home and sobbed my heart out. Lillian died that night, thankfully surrounded by her loved ones. Although I made an official complaint, I was informed that, because I wasn't a relative, the hospital wasn't prepared to take the matter further. Of course, Margaret was too distressed at the time to even consider making a complaint herself and, when she did eventually recover, she felt that it was too late to cause a fuss and, as usual, no action was ever taken.

I still find it difficult to express my emotions about the incident as they veer from disgust to despair. How any nurse could possibly sit there doing paperwork when a vulnerable, elderly patient needed assistance is beyond my comprehension, although, the real blame must lie with the sister in charge who didn't act to prevent the situation arising in the first place. It beggars belief that staff with such low standards themselves could ever be appointed to train and supervise junior staff, and it raises serious questions as to where any future improvement in nursing standards will come from.

Only a few months ago a colleague who is a senior sister in a hospice asked a graduate student nurse for her help to change a dying middle-aged lady who had been doubly incontinent. The student looked disgusted and replied, 'I don't do mess.'

From my point of view, that person has very

definitely chosen the wrong career. But, then again, perhaps my opinions are still rooted in an outdated concept of patient care? In the forty-one years that I worked as a nurse I witnessed some amazing examples of good, old-fashioned nursing and perhaps, because of this, I am even more shocked by how things have changed. Once when I was working in Casualty, two ambulance men brought in a bedraggled elderly tramp, who had been found collapsed in the local park. He appeared to have had a stroke and, although conscious, was unable to speak. Valerie, an Irish staff nurse, went over to his stretcher and said, 'Hello,' and reassured him that he was now in safe hands. It was soon obvious that he had been doubly incontinent and the smell was overpowering. It was also very visibly clear that he had head and body lice; even his beard was crawling with wildlife. Without further ado, she volunteered my services to help her bathe him so that he would be nice and clean for the doctor. The two ambulance men grimaced but helped us to lift him into the bath and then very quickly made their exit, wishing us good luck as they backed away.

Valerie spoke to the man as if he were her father. She washed and scrubbed him and even gave him a haircut. The beard disappeared and even his fingernails were clipped and scrubbed spotlessly clean by the time she had finished with him. (My only task had been to keep him afloat, while dodging the fleas and lice.) Amazingly, under all the layers of dirt and hair there was a reasonably normal middle-aged human being.

He wasn't too happy, though, as he probably hadn't had the pleasure of soap and water for many years and the water in the bath had to be changed several times before Valerie completed his transformation. Once she was satisfied with her efforts, two porters were summoned to help get him out of the bath and on to a trolley ready for the doctor to examine him. (There were no hoists in those days.) I will never forget Valerie's kindness that evening. If that tramp had been a member of the royal family he couldn't have received better care. To me that is what nursing should be all about.

My friend Bernie was small in stature but extremely strong-willed (probably best described as feisty). She was a fearlessly determined advocate for the patients in her care and she didn't suffer fools gladly. She was one of the most caring, hard-working nurses I have ever come across. Bernie was senior sister on one of the old-fashioned wards at Queens Park Hospital, Blackburn. The wards were single-storey, ground-floor extensions linked to the main hospital by a long, draughty corridor running on the outside of the main buildings and were notoriously difficult to keep heated in the winter. The plastic swing doors to her ward were old and didn't close properly, and they let the wind howl through at times. During a particularly cold spell, the patients were all complaining and, despite repeated requests over an extended period to replace the doors, the hospital administrators had taken no action. Late one night, Bernie produced a screwdriver and the faulty doors found their way into a skip. Administration staff were purple with rage but she didn't care; her patients needed to be warm and comfortable. New doors were fitted soon afterwards and Bernie was applauded by both staff and patients when she next came on duty. She was prepared to argue the point with anyone when it came down to the welfare of her patients.

In today's politically correct and budget-conscious climate I have little doubt that Bernie would have been suspended, if not dismissed, for such behaviour. I often wonder how she got away with it. It was probably because she was right. And also because she was held in such high regard by both nursing and medical staff, especially the two consultants in charge of patient care on the ward. Bernie was diagnosed with breast cancer and sadly died aged just forty-five, but I like to think her spirit influenced the way I have always tried to stand up for my own patients' interests over the years.

★ ★ ★

In my forty-one-year nursing career I have seen advances in research and technology that have changed the face of medicine and will continue to do so in the future. I remember when there was no disposable equipment — when syringes, needles, bedpans and urinals had to be meticulously cleaned, dried and re-sterilised, much of it by hand. Matron or Sister came down hard on us if everything wasn't spotlessly clean and tidy, including our uniforms. Hair had to be kept off the collar and jewellery was banned. In those days, the hospital provided your uniform and you wore it with pride because it was a symbol of professionalism and trust, and couldn't be acquired anywhere else. Now a healthcare assistant in a rest home can buy what used to be universally recognised as a ward sister's navy blue uniform over the counter and the public wouldn't necessarily know the difference.

Hospitals used to employ their own domestic staff and every nook and cranny of each ward and corridor was expected to be spotlessly clean. Every member of staff took great pride in their own section of the hospital and Sister watched their work like a hawk, knowing that Matron would have apoplexy if any square inch was less than pristine. I find it a damning indictment of the NHS that private hospitals now feel able to use the prospect of a patient receiving treatment in a clean room as a marketing strategy.

Targets and financial controls are, of course, important, but so much time and effort today is spent on administration and paperwork that management and senior nursing staff have lost sight of the real purpose of nursing — looking after sick people. Caring for patients and saving lives is the primary reason for the existence of hospitals, and patients are people not commodities in a supermarket. Management skills acquired in banks and retail businesses don't necessarily transfer to the running of NHS hospitals.

From 2013 all student nurses must possess a degree-level qualification in order to be allowed to train and yet, to date, I have never seen any evidence that such graduates make better nurses. The new recruits may be much more intellectually gifted and educationally accomplished than a person such as myself, but a good nurse also needs to be a caring, compassionate individual who has an awareness of their patients' needs at all times. No task should be too basic or unpalatable for a nurse to deal with, whether it be cleaning up an incontinent patient or simply taking the time to observe whether a patient is cold, hungry or in pain, and acting upon it. This was the philosophy instilled into me as a student nurse and I sincerely hope I have always managed to follow it throughout my career.

Society itself has changed and people's expectations have quite legitimately grown along with that change. Miracles are regularly performed by life-saving operations and wonderful new machines are installed at enormous expense to us all, because it is mainly public money that pays for it. Somewhere among all these soaring costs patients still require good nursing. At some point along the line, this seems to have been forgotten.

Other titles published by
The House of Ulverscroft:

THE GIRL IN THE PAINTED CARAVAN

Eva Petulengro

Born into a Romany gypsy family in 1939, Eva Petulengro's childhood seemed idyllic. They travelled the country in their painted caravan, spending their evenings singing and telling stories by the fire. She didn't go to school. When she was unwell her family would gather wild herbs to make remedies. They would hunt game and rabbits for food, and to make a living, the men tended horses while the women would read palms. But in the post-war era, her perfect world was turned upside down . . . Eva describes the characters in her family, including her grandfather 'Naughty' Petulengro and her five beautiful aunts who entranced everyone they met. *The Girl in the Painted Caravan* vividly captures a way of life that has now, sadly, all but disappeared.

DAFFODIL GIRLS

Kitty Dimbleby

For every brave soldier risking their life for Queen and country, there is the subtle heroism of the women back at base in Britain. *Daffodil Girls* is the story of the women behind the soldiers of the 2nd Battalion Royal Welsh. Kitty Dimbleby describes the lot of a soldier's wife: a long-distance relationship with someone who, daily, is in danger. When he's away, having to deal with everyday family life. Then having to readjust to your partner's return; perhaps come to terms with the horrors they have encountered. And how do you cope if he doesn't come back at all? Kitty Dimbleby follows these women though the cycle of a regiment's tour of duty: the preparation for departure, the six months of action and the emotional renunion.

CONFESSIONS OF A GP

Benjamin Daniels

Just who are the people sitting alongside you in the doctor's waiting room? Could they be the sort of patients Dr. Benjamin Daniels has to see every day? The middle-aged woman troubled by pornographic dreams about Tom Jones. An adulterous husband who wants the doctor to secretly administer antibiotics to his wife, as he thinks he might have given her chlamydia after an office affair. The woman with a botched boob job wanting it fixed on the NHS. A schoolboy with 'tummy aches' that don't really exist. An eighty-year-old man who can't remember why he's come to see the doctor in the first place. The flirtatious transvestite. And that's without mentioning the home visits. The life of a family doctor is funny and moving in equal measure.

BEFORE I FORGET

Fiona Phillips

In August 2008, television presenter Fiona Phillips quit the job she loved, after twelve years in GMTV, interviewing the most famous and influential people on the planet. She was going to devote more time to her father, Phil, who had been diagnosed with Alzheimer's — a year after her mother had died of the same disease. *Before I Forget* is an account of growing up in the 1960s and '70s within a complex family. Fiona reveals her parents' pride when she landed the job at GMTV. She describes watching them fade away as both parents succumb to Alzheimer's: one moment interviewing George Clooney, the next taking a call from Pembrokeshire Social Services to say that there was trouble at her parents' house, hundreds of miles away.

GLORIOUS GRANDPARENTING

Gloria Hunniford

Grandparenting is not what it used to be, but as the grandmother to nine wonderful grandchildren, Gloria Hunniford knows about keeping up with them. In *Glorious Grandparenting* she shares her ideas on what to do when the grandchildren come to stay, and how to keep pace with them as they grow older. For many grandparents these days, life isn't always easy. In this book Gloria speaks to those who feel 'taken for granted' as a child-minder, have conflicting views on childcare or, sadly, have become separated from their grandchildren. She looks at the controversial lack of legal rights for grandparents and offers advice and guidance on handling these emotive issues.

THE RELUCTANT TOMMY

Ronald Skirth and Duncan Barrett

In the First World War, like many other Tommies, Ronald Skirth fought in the trenches, endured shell shock and somehow survived. But Skirth's story is extraordinary: on the Flanders battlefield he came across the dead body of a teenaged German soldier. The boy was just like him; in his hand, a photo of his girlfriend who looked just like Skirth's sweetheart, Ella . . . Skirth resolved never again to help take a human life. He altered the trajectory of guns to fire harmlessly, and, at great risk, carried out smaller acts of sabotage. Despite suffering breakdowns and amnesia, Skirth continued his peaceful campaign, lived out the war, and returned to marry Ella. *The Reluctant Tommy* is the story of a man who stuck by his principles in impossible circumstances.